The JOY of Knowing GOD

The JOY of Knowing GOD

Richard L. Strauss

LOIZEAUX BROTHERS
Neptune, New Jersey

First Edition, July 1984

Copyright © 1984, by Richard L. Strauss
A publication of Loizeaux Brothers, Inc.
*A Nonprofit Organization Devoted to the Lord's Work
and to the Spread of His Truth*

Library of Congress Cataloging in Publication Data

Strauss, Richard L.
  The joy of knowing God.

  Bibliography: p. 289
  Includes index.
  1. God—Attributes.   2. God—Knowableness.
I. Title.
BT130.S87   1984   231'.4   84-3889
ISBN 0-87213-834-8

PRINTED IN THE UNITED STATES OF AMERICA

To
the dearest person on earth to me
whose intimate knowledge of God
and simple trust in God
have been a constant inspiration
my best friend and loving wife
Mary

CONTENTS

1

SHOW ME THY GLORY

SOME PEOPLE thoroughly fascinate me. Soon after I meet them I sense that there is something extraordinary about them. They think deeply and profoundly about things. Their ideas are creative and interesting. Their suggestions are practical and profitable. They exude an unusual radiance and concern for others. I find myself asking them questions and listening intently to the answers because I want to get to know them better, find out what they think, how they feel, and what makes them the people they are. Getting to know them is immeasurably helpful to me.

One day it occurred to me that God is the most fascinating person alive and that getting to know Him could well be the most helpful thing that ever happened to me. The more I probed His nature the more convinced I became that knowing Him is the solution to most of my problems. And as I listened to others share their burdens with me as their pastor, I became convinced that knowing God better was the answer to many of their problems as well. I decided that I want to get to know God intimately, and that I want to help others get to know Him as well, if I possibly can.

Many Bible students believe as a result of their examination of Scripture that the Christian's most important occupation is getting to know God. Would you say that you know God personally? If so, how well? Barely? Casually? Intimately? Polls reveal that, in spite of the increased secularization of our society, the great majority of Americans still believe in the existence of God. Nearly everyone has had doubts about it at some time or other, but when the average person considers the evidence thoughtfully, he comes to the convinced persuasion that there is no other logical explanation for things as they are or life as we know it. There must be a personal God.

But if those same people were asked, "Do you know God personally?" many would admit that they had never actually thought about it. Having a personal and intimate relationship with God is something that has never occurred to them. In fact, they are not even sure that God is knowable, or that they would want to know Him if they thought they could.

All of us have our own mental image of what God is like. Psychologists tell us that it is formed largely through our relationships with our earthly fathers. For some, God is an angry tyrant who is upset with them most of the time. Who wants to know a god like that? For others, God is a strict disciplinarian who is always watching over their shoulders, ready to rap them on the knuckles if they step out of line. They want to get as far as they can from a god like that. For still others, God is an absentee father who is too busy or too aloof to care about them. He created them but now He has more important things to do. There isn't much sense in trying to get to know a god like that. And for yet others, God is like an old-fashioned great-grandfather who might be nice to know, but who really wouldn't understand them or have much in common with them if they did know Him. So why bother to make the effort?

Most people would like to feel that God is on their side rather than against them, or that He will be there when they need Him. But know Him personally? That concept is foreign to them. I have often wondered what God thinks about all this. He *is* a person, you know. He does think. And He does have feelings. How would you feel if you kept sharing your-self with others in overtures of friendship, but most everybody to whom you reached out refused to accept you or refused to believe what you had to say about yourself? They insisted instead on perpetuating their own preconceived notions about you and went on ignoring you. That may be how God feels about the situation.

God is knowable, and He does want to be known. As a matter of fact, He tells us that our eternal state depends upon knowing Him. Jesus said, "And this is eternal life, that they may know Thee, the only true God, and Jesus Christ whom Thou hast sent" (John 17:3). Knowing God and His Son Jesus is the heart of the whole matter of eternal life. The word *know* in this verse does not refer to a casual acquaintance either. It is the kind of knowledge that comes through living contact and personal relationship. If knowing God is that important, maybe we ought to talk about how we can get to know Him.

The One To Be Known Must Reveal Himself

What does it mean to know somebody? Obviously, we must first know something about him, what he is like, how he thinks, and how he is likely to act under certain circumstances. And that can only happen when he reveals himself to us.

If I want to get to know you, I need to make myself available to you, reach out to you in a friendly way, and show an interest in you. But that will accomplish very little unless you are willing to reveal yourself to me. *You* are the key. You decide whether or not I will ever get to know you. If you want me to know you, you will open up and tell me about yourself—what you are thinking, what you really believe, what you are feeling. You will be yourself in my presence, that is, act in a normal manner consistent with your true personality. You won't put on airs, wear a facade, mask your true self, or always put your best foot forward.

One reason some Christians enjoy so few genuine friendships is that they are afraid to let people know them, afraid they wouldn't be liked or trusted if anybody knew the real person inside. So they play the old game of cover-up. God is not like that. He wants to be known. He is confident that the better we know Him, the more we will love Him, trust Him, worship Him, and serve Him. So He takes the initiative and opens up. He tells us about Himself. He reveals Himself to us. It has to be that way. There can be no personal knowledge of God unless He makes Himself known.

How does God reveal Himself? One way is in nature. "The heavens are telling of the glory of God" (Psalm 19:1). He also reveals Himself in history. As King Nebuchadnezzar of Baby-lon learned, "the Most High is ruler over the realm of man-kind" (Daniel 4:17). The Apostle Paul taught us that God reveals something about His holy standards through man's conscience (Romans 2:14-16). But none of these give us very many particulars about God's personality or nature. We need something more. We need to have Him talk with us. And He does that, not through spooky voices or mystical experiences, but through Scripture. They are God's words to us. They were given by the breath of His mouth (cf. 2 Timothy 3:16; Matthew 4:4). In the Bible God tells us what He is like. We learn how He thinks, how He feels, and how we can expect Him to act. If we want to know God, we must begin by opening the Bible and reading what He has to say about Himself.

But God is infinite, and we are finite human beings. How can the finite ever really understand the infinite? How can the human ever truly know the divine? It seems that God must reveal Himself to us in some way more personal than mere written words if we are ever to know Him genuinely. And that is exactly what He did. "God, after He spoke long ago to the fathers in the prophets in many portions and in many ways, in these last days has spoken to us in His Son, whom He appointed heir of all things, through whom also He made the world. And He is the radiance of His glory and the exact representation of His nature, and upholds all things by the

word of His power" (Hebrews 1:1-3). Jesus Christ is the out-
shining of God's glory and the perfect expression of God's
essential being. To know Him is to know God. Jesus Himself
made that claim when He said, "If you had known Me, you
would have known My Father also; from now on you know
Him, and have seen Him" (John 14:7).

While Jesus has returned bodily to Heaven, God has given
us both the inspired record of His life as well as the spiritual
faculties we need to know Him personally. We can know
Christ just as intimately as if we walked with Him on earth
as His first disciples did. And to know Him is to know God.

Of course, the spiritual faculties we need are not operative
when we are born. Scripture says they are dead. They need
to be made alive toward God (cf. Ephesians 2:1). God does
that for us when we acknowledge our guilt and put our trust
in Christ's payment for our sins at Calvary. In a second birth,
a spiritual birth, a birth from above, He gives us eternal,
spiritual life (cf. John 3:3,16). He enters our being in the
person of His Spirit and brings us into a personal relationship
with Himself. Then we can confidently say, "I know the
Lord." The knowledge of God begins at the cross of Jesus
Christ. This is the knowledge He was referring to when He
claimed that eternal life was a matter of knowing His Father
and Himself. Knowing God in this sense means becoming a
true Christian.

From that point on we have the spiritual resources to get
to know Him better. And that is what He wants us to do. He
encourages us to grow in His knowledge (2 Peter 3:18). But
how is that going to happen? He has taken the initiative and
has revealed Himself. The next step is ours.

The One Who Wants To Know Must Respond

Cultivate a Desire.   Let's go back to our human illustration
for a moment. If I want to know you, first you must open up
to me and share yourself with me. But I am still not going to

know you very well unless I respond to your self-revelation. The quality of my response will depend to a large degree on the intensity of my desire. Has my first insight into your personality whet my appetite to know more? Do I wish to pursue the relationship and carry it to a deeper level? While you were the key originally, now I am the key. I decide whether or not I will ever know you better.

Some Christians have not made much of a response in their relationship with God. They have learned enough about Him to acknowledge their need for salvation, and they have met Him personally and experientially in a saving relationship, but they have never moved on from there. Unfortunately they have gotten busily entangled in too many other pursuits, and their time for getting to know God better has been crowded out. Though they know Him, it is not a very intimate and thorough knowledge. That could explain some of the problems in their lives, things such as nagging worries, endless fears, stifling guilt, a sour disposition, a gloomy outlook, and spiritual or emotional depression, since an inadequate knowledge of God will affect all these areas of life. And things will probably not change very much until they do develop a burning desire to know God more intimately.

Getting to know God better could well be the single most important issue in the Christian's life. It affects so many aspects of our spiritual walk. For example, most believers who desire to please God want to know His will. They are asking, "What does God want me to do?" Knowing Him better will provide the answer to that question. As our knowledge grows, we will begin to think as He thinks, see things as He sees them, be burdened about the same things that burden Him. We will not need to ask what He wants us to do. We will know. And that is a good reason to begin cultivating a desire to know Him.

Moses had that desire. We read about it shortly after Israel's idolatrous worship of the golden calf. Moses had pitched a tent outside the camp and was meeting there with God regularly. God was speaking to him face to face as a man speaks to his friend, and Moses was getting to know Him. But he wanted to know Him much better. "Now therefore, I pray Thee, if I have found favor in Thy sight, let me know Thy ways, that I may know Thee" (Exodus 33:13). That was the desire of his heart—to truly know God. His request resulted in a great promise from God: "My presence shall go with you, and I will give you rest" (Exodus 33:14). It was a beautiful assurance of God's perpetual guidance and care.

But even that was not enough for Moses. Every new revelation of God stirred a hunger in his heart for more. With a longing in his soul he cried, "I pray Thee, show me Thy glory!" (Exodus 33:18) God's glory is the sum total of all his attributes. Moses yearned to know all that a human being can possibly absorb about an infinite God. His soul thirsted for a knowledge of God. That is how a person gets to know Him. He realizes that life in this world is empty and meaningless apart from an intimate and thorough knowledge of the living God who made the world and controls it, who made him and gave him life. He longs to know God and he cries out from the depths of his soul, "Show me Thy glory." That person is ready for an earthshaking, life-changing, experiential knowledge of God.

David had the same desire. We see it repeated throughout the Psalms:

> One thing I have asked from the LORD,
>   that I shall seek:
> That I may dwell in the house of the LORD
>   all the days of my life,
> To behold the beauty of the LORD,
> And to meditate in His temple (Psalm 27:4).

To dwell in the house of the Lord was to live in intimate fellowship with the Lord. That was David's passion:

As the deer pants for the water brooks,
So my soul pants for Thee, O God.
My soul thirsts for God, for the living
　　God;
When shall I come and appear before
　　God? (Psalm 42:1-2)

O GOD, Thou art my God; I shall seek
　　Thee earnestly;
My soul thirsts for Thee, my flesh
　　yearns for Thee,
In a dry and weary land where there is
　　no water (Psalm 63:1).

Paul had the desire as well: "But whatever things were gain to me, those things I have counted as loss for the sake of Christ. More than that, I count all things to be loss in view of the surpassing value of knowing Christ Jesus my Lord, for whom I have suffered the loss of all things, and count them but rubbish in order that I may gain Christ" (Philippians 3:7-8). All the position, praise, power, prestige, and possessions of earth were like trash compared to the excellency of knowing Christ because those things have no eternal value. They were not worth occupying his mind.

Why would anyone want to sit around and long after trash? Yet that is exactly what some believers are doing. They crave the things of the world instead of the knowledge of God; they long for the debris at the city dump when they can have the best life has to offer—an intimate relationship with the living God. The overpowering passion of Paul's life was to know Christ (Philippians 3:10). That may have been one of the prime reasons God used him so powerfully. The desire was there. Ask God to give you that same desire, to help you cultivate a thirst for Him. Then begin reading His Word with an eye open to what He says about Himself. Each new revelation will create a desire to know more.

Accept What God Reveals. After cultivating the desire, the next step in our response to God's self-revelation is to accept what He makes known about Himself. That is the body of information we call the attributes of God. An attribute is an inherent characteristic, whatever God reveals as being true of Himself. It is not so much a part of God or a quality that He possesses as how He is or what He is—the essence of His being, His nature, His character. God and His attributes are actually one. As we study these attributes we are going to learn not only what God is like, but who God is.

Some theologians draw a sharp distinction between God's essence and His attributes, but that seems to be unnecessary. The sum of His attributes constitutes who He is, His essential being. If you described all the properties of something you would be describing what it is, its essence. Just so, if you could describe all of God's attributes you would be describing His essence, who He is.

Obviously, we do not know everything there is to know about God. We are limited to what He has revealed about Himself in His Word. And with our finite minds we cannot even comprehend all of that. But what we do grasp of what He has revealed can enrich our existence on earth immeasurably and provide us greater pleasure than any other pursuit in life. It brings us into personal touch with the living God.

There is also a debate among theologians concerning how the attributes of God are to be classified and cataloged. Some distinguish His *natural* attributes from His *moral* attributes, that is, those that belong to his constitutional nature in contrast to those that qualify him as a personal, moral being. Others separate the *communicable* attributes from the *incommunicable,* that is, those that can be understood by comparing them to something in human life in contrast to those that have no human counterpart. Others insist there are *immanent* attributes that relate to God as He is, and *transitive* attributes by which He reveals Himself to His creation. Why do we need to classify God's attributes? He is who He is. I would prefer simply to know Him as He is and not try to pigeonhole each attribute.

As we see God reveal Himself in His Word we may say at times, "That is not the way I have always thought about God." But what we have always thought is not particularly important. Concentrating on that may only confuse us. We need to focus on what God has told us about Himself. For example, if I have preconceived ideas about you that are inaccurate, yet I continue to hold on to those ideas after you tell me the truth about yourself, I will obviously never get to know you. I must accept what you tell me about yourself. Just so, when God tells us who He is and how He acts we need to believe Him. That is essential to knowing Him. But there is still something more that we need to understand.

Involve Your Entire Being.   After the desire has been culti-vated, and the decision to accept what He reveals has been made, there must be a definite commitment to Him that involves our total being. In our human illustration, I cannot get to know you intimately unless I commit myself to spend time with you, take an interest in what interests you, get concerned about what concerns you, and rejoice in what brings joy to you. I must become totally involved in your life. Unfortunately, many of us have stopped short of that point in our knowledge of God.

If we really want to know Him, it is going to involve our total person—intellect, emotions, and will. Unfortunately, we live in a day of extremes. On one hand are the superintellec-tuals who know all the doctrines about God, yet feel nothing in their relationship with Him. On the other hand are the supersentimentalists who can drum up a great emotional religious experience, but do not know the facts about God. In between are all kinds of people who say they know God yet do not exercise their wills to obey Him.

All three parts of our personality are involved in knowing God. First, we learn about Him with our intellects. We study the Word, absorb the information He reveals about Himself, meditate on it, then think through its implications and appli-cations to our way of living. That is all the function of the mind. The mind must be involved in knowing God. If we do not have accurate information about Him, we cannot say we know Him.

But we must not stop with the mind. As we learn more about Him we become more emotionally involved with Him. And that is nothing to be afraid of. There is no reason to back away from the emotional expression of our faith. When we see the depths of His love for us it might well bring tears to our eyes or shouts of joy to our lips. It will certainly inspire greater love for Him. When we understand the far-reaching implications of His goodness and grace toward unworthy sinners such as we are, we may burst into song, even if we cannot carry a tune. When we realize how deeply we have hurt Him by our sin we will feel grief. When we experience the reality of His forgiveness we will feel relief, and love, and joy, and a sense of security. When we see people spurn Him our hearts will be saddened. These are all emotions, and a true knowledge of God cannot eliminate them.

But we do not stop with an intellectual knowledge of the facts and some exciting emotional experiences. We must do something about what we have discovered. We must choose by an act of our wills to live in a manner consistent with the information we have received and the feelings we have encountered. Not everyone does that. Paul told us about people who professed to know God but denied Him by their deeds (Titus 1:16). John went so far as to say that the person who says he knows God but refuses to obey Him is a liar (1 John 2:4).

Let's go back to the human illustration again. If I have gotten to know you intimately, you will expect certain things from me, things such as loyalty, faithfulness, trust, fellowship, an open sharing of myself with you, and a desire to please you. Those are things I must choose to do by an act of my will.

We cannot really say we know God just because we have accumulated some facts about Him or had an emotional experience with Him. If we truly know Him we will choose to do what He wants us to do. We will talk with Him, freely tell Him what is going on inside us, honestly admit where we fall short of His expectations, implicitly trust what He tells us, depend on Him, submit ourselves to Him, obey Him, and worship Him all because of who we have discovered Him to be. As we relate to Him in that way our personal knowledge of Him will grow even more meaningful and fulfilling.

Our willingness to obey God can increase our understanding of Him immensely. For example, if I express my willingness to obey your instructions, I am going to learn a great deal about you from the things you ask me to do. The more I obey, the more you will instruct me, and the more I will learn. When I stop listening to what you want me to do I will stop growing in my knowledge.

Anne Sullivan, who tutored the blind and deaf Helen Keller, recognized that it was useless to try to teach her anything until the young girl learned to obey her. She became convinced that obedience is the gateway through which knowledge enters the mind of a child. The same is true for the child of God. Obedience is the gateway to our knowledge of Him. Some of us have reached a roadblock in our relationship with God. Knowing Him better will first require yielding our wills to Him fully and deciding to obey Him unreservedly.

If that issue is settled and you want to go on growing in your knowledge of God, I would like to help by bringing together some of the information He has revealed about Himself in His Word. I feel most inadequate to do that, but I want to try. The rest is up to you. You will need to believe what God says, then commit yourself to total involvement with Him. It may mean some changes in the way you live, but the benefits will be enormous. Maybe it would be profitable to review a few of those benefits before we go on to explore God's attributes. That is the purpose of the next chapter.

Action To Take:

Determine first that you will ask God daily to show you something about Himself, and secondly that you will read some portion of Scripture daily, looking for some truth about Him. Begin right now.

2

THE PEOPLE WHO KNOW THEIR GOD

WHAT'S WRONG with my spiritual life? Why don't I have the peace and joy that other Christians have?" I couldn't begin to count the number of people who have asked questions like those through the years of my pastoral ministry. They have read in the Bible that Christians are supposed to have "joy inexpressible and full of glory" (1 Peter 1:8), but they cannot even begin to imagine what that kind of a Christian experience must be like. If they were writing a treatise on the Christian life it would be more like "gloom irrepressible and full of worry."

No Magic Formula

I do not have any magic formula to put the sparkle into your Christian life. There are many factors in Scripture that affect our spiritual well-being, but one thing is certain—our personal, intimate, experiential knowledge of God is one major factor. The spiritual benefits of knowing God are literally exciting. We shall be talking more about them in conjunction with each individual attribute, but let us consider a few general advantages as we get started, in order that we might sharpen our spiritual appetite and arouse our thirst for God. Here are some of the good things we will enjoy as our knowledge of God grows.

Power

Scripture declares that "the people who know their God will display strength and take action" (Daniel 11:32). That is a great promise. But in order to understand it we need to know a little Jewish history. The Jewish people have experienced some fierce persecutions through the centuries, but none worse than under Antiochus Epiphanes, the Syrian king who reigned from 175 to 164 B.C. He assumed the name Theos Epiphanes which means "the manifest God," but the Jews changed one letter in his name (in their language) and called him Epimanes, which means "mad man." And mad he was! His hatred for the Jews was literally insane.

Daniel anticipated his reign prophetically in this eleventh chapter of the book. And he did exactly what Daniel predicted. He ordered the Jewish sacrifices to cease and polluted the temple of God by offering swine's flesh on the altar. In addition to that, he prohibited the observance of the sabbath and the circumcision of children, ordered all copies of Scripture destroyed, set up idolatrous altars, commanded the Jews to offer unclean sacrifices, and insisted that they eat swine's flesh. Anyone who disobeyed his edicts was sentenced to death. It was an ancient holocaust. As Daniel anticipated this atrocity he asked himself how these people would ever be able to survive. The answer was not long in coming: "the people who know their God will display strength and take action" (11:32).

And that is exactly what they did. A group of courageous men called the Maccabees led a heroic revolt against Antiochus. Their exploits, against insuperable odds, were nothing short of phenomenal. They knew their God, laid hold of His sovereign power and might, took action, and broke the grip of Antiochus on Israel. Their story is a saga of strength, the mighty power of people who know God. People today who truly know God have the same degree of courage and strength. They stand for righteousness, oppose wickedness, endure persecution when necessary, triumph through suffering, and accomplish great things for God's glory. There is no other way to have spiritual power except through the knowledge of God.

Daniel himself was a man who knew God. When the presidents and princes of the Medo-Persian Empire prevailed upon King Darius to issue a decree prohibiting anybody from making petitions to any god or man except the king, or be cast into the lion's den, Daniel went right on praying to the God of Heaven (Daniel 6:4-15). Not even the threat of death could keep him from it. He knew his God, and people who know God have the courage and strength to do His will even though the whole world be against them and everybody around them be giving in to sin. We too can have the spiritual power to do God's will and to make a significant impact on the godless world in which we live. As our knowledge of Him increases and our friendship with Him grows more intimate, He makes His power more readily available to us.

Peace

Peter tells us something about people who know God. He says, "Grace and peace be multipled to you in the knowledge of God and of Jesus our Lord" (2 Peter 1:2). His statement reveals that both grace and peace are increased in the believer's life by the full or thorough knowledge of God. *Grace* is God's favor, His gracious care, faithful assistance, and help. We enjoy God's help to the extent that we know Him. That should be easy to understand. If we do not know Him very well, we will not know what help He has available, or even that He is offering us any help. We must know Him in order to be able to accept the benefits He extends to us.

But it is the *peace* that I want to address here—an inner tranquility, a quiet confidence, a stability and control in the face of difficult circumstances. It multiples in us through the knowledge of God who controls our circumstances. How desperately we need peace in our up-tight world! When we have peace, we realize that there is no reason to worry over every new problem. The all-powerful God who loves us and cares about every detail in our lives is going to see that it turns out best. The better we get to know Him, the more we rest in His wise plans for our future.

There is a great illustration in the book of Daniel of the peace that comes from knowing God. King Nebuchadnezzar had erected a ninety-foot statue of himself before which all his subjects were commanded to bow. To refuse meant death in the fiery furnace. But Shadrach, Meshach, and Abednego were men who knew God. They could not bow before that golden image. When it became obvious that they had refused, they were brought before the king and given one last chance. Nebuchadnezzar proudly announced, "if you will not worship, you will immediately be cast into the midst of a furnace of blazing fire; and what god is there who can deliver you out of my hands?" (Daniel 3:15)

The answer of those three men of God is one of the classic Biblical expressions of faith. They began by saying, "O Nebuchadnezzar, we do not need to give you an answer concerning this" (verse 16). There was no disrespect in their words. They were merely admitting that the accusation was correct and that they had no defense. They did what they had to do. But they continued, "If it be so, [that is, if we are thrown into the fire] our God whom we serve is able to deliver us from the furnace of blazing fire; and He will deliver us out of your hand, O king. But even if He does not, let it be known to you, O king, that we are not going to serve your gods or worship the golden image that you have set up" (verses 17-18).

They knew an all-powerful God who was able to deliver them. He who created fire and who made their bodies could certainly keep them from being burned. And they believed He would. But even if they did not fully understand God's plan and purpose for them at that time and He did not deliver them, it really did not matter! They would be better off in His presence anyway. In either case, they would not disobey Him by bowing before the image. They had perfect peace and tranquility in the face of a torturous death because they knew God.

Wouldn't you like to have peace like that? Wouldn't you like to stand up to any trial, any problem, any danger, or any threat, and be able to say confidently, "It really doesn't matter what happens to me. I know that God will work it together for good. I want only to do His will and glorify Him." That degree of peace depends on an intimate knowledge of God. As we learn to know Him better and begin to sense His unlimited power coupled with His undying love, we will learn to relax in Him—just as a little child relaxes peacefully in his father's arms while a storm rages outside.

Wisdom

Paul was a man who enjoyed the benefits of knowing God, and he longed for his converts to share those same blessings. He often prayed to that end, and in those prayers we learn more about the advantages of knowing God. For the Ephesians he prayed, "that the God of our Lord Jesus Christ, the Father of glory, may give to you a spirit of wisdom and of revelation in the knowledge of Him" (Ephesians 1:17). The word *spirit* is not a reference to the Holy Spirit. The Ephesians already had Him dwelling in their lives. Paul was referring to a mental attitude or disposition of true spiritual understanding which the Holy Spirit alone could produce in them, that is, the ability to comprehend God's truth and appropriate it. He wanted them to be able to grasp spiritual realities and the application of those truths to their lives.

Some of us have a deficiency in spiritual understanding. We read the Word of God without comprehending what it says, and we totally miss its implications for us. We would like to have what Paul prayed for, a spirit of wisdom and revelation, the ability to discern divine truth, but we never seem to attain it. Where is it to be found? How can we get it? Does it require a degree in theology? Paul tells us where it is located—in the knowledge of Him. The people who intimately know their God have spiritual understanding that far surpasses their formal education. The time they have spent with Him has given them more insight into the purpose of life than any of the world's great universities could ever provide.

Peter and John were men like that. They were preaching Christ in the temple courtyard and the Jewish religious leaders were furious. They took the two disciples into custody and questioned them about their activities, insisting that they reveal by what power they performed their miracles. Then Peter, filled with the Holy Spirit, delivered a powerful testimony to the person of Christ that demonstrated not only his familiarity with recent events in Jerusalem, but also his grasp of Old Testament Scripture (Acts 4:8-12). It was an amazingly articulate expression of faith from an uneducated fisherman. Where did he get that kind of wisdom? The record goes on to tell us: the Jews "began to recognize them as having been with Jesus" (Acts 4:13). They had come into a personal and intimate knowledge of the living God through His Son Jesus Christ. They had walked with Him and talked with Him for three and one-half years. As a result they had an understanding of spiritual truth that those religious rulers could not begin to match with all their theological training and sanctimonious religiosity. People who know God have wisdom.

Your Real Purpose

Isn't that what you really want? Not so you can amaze your friends with your knowledge of Scripture or your grasp of theological truth. But so that you can know what life is all about, and make an impact on their lives for the glory of God as they observe the reality of Christ in you. It will happen when you get to know Him intimately.

Growth

Paul's prayer for the Colossians describes another advantage of knowing God: "For this reason also, since the day we heard of it, we have not ceased to pray for you and to ask that you may be filled with the knowledge of His will in all spiritual wisdom and understanding, so that you may walk in a manner worthy of the Lord, to please Him in all respects, bearing fruit in every good work and increasing in the knowledge of God" (Colossians 1:9-10). There is some difference of opinion as to how this should be translated. While most of our popular translations render it as a prayer for the Colossians to increase in the knowledge of God, most commentators understand it to mean that the knowledge of God is the means by which we bear fruit and increase in every good work. They would translate it something like this: "bearing fruit and increasing in every good work by the knowledge of God."

Now that is a thought for believers to mull over. Some are asking, "Why can't I do what is right? Why don't I have the love and joy and peace that I crave?" Here is one reason. Our fruitfulness and our growth depend on our knowledge of God. We ought to be able to understand that since it works the same way in the human realm. As I grow in my knowledge of my friends I enjoy being with them more and I have a greater desire to please them. That is what occurs in our relationship with the Lord. The more we know of His love for us the more we love Him in return (1 John 4:19). And the more we love Him the more we want to please Him (1 John 5:3; John 14:15).

There is another human analogy that will help us understand this truth. Psychologists tell us that we acquire similarities to the people we get to know intimately and with whom we spend much time. As we spend time with our Lord and grow in our knowledge of Him we begin to develop Christlike traits, the very things which the New Testament refers to as fruit. In other words, we will bear fruit and increase in every good work *by* the knowledge of God. Try getting to know Him better. You will enjoy it.

A Psalm writer named Asaph did. He was in bad shape spiritually. He says he came close to stumbling; his steps had almost slipped (Psalm 73:2). He was on the verge of a serious spiritual defeat, angry with God because ungodly people were doing better than he was. He certainly was not growing until, he says,

> I came into the sanctuary of God;
> Then I perceived their end (verse 17).

Being in the sanctuary of God was an Old Testament way of expressing fellowship with Him. Asaph got to know God— His love, His care, His guidance, and His all-sufficiency. Then he went on to say,

> Nevertheless I am continually with Thee;
> Thou hast taken hold of my right hand.
> With Thy counsel Thou wilt guide me,
> And afterward receive me to glory.
> Whom have I in heaven but Thee?
> And besides Thee, I desire nothing on earth.
> My flesh and my heart may fail,
> But God is the strength of my heart and my
>   portion forever (verses 23-26).

His knowledge of God changed his life and gave him a growing delight in walking with Him. He could say, "But as for me, the nearness of God is my good" (verse 28). The closer he got to God the more he grew and the better he enjoyed his spiritual experience. It can be our good too. We will experience new growth and fruitfulness when we get to know Him.

Freedom

There is one more general blessing of knowing God that I would like to point out. It is found in Paul's letter to the Galatians. Those Galatians had a problem with legalism. Their Christian lives were a grind: "I've got to do this, I've got to do that, I can't go here, I can't say that." They lived in constant fear that they had not done enough to please God and that led to overwhelming feelings of guilt. The only way to compensate for their guilt was to try harder. They were probably saying, "I must grit my teeth and give it all I've got. But I really don't feel like it. I wish God would get off my back." So along with the fear and guilt there was probably resentment against God for the pressure they were feeling. One word sums up that kind of Christian life—*bondage!*

God never intended us to live like that. Knowing Him truly, personally, and intimately delivers us from bondage. Paul wrote to them, "But now that you have come to know God, or rather to be known by God, how is it that you turn back again to the weak and worthless elemental things, to which you desire to be enslaved all over again?" (Galatians 4:9) They came to know God and their knowledge had delivered them from bondage. But as sad as it was, they had willfully chosen to put themselves back under the very bondage from which they had been delivered. Why? What was their problem?

Trying to please God without growing in our knowledge of Him will put us under bondage every time. We think we have to perform to be accepted. So we struggle and strive to please Him, never sure we have succeeded, frustrated over the pressure we think He is putting on us, and yet afraid to stop trying. That kind of life is sheer misery.

When we understand His love, His grace, His forgiveness, and His unconditional acceptance of us in Christ, obedience is no longer a struggle or a grind. It is free, natural, and joyful. In fact, it is actually fun. We obey Him not because we think we must do it in order to gain His approval, but because we want to. We consider it a delightful privilege. We love the one who has already accepted us, undeserving though we are, and we enjoy pleasing Him. Paul pleads with the Galatians and with us, "Stand fast therefore in the liberty wherewith Christ hath made us free, and be not entangled again with the yoke of bondage" (Galatians 5:1 KJV). The only way we can do that is to get to know Him better.

There is actually no end to the blessings of knowing God. As Peter put it, "His divine power has granted to us everything pertaining to life and godliness, through the true knowledge of Him who called us by His own glory and excellence" (2 Peter 1:3). Everything we need to assure us of eternity in God's presence is found in our knowledge of Him. Everything we need to help us live godly lives here and now is found in our knowledge of Him. *Everything!* It sounds again as though getting to know God could be the most important aspect of our Christian lives. What are we waiting for? Let's begin to grow in our knowledge of Him.

Action To Take:

Begin to think about God at frequent intervals throughout the day. In each new situation ask yourself, "What difference would it make if I knew God's perspective on this? How would I respond if I really knew God?"

3

THREE IN ONE

IT IS ESSENTIAL for us to understand from the outset that our one great God exists in three persons. Admittedly, the typical nonbeliever views the doctrine of the trinity as one of the most ridiculous things he has ever heard. He is convinced that Christians must be out of their minds to accept it. God is one yet God is three? That's absurd! One plus one plus one equals one? That's nonsense—a blatant contradiction of simple, self-evident arithmetic. It stretches the credulity of reasonable people. "Three-in-One" may be a good name for sewing machine oil, but as a description of God the unbeliever sees it as sheer, unmitigated gibberish.

Where did such an idea ever come from? It is so utterly outlandish by human standards, it would seem unlikely that any man would have ever thought it up. That leads us to suspect that God Himself might have revealed it, and that is exactly what we find in Scripture. While the word *trinity* nowhere appears in the Bible, the idea is found there from beginning to end. There is no question about it—the doctrine of the trinity is divinely revealed Biblical truth. Our one God exists in three persons.

That is not to say that the authors of Scripture understood it clearly at first. When Peter, John, and the other disciples first saw Jesus they did not say, "Oh look, there goes God in flesh, the second person of the holy trinity." Yet as they heard Him claim to be the revelation of the Father with the prerogatives of deity, and as they watched Him perform the supernatural works of deity, they came to the convinced persuasion that He was God the Son.

Likewise, they probably gave very little thought at first to the Holy Spirit being the third person of the eternal Godhead. But when the events of the day of Pentecost had ended, it was obvious to them that the power they had witnessed working in them and through them was not their own. It was the power of God. The Spirit who indwelled them was none other than God Himself. So then, led by that same divine Spirit they revealed to us in their writings the triunity of the eternal God.

Men may object to it, but their objections arise primarily because they seek to understand the Creator in terms of the creature, to see God as merely a bigger and better version of man when in reality He is a totally different kind of being, an infinite being whom our finite minds cannot fully comprehend. We believe the doctrine of the trinity not because we understand it, but because God has revealed it. It is not incidental or unimportant. It is the very essence of His being, the way He is. And it is necessary for us to know it if we hope to grow in our understanding of His nature and perfections. What then does it mean that God exists in triunity?

An Explanation of the Triune God

It is a basic tenet of our Biblical faith that there is but one God. "Hear, O Israel! The LORD is our God, the LORD is one!" (Deuteronomy 6:4) The unity of the Godhead cannot be questioned. God does not consist of parts so He cannot be divided into parts. He is one. Polytheism is sinful man's feeble attempt to break God down into lesser gods and so weaken Him, to get rid of that one supreme, sovereign ruler whose will is absolute and who demands our total allegiance. But it cannot be done. There is one God, undivided and indivisible, who has one mind, one plan, one purpose, and one ultimate goal. We can be thankful for that. Trying to please many gods would only lead to mental confusion and turmoil. Missionaries testify to the utter relief expressed by animistic and polytheistic peoples when they discover that there is but one God. Submitting to the will of one God brings wholeness and unity of purpose to life.

But Scripture reveals that there are, in that one divine essence, three eternal distinctions. Those distinctions seem best described as *persons*, known as the Father, the Son, and the Holy Spirit. All three have identical attributes, however, and therefore they are one—not merely one in purpose, but one in substance. To possess all the exact same attributes is to be one in essential nature. Three persons with identical sovereignty, for example, would be one sovereign. Three persons with identical omnipotence would be one omnipotent being. We humans may have characteristics similar to others, but not identical to them. If we were absolutely identical to another person in every way, the two of us would actually be one. The three persons of the Godhead possess identical attributes. They are one in substance and one in essence, and therefore they are one God.

Many attempts have been made to illustrate the doctrine of the trinity: a three-leaf clover; an egg with its yolk, white, and shell; H_2O which can be either water, ice, or steam; the sun which embodies heat, light, and time; a man who is at one time a father, a son, and a brother; the space in a cube which is one entity, yet composed of length, breadth, and heighth, each equal to the other and part of the other. But in the final analysis every illustration breaks down somehow. We cannot find any finite analogy which fully explains the doctrine of the trinity. We simply believe it because God has revealed it. Our one God exists in three persons.

It seems to have been a man named Theophilus of Antioch who first applied the term *trinity* to this Biblical concept as early as 181 A.D. But it was the Anathasian Creed, completed some time in the fifth century, which stated it most clearly:

"We worship one God in trinity, and trinity in unity, neither confounding the persons, nor separating the substance."

Some Evidence for the Triune God

It is one thing to say that God is three in one, but some-thing altogether different to prove it. What is the Biblical testimony to the doctrine of the trinity? While the primary emphasis of the Old Testament is on the unity of God, the indications of His trunity are clearly seen even there. We need not read very far to find the first one: "In the beginning God created the heavens and the earth" (Genesis 1:1). While the verb *create* is singular and thus should have a singular subject, *Elohim,* the Hebrew name for God in this verse, is plural. That may not prove the Trinity, but it definitely points to plurality of persons in the Godhead. There was no other logical reason to choose a plural name. Some have main-tained that it is a plural of majesty, but that projects some-thing to ancient Hebrew minds that they never considered. They addressed their kings in the singular. So, as startling as it may seem, the first time we meet God in the Old Testament there is evidence of plural personal distinctions in Him.

We are not surprised, then, to hear Him say a short time later, "Let *Us* make man in *Our* image" (Genesis 1:26). The plural pronouns could not refer to angels because they were never associated with God in His creative activity. Conse-quently, more than one divine person was evidently involved. The plural pronouns make no sense otherwise (cf. Genesis 3:22; 11:7).

There are other Old Testament indications of plurality in the Godhead, such as references to the Angel of Jehovah, who is sometimes identified with Jehovah and yet at other times distinguished from Him. But one of the clearest statements was recorded by the prophet Isaiah. The Lord is speaking, the one who calls Himself the first and the last, the one who created the heavens and the earth (Isaiah 48:12-13). Here is what He says:

> Come near to Me, listen to this:
> From the first I have not spoken in secret,
> From the time it took place, I was there.
> And now the Lord GOD has sent Me,
>   and His Spirit (verse 16).

Do you see the implication of that? The Lord said that the Lord God and His Spirit sent Him. It looks very much like our one God exists in three persons.

But the unanswerable Biblical testimony to the Trinity is simply that all three persons are referred to as divine. First, the Father is called God. For instance, He is referred to as "God the Father" (Galatians 1:1), or "God our Father" (Galatians 1:3; Ephesians 1:2), or "the God and Father of our Lord Jesus Christ" (Ephesians 1:3). His deity is unquestioned.

But the Son is likewise referred to as God. He possesses the attributes of deity such as eternity, immutability, omnipotence, omniscience, and omnipresence. He bears the names of deity such as Jehovah, Lord, Immanuel, and the Word. He even permitted Thomas to call Him "my Lord and my God" (John 20:28). He exercises the prerogatives of deity such as forgiving sins, raising the dead, and judging all men. And He accepts worship reserved only for God.

Nobody can deny that He was claiming equality with the Father when He said, "In order that all may honor the Son, even as they honor the Father. He who does not honor the Son does not honor the Father who sent Him" (John 5:23). He insisted that He deserved the very same reverence that was reserved for God the Father. He did not seem to be the kind of man who was a lunatic. He must have been who He claimed to be—God the Son, equal with the Father and worthy of the same honor as the Father. The Father Himself addressed His Son as God: "But of the Son He says, THY THRONE, O GOD, IS FOREVER AND EVER" (Hebrews 1:8).

The prologue to John's Gospel tells us one reason Christ came to earth: to make the Father known, to reveal God to men (John 1:18). We can know more of what God is like by examining the person of Jesus Christ. He was God in flesh. As we explore Scripture and seek to discover who God is, we cannot neglect the earthly life of Jesus Christ. He is God the Son.

But the Holy Spirit is also called God. His name is "the Spirit of God" (Genesis 1:2). He too possesses the attributes of deity and performs the works of deity. While He is the Spirit who proceeds from the Father (John 15:26), He is at the same time called "the Spirit of Christ" (Romans 8:9). He is coequal with both the Father and the Son. The Apostle Peter clearly viewed Him as God when he said to Ananias, "Why has Satan filled your heart to lie to the Holy Spirit? . . . You have not lied to men, but to God" (Acts 5:3-4).

If the Father, the Son, and the Spirit all bear the names of God, possess the attributes of God, and perform the works of God, then there is no alternative but to acknowledge that our one God exists in three persons.

The Ministry of the Triune God

Scripture links these three persons of the Godhead together so closely in so many divine activities that it would be foolish to deny that any one of them is God. Observe some of those activities.

Creating the World. All three were involved in creation: the Father (Genesis 1:1); the Son (John 1:3,10; Colossians 1:16); and the Spirit (Genesis 1:2, Psalm 104:30). If all three created, then God the Creator must exist in three persons.

Sending the Son. All three members of the Trinity were active in the incarnation. When Mary questioned the angel about the possibility of a virgin birth, the angel answered her, "The Holy Spirit will come upon you, and the power of the Most High will overshadow you; and for that reason the holy offspring shall be called the Son of God" (Luke 1:35). The power of the Father, ministered through the agency of the

Spirit, resulted in the birth of the Son into the world. This close association in the birth of the Saviour is further indication of their oneness.

Identifying the Messiah. At precisely the proper moment, Jesus Christ was revealed to Israel as her Messiah. John the Baptist was the chosen instrument and the act of baptism was the chosen means. "After being baptized, Jesus went up immediately from the water; and behold, the heavens were opened, and he saw the Spirit of God descending as a dove, and coming upon Him, and behold, a voice out of the heavens, saying, 'This is My beloved Son, in whom I am well-pleased' " (Matthew 3:16-17). As the Spirit came upon the Son, the Father's voice was heard from Heaven expressing His approval. It was another powerful testimony to the eternal triune Godhead.

Providing Redemption. Two central passages bring the three members of the Godhead together in providing for man's eternal salvation. "How much more will the blood of Christ, who through the eternal Spirit offered Himself without blemish to God, cleanse your conscience from dead works to serve the living God?" (Hebrews 9:14) It was the offering of the Son to the Father by the power of the Spirit. The Apostle Peter taught, furthermore, that God the Father chose us to salvation, God the Son paid for it by shedding His blood, and God the Spirit set us apart unto the obedience of faith (1 Peter 1:1-2). Without each person of the Trinity doing His part we would yet be in our sins.

Proclaiming Salvation. In the early years of the Church God did some spectacular things to verify the gospel message which the apostles were preaching. The writer to the Hebrews tells us: "How shall we escape if we neglect so great a salvation? After it was at the first spoken through the Lord, it was confirmed to us by those who heard, God also bearing witness with them, both by signs and wonders and by various miracles and by gifts of the Holy Spirit according to His own will" (Hebrews 2:3-4). It was the same message that was first spoken by the Son Himself. When the apostles proclaimed it, the Father bore witness to its truthfulness by bestowing miraculous gifts through the Spirit. It was not only a powerful witness to the truth of the message, but another demonstration of the triune God at work.

Sending the Spirit. The three persons of the Trinity are so interwoven in sending the Spirit into the world that it is difficult to distinguish between them. In one passage it is stated that the Father would send Him in Christ's name and that He would testify concerning Christ (John 14:26). In another it is said that the Son would send Him from the Father (John 15:26). In yet another the Father sends Him and calls Him the Spirit of His Son (Galatians 4:6). What a picture of unity—such perfect unity that the actions of one are considered to be the actions of the other. Orthodox Christian doctrine has long taught that the Spirit proceeds from both the Father and the Son. But all three are vitally involved in His coming.

Indwelling Believers. Jesus taught His disciples that both He and His Father would make Their abode with them (John 14:23). But their indwelling would be in the person of the Comforter, the Spirit of truth (John 14:16-17). As the Spirit of both the Father and the Son His indwelling is the indwelling of the triune God. That would not be possible unless the three were one.

Baptizing Believers. In our Lord's commission to His disciples He said, "Go therefore and make disciples of all nations, baptizing them in the name of the Father and the Son and the Holy Spirit" (Matthew 28:19). The unity of the Godhead is declared by combining them in one *name* (singular). Yet the distinctiveness of the persons is maintained by listing them separately. It is another link in the long chain of evidence that the Father, the Son, and the Spirit are one God.

Entering God's Presence. All three members of the Godhead are intimately involved in the believer's access into the presence of God. Speaking of Christ, the Apostle Paul taught, "For through Him we both have our access in one Spirit to the Father" (Ephesians 2:18). Both Jews and Gentiles can approach the Father through the merits of the Son with the help of the Spirit.

Blessing Believers. In Paul's final remarks to the Corinthian Christians he linked the three members of the Godhead together in a beautiful benediction: "The grace of the Lord Jesus Christ, and the love of God, and the fellowship of the Holy Spirit, be with you all" (2 Corinthians 13:14). Unless the three are one, eternally and equally supreme, there would be little reason to put them together on an equal basis like this in a divine blessing. The apostle certainly considered them to be one.

The Bible Proclaims the Trinity

People who oppose the doctrine of the trinity like to say that it is nowhere found in the Bible. As we have seen, nothing could be further from the truth. How thankful we can be that it is there. We have a loving Father who has given us His eternal life, who provides our needs, and trains us in productive and satisfying living. We have a gracious Saviour who became a man like us, who paid the eternal debt of our sin, who sympathizes with us in our weaknesses, who feels with us in our sorrows, and who intercedes for us at the Father's right hand. We have the Holy Spirit who indwells us, who binds us together in one body, who comforts us, teaches us, guides us, and makes available to us all the resources of the eternal, omnipotent Godhead.

How could we live the Christian life if any one of them were less than God? We would be far poorer, and our lives would be less than complete. As it is, He is all that we need— an almighty triune God in the heavens, who rules and controls all things; a gracious triune God in our hearts, who loves us, cares for us, and ministers to our needs. What more can we ask?

Action To Take:

Express to God your desire to get to know Him in the fullness of His triunity—Father, Son, and Holy Spirit. Remind yourself regularly through the day that the triune God dwells in your body in the person of the Holy Spirit.

4

GOD IS SPIRIT

THE LORD JESUS was on His way to Galilee with His disciples. He had not taken the usual route for a Jew of His day—across the Jordan at Jericho, north along the east side of the river, then back into Galilee. Instead, He said that He had to go through Samaria (John 4:4). The disciples did not understand that but they went along without grumbling. They would soon learn why it was necessary to go that way. There were thirsty souls who were ready to receive Him.

It was during that trip through Samaria that Jesus taught one of the most basic truths about God found anywhere in the Bible. Picture yourself at a well by the side of the road near the little village of Sychar and listen to our Lord's conversation with a Samaritan woman, a rather unsavory character, to say the least. She had been married five times, and was at that moment living with a man to whom she was not married.

Jesus had worked the conversation around to spiritual things and was responding to the woman's comment about where people ought to worship: "Woman, believe Me, an hour is coming when neither in this mountain, nor in Jerusalem, shall you worship the Father. You worship that which you do not know; we worship that which we know, for salvation is from the Jews. But an hour is coming, and now is, when the true worshipers shall worship the Father in spirit and truth; for such people the Father seeks to be His worshipers" (John

4:21-23). It was at that point in the conversation that Jesus said something about God which had never been clearly stated before. The truth was apparent from what had been revealed in the Old Testament, but it had never been put into plain words. "God is spirit," He declared, "and those who worship Him must worship in spirit and in truth" (John 4:24).

God is spirit. There is no article in the Greek text before the word *spirit*, and that emphasizes the quality or essence of the word. Furthermore, the word *spirit* occurs first in the sentence for emphasis. The literal idea would be something like, "Absolutely spirit in His essence is God." Jesus did not leave any doubt about this truth. God is spirit!

But what does that mean? Some have a strange idea about what a spirit is. That is particularly true of children. To them spirits mean ghosts. When two of my sons were small we overhead them talking about ghosts. The five-year-old said, "Did you know that God is a ghost? He's the Holy *Ghost*." His four-year-old brother answered with great theological insight, "Yes, but he's like Casper, the friendly ghost" (a popular television cartoon character of the day). Is that really what it means for God to be spirit? Let us examine what it does mean, as well as how it applies to our lives.

He Is a Living Person

We can know Him

It is quite obvious that a spirit is alive. Our God is not an inanimate object, like a pagan idol with a mouth that cannot speak, eyes that cannot see, ears that cannot hear, and hands that cannot accomplish anything (cf. Psalm 115:4-7). He is alive. The very word *spirit* also means "breath," and breath is the evidence of life. Throughout Scripture He is called the living God (e.g. Joshua 3:10; Psalm 84:2; 1 Thessalonians 1:9).

But a spirit is also a person, not an impersonal force which acts without purpose or reason. I read in the newspaper that the British Columbia Appeal Court has ruled God to be a nonperson. A suspect was observed by hidden camera praying, and in his prayer he admitted that he was guilty. The court ruled that privileged communication, which would be inadmissible in court, must take place between two people, but that since God is not a person, comments made to Him are considered to be admissible evidence.

The judges who rendered that decision would seem to be rather unfamiliar with God's revelation of Himself. The essential nature of personality is self-consciousness and self-determination, and God has both. He is conscious of His own being. He told Moses that His name was, "I AM WHO I AM" (Exodus 3:14). Only a person who is aware of Himself could make that statement. He also has the freedom to choose His own course of action according to what He considers best. He demonstrated it when He subsequently told Moses to return to Egypt, gather the elders together, and inform them that the nation was about to be delivered from Egyptian bondage (Exodus 3:15-17). An impersonal force does not speak and give logical directions like that.

God also has the basic characteristics of personality—intellect, emotions, and will. He thinks, He feels, and He acts. And that is good news. Because He is a living person we can get to know Him personally and communicate with Him freely. If He were an inanimate object or an impersonal force there would be no hope of a personal relationship with Him.

He Is Invisible

We can know Him apart from our physical senses

Just about everybody knows that a spirit cannot be seen. We cannot even see a human spirit. The most intimate of friends cannot see each other's spirit and none of us can see God. Paul called Him "the invisible God" (Colossians 1:15), and "the King eternal, immortal, invisible" (1 Timothy 1:17).

John assured us that "no man has seen God at any time" (John 1:18). Mortal men have seen visible manifestations which God used to reveal Himself to them and to communicate with them, as when God the Son took human form in a Bethlehem manger. But they have never seen Him fully in His spiritual being. There is no way they could. Spirits are invisible.

Rather than spooking us out, that can be a very comforting truth. Because God is invisible, not only can we know Him, but we can know Him apart from our physical senses. We do not have to see Him or feel Him to know Him. We have spirits too, you see. God *is* spirit, but we *have* spirits housed within our physical bodies. And when our spirits are made alive toward God through the new birth, we have the capacity to commune with Him in our spirits, anytime, anywhere, and under any circumstances.

Communion with God does not depend on external things because it takes place internally in the spiritual part of our being. That was the point of Jesus' comment to the woman at the well. Since God is spirit we must worship Him in spirit. Worship is not primarily a matter of physical location, surroundings, form, ritual, liturgy, or ceremony. It is not a matter of creating a certain kind of mood or atmosphere. It is a matter of spirit. Worship is the response of our spirits to God's revelation of Himself.

It is difficult for us to grasp this truth since our spirits live in physical bodies and our physical bodies inhabit a physical universe. Our occupation with the physical makes us try to put our relationship with God into that same realm. We want to be inspired to worship Him by lavish cathedrals, great art, pleasant sounds, lovely aromas, and beautifully worded liturgies. Our human natures cry out for religious symbols, images, and pictures to help us create a mood for worship. We think we have to be in a church building and follow certain prescribed procedures. God says, "You cannot reduce me to physical things that can be experienced with your senses. I dwell in the realm of spirit and that is where I want to meet with you." Physical things may direct our attention to God, particularly things *He* has made. But we meet with Him in our spirits. We can enjoy Him riding to work in the car, pushing the vacuum cleaner through the living room, walking from one class to another, or anywhere else. We know Him and enjoy Him in the spiritual realm, apart from the physical senses.

He Is Immaterial

Knowing Him delivers us from bondage to material things

The major thing we learn about God as spirit is that He is immaterial. By that we do not mean He is insignificant or unimportant, but rather, incorporeal. He does not have a body. Jesus reaffirmed that fact to His frightened disciples shortly after the resurrection. When He entered the room in His glorified body they thought they had seen a spirit. He calmed them by saying, "See My hands and My feet, that it is I Myself; touch Me and see, for a spirit does not have flesh and bones as you see that I have" (Luke 24:39). Spirits do not have bodies.

This seems to present a problem, however, since Scripture does refer to God at times as though He has a body. For example, it mentions His hand and His ear (Isaiah 59:1), His eye (2 Chronicles 16:9), and His mouth (Matthew 4:4). Theologians call these *anthropomorphisms,* a word meaning "human form." They are symbolic representations used to make God's actions more understandable to our finite minds. But God has no material substance and He is not dependent on any material thing. He dwells in the realm of spirit.

That has some pertinent implications for our lives. If we know, love, and serve a God who does not have material substance, that should diminish our interest in material things. And that would make us different from the people around us, wouldn't it? We live in a culture that continually tries to feed our desire for the things money can buy and the security money can provide. It is nearly impossible to escape that influence. Yesterday's luxuries become today's necessities. And the more we get, the less it satisfies. If we ever get everything we want, we will find that none of it brings any real contentment.

I have a close friend who established as his goal in life to be a millionaire by the time he was forty-five years of age. He made it two years early, but it did not satisfy. His business had crowded out his time for God and left him empty and unfulfilled. I got to know him as the result of a funeral. His oldest son had been killed in an automobile accident, and it had left him despondent and disheartened. He had decided to let God have a place in his life again, but as he drove to church one Sunday after the tragedy, he admitted to himself that he really didn't want to go to church. But he didn't want to stay home either. In fact there was only one thing he could think of that he wanted in life, and that was to know God better. To his amazement, I announced that morning that I was beginning a series of messages on the attributes of God. His growing knowledge of God has brought him gratification that his money could never provide.

We hear stories like that, yet because our knowledge of God is so inadequate we find it difficult to believe that material things cannot satisfy. We keep trying to acquire more and more simply because that has become our way of life. We continually ask ourselves, "How can I invest this money so it will make me more money?" There are literally hundreds of thousands of millionaires in our country, many of whom are Christians. Their Christian friends sometimes invite them to meetings to tell folks how God has blessed them. They seem to be equating God's blessing with net worth. But that does not seem to be consistent with a God who is spirit.

God is not opposed to money. He allows us to earn the money we have. He gives us the health, the strength, the brains, and the opportunities to acquire it. But a God whose being is spirit cannot measure blessing in terms of bank accounts, investment portfolios, or land holdings. He measures it in terms of inner peace, contentment, satisfaction, meaning, purpose, loving and joyful relationships with other people who have eternal souls, as well as a meaningful relationship with Himself. Money cannot buy those things.

There are people talking about how much God has blessed them who know very little of what true blessing really is. Unfortunately, they confuse many of God's people who are not wealthy and leave them feeling as though God doesn't love them or care about them. It would be more helpful to testify about how little satisfaction money and material things can bring compared to the satisfaction which a personal relationship with God brings. Some unbelievers make lots of money too, but that does not necessarily mean that God's blessing is on their lives. If money is the measure of blessing, then the crime syndicates and drug traffickers must be blessed above all. A God whose being is spirit does not measure blessing by the amount of material things we possess.

Neither does He measure security in terms of how much we have stored up for the future. He can wipe out million dollar reserves as quickly as hundred dollar reserves (or ten dollar reserves, if that is closer to your financial situation). He wants us to find our security in Him, not in money or material things. He wants everything we have to be available to Him. He may not ask for all of it, but He has the right to do so if He so desires. He asked everything of a rich, young ruler, and that misguided man gave up the opportunity to receive eternal life because he was afraid of what discipleship would cost him (Luke 18:18-27). God would like us to be willing to give up any possession, any investment, anything he asks, and to trust Him fully with our future. We will be able to do that as we get to know the God who is spirit.

The most important question we should be asking is not, "How can I invest my money to make more money?" or even, "How can I provide greater financial security for myself and my family?" A better question might be, "How can I use my spendable income and my available capital to glorify the Lord, to advance His cause, and to help others in need?" God gives us our money. To some He gives more than others. Nothing in Scripture would forbid modest savings or invest-ments. But the clear emphasis of God's Word is that money is not primarily to store up or spend for our own comforts. It is to use for God's glory.

That is the emphasis of Christ's parable of the rich fool (Luke 12:16-21). That man hoarded riches for himself, but God never let him live to enjoy them. God said he was a fool, and his soul was required of him that very night. After telling the story Jesus added, "So is the man who lays up treasures for himself, and is not rich toward God" (Luke 12:21). To be rich toward God is to invest what we have over and above our needs for the salvation of souls, for the spiritual strength-ening of God's people, and for the alleviation of human suffering. That is real blessing and real security.

The Lord Jesus summed up this subject beautifully in the Sermon on the Mount: "Do not lay up for yourselves trea-sures upon earth, where moth and rust destroy, and where thieves break in and steal. But lay up for yourselves treasures in heaven, where neither moth nor rust destroys, and where thieves do not break in or steal; for where your treasure is, there will your heart be also" (Matthew 6:19-21). We can read that, nod our agreement, then go right on laying up treasures on earth. Do you know why that is? It's because we have not gotten to know God very intimately. We have not fully learned that, while He is interested in material things and while He can provide all that we need, He Himself is spirit, and the things on the top of His priority list relate to the spirit. Are you giving as much attention to developing your spiritual life as you are to increasing your net worth?

Shortly after the Sermon on the Mount the Lord Jesus gave His disciples an opportunity to put His instruction into prac-tice. He sent them out to minister two by two without money or extra supplies (Matthew 10:9-10). They learned that when they put His work first He takes care of their physical needs. We have opportunities to put His instructions into practice as well. There are needs all around us. How will we respond? Those who intimately know the God who is spirit will give more and more of their attention to the spiritual realm and, consequently, demonstrate a growing willingness to share their material substance with spiritual ministries and people in need. In that, the God who is spirit will be glorified.

Action To Take:

Since God is a living person, begin to talk with Him throughout the day. Share every detail of living with Him—joys, sorrows, victories, defeats, problems, pleasures, fears, frustrations, etc.

In view of God's spiritual nature, what changes do you think you should make in your priorities? In the use of your money?

5

FROM EVERLASTING TO EVERLASTING

A BUS TRIP through modern Israel will transport you back more than four thousand years and give you a glimpse of an unusual ancient phenomenon—the black goatskin tents of Arab desert dwellers known as Bedouins. Except for a periodic pickup truck, tractor, or television antenna, what you see has remained largely unchanged through the centuries. It is the same basic lifestyle as that of a godly old nomad named Abraham.

Uprooted from his ancestral home in Ur near the shores of the Persian Gulf, he wandered from one place to another, dwelling in tents, facing one adversity after another, never sure of what the next day would bring. His life was filled with uncertainty and insecurity, and he longed for something permanent (cf. Hebrews 11:9-10). It was near a well in the town of Beersheba that he found what he was looking for. There God revealed Himself by the name of El Olam, which means "the eternal God," the first time that name is mentioned in Scripture (Genesis 21:33). What an encouragement it was for Abraham to learn that in spite of the unsettled, unstable, and transitory character of his life, the God whom he knew and loved, who controlled every circumstance of life, had been around from eternity past and would be around for eternity to come.

Another godly Old Testament person named Moses lived

to the ripe old age of 120, considerably more than the insurance tables would predict for him if he were alive today. But as he neared the end of his life, he became deeply impressed with the impermanence and brevity of life on this earth. He found his mind turning more and more to the same truth God had revealed to Abraham years before. He wrote a psalm about it, probably the clearest statement of God's eternity found in the Bible.

> LORD, Thou hast been our dwelling place
>   in all generations.
> Before the mountains were born,
> Or Thou didst give birth to the earth
>   and the world,
> Even from everlasting to everlasting,
> Thou art God (Psalm 90:1-2).

Other Biblical writers picked up the same theme and we find it repeated throughout the pages of Scripture. Isaiah called God "the high and exalted One who lives forever" (Isaiah 57:15). Paul referred to Him as "the King eternal" (1 Timothy 1:17). What does that mean? What are the implications of God's eternity? What difference should it make to us that our God is eternal?

We shall learn as we progress through the study of God's attributes that everything God is, He is to a perfect and ultimate degree. In other words, he is infinite—without limitation and without termination. Some consider eternity to be simply infinity in relation to time. That is true, but it seems to involve more than that. An eternal God is not only without beginning or end, but is also free from the succession of events and is totally sufficient in and of Himself. If we really want to know God and enjoy His fellowship it would be helpful for us to understand these truths which He has revealed about Himself.

He Is Without Beginning or End

Moses said, ". . . from everlasting to everlasting, Thou art God." Let us examine the first part of that statement, "from everlasting." Periodically, children will come to me and ask, "Where did God come from?" We have all been taught to believe that everything comes from someplace. Every physical object has a maker. Every effect has a cause. Somebody made my watch. Somebody built my house. Humanly speaking, somebody was even responsible for bringing me into existence, a man and a woman I call my father and mother. We teach our children from their earliest days of understanding that the ultimate builder and maker of all things is God. He created the universe, of which every other tangible thing we know about is a part. The next question is a natural one. We set them up for it. They are surely going to ask it. They really cannot help themselves. "Who made God?"

The answer is difficult for them to accept. They have no frame of reference to which they can relate it. They have never heard an answer like this before. It may leave them puzzled and confused at first, but there is no other possible explanation. Nobody made God. He always was. The Bible never tries to prove His existence or explain where He came from. It merely assumes that He is there and that He has always been there. He had no beginning.

When we open the first page of the Bible, we read simply, "In the beginning God." He is just there! And look at what He is doing—creating the heavens and the earth. He existed before all things and He Himself brought everything else into existence. If anybody existed before God and was responsible for making God, then He would be God, and we would have to begin our questioning all over again. Who made Him?

What we are really saying is that because God is eternal He is self-existent, the only being there is who does not owe His existence to somebody else. He is independent of any other being or cause. He is over and above the whole chain of causes and effects. He is uncreated, unoriginated, without beginning, owing His existence to no one outside Himself. He has life in and of Himself. As Jesus put it, "For just as the Father has life in Himself, even so He gave to the Son also to have life in Himself" (John 5:26). Were it any other way He would not be God. An eternal being must be self-existent.

Even our common sense tells us that ultimately, behind every other cause and effect, there has to be One who Himself is uncaused and self-existent. The Israelites in their Egyptian bondage, feeling oppressed, forgotten, and hopeless, knew that in spite of their distress it had to be so, that behind all their caused circumstances, somewhere, somehow, there had to be a God who Himself was uncaused, who could make sense out of what seemed to be senseless suffering. When God told Moses to go back to Egypt and deliver them from their bondage, Moses hedged. "Who shall I say sent me?" he asked. "And God said to Moses, I AM WHO I AM; and He said, Thus you shall say to the sons of Israel, I AM has sent me to you" (Exodus 3:14). When the children of Israel would hear that the One who sent Moses was the self-existent God who simply is, they would recognize Him and follow Moses' leadership. That would make sense to them.

Not everyone is that sensible, however. Some philosophers and scientists reject an eternal, self-existent God because they cannot put Him in a test tube and examine Him or explain all His ways. But that is just subterfuge. If they *could* examine Him scientifically or explain Him fully, then He would not be God, and they know that full well. Their major problem is pride. To believe in an eternal, self-existent, uncaused cause, we must admit that everything else owes its existence to Him. And that would include us. We too are then totally dependent on Him for everything right down to life and breath itself. Egotistical, self-sufficient, self-made men are not willing to admit that. They like to believe they need nobody but themselves.

Maybe they need to be reminded that the God who has no

beginning also has no end. He is not only "from everlasting" but also "to everlasting" (cf. Psalm 102:25-27). He has brought some other things into existence as well that will have no end, such as angels and human souls. That is great news for believers. We shall someday enter fully into the eternal life we already possess in Christ. All time pressures will be gone and we shall be able to relax with total joy and delight in the presence of the eternal God who made us for Himself. People who are rightly related to an eternal God will obviously enjoy Him eternally. As the Psalmist put it, "For this God is our God for ever and ever" (Psalm 48:14 KJV).

But eternity is not such good news for the unbeliever. The eternal God who made people with no end also made places with no end. One of them was prepared especially for the devil and his angels, a place of "eternal fire" (Matthew 25:41), a place of "torment day and night forever and ever" (Revelation 20:10). While God did not make this place for people, unbelieving people who reject His gracious offer of salvation will spend eternity there. "And if anyone's name was not found written in the book of life, he was thrown into the lake of fire" (Revelation 20:15). There is no way to escape it other than by bowing before the eternal, self-existent God, admitting that we are unworthy of His favor, acknowledging our sin and our need for His forgiveness, and accepting the salvation He provided when He sent His Son to the cross. We are totally dependent on Him, totally at His mercy. It cannot be otherwise with a God who has no beginning or end.

He Is Free From the Succession of Events

One of the basic characteristics of time is the sequence of events: past, present, and future; yesterday, today, and tomorrow. We are bound to the fleeting succession of present moments. The moments before are but a memory with lingering results, and the moments to come are still an expectation which we cannot fully predict. We measure these succeeding moments by the rotation of heavenly bodies. We use clocks to help us and on some occasions, such as a hundred meter dash in the Olympic games, we break the succession of moments down into hundredths of a second. But we cannot escape the limitations of time, our bondage to the succession of moments, and the events that fill them.

We need to understand that eternity is more than the endless extension of time backward and forward. For convenience, we speak of eternity past and eternity future, but in actuality eternity supercedes time. It is a mode of existence that is not bound by this succession. There are no such things as past, present, and future with God. He created time and He can work within its framework, but He Himself is over and above it. He lives in one eternal *now*. Our tomorrows are just as real and present to Him as our yesterdays and todays because He has already experienced them.

Any human illustration of this truth will break down somewhere, but it might be helpful to try one. Imagine yourself watching the Rose Parade on a street corner in Pasadena. You view the parade one float and one band at a time—a succession of events. When it is finished you can look back on your experience and say, "I saw the parade." Now imagine yourself in the Goodyear blimp, viewing the parade from start to finish. You are aware of the sequence, but you can see the end from the beginning. It is all part of your consciousness at once rather than merely a succession of events. That is the way God views our lives and, in fact, all of human history from the beginning to the end of time.

> Remember the former things long past,
> For I am God, and there is no other;
> I am God, and there is no one like Me,
> Declaring the end from the beginning
> And from ancient times things which
>   have not been done (Isaiah 46:9-10a).

He does not acquire His knowledge from a succession of events as we do, (float by float, band by band). He knows the end as thoroughly as the beginning because He has already lived it. It is eternally present with Him.

This is a truth for believers to rest in. God knows all our tomorrows. There are no surprises with Him. We may experience a great many surprises in life, but there are none with God. He already knows the pleasures that are in store for us. He knows the tragedies we shall face. He even knows the sins we shall commit and He is already grieved over them. But He has a plan that will work them all together for good. Knowing a God like that not only helps us want to please Him, but it helps us face our future with confidence and courage. God is going to be there tomorrow, whatever it holds, with the next page of our lives open, ready to reveal the next step He wants us to take in the perfect plan He has arranged for us.

He Is Sufficient In Himself

There is at least one more element of an eternal being that we need to discuss. Since He existed before time and space, before any created thing or created being, then obviously He can exist without anything or anybody outside of Himself. We know He can do it because He did it. He existed when there was nothing else in existence. God does not need anything or anybody. He is totally self-sufficient. He is in Himself and has within His own being all that He needs.

That is not true of any other living organism. For example, we need things outside ourselves, things such as air, food, and water. Not God! If He needed anybody or anything outside Himself then He would not be complete, and if He were not complete He could hardly be God. But He is complete and He needs absolutely nothing. When Paul preached to the philosophers in Athens he declared, "The God who made the world and all things in it, since He is Lord of heaven and earth, does not dwell in temples made with hands; neither is

He served by human hands, as though He needed anything, since He Himself gives to all life and breath and all things" (Acts 17:24-25). God needs nothing outside of Himself.

It came as somewhat of a shock to me when I first realized that God did not need me. And you might as well face it too. God does not need you. He does not need our worship, our fellowship, or even our witness. He loves us and He wants us. In His grace He desires to use us and allow us to experience the satisfaction and excitement of being part of His eternal plan. But He does not need us. He did not create us because He needed us, but rather because He decided in His sovereign wisdom and good pleasure that creating us would be the best way to demonstrate His glory and grace (cf. Isaiah 43:7). That is no affront to our worth. Loving us and wanting us gives us more significance and security than needing us could ever provide. Rather than God needing us, we need Him. We are incomplete and unfulfilled apart from a personal relationship with Him. We can find true meaning only when we allow Him to have His proper place in our lives. We need God, but only God is complete in Himself.

God's self-sufficiency has practical application to our lives. If He possesses everything needful, and He has offered to come into our lives and share Himself with us, then obviously we can find all that we need in Him. That is exactly what the Apostle Paul stated about Him. Speaking of God the Son, he said, "For in Him all the fulness of Deity dwells in bodily form, and in Him you have been made complete" (Colossians 2:9-10). Jesus Christ is the God-man, and thus is eternal as well. The prophet Micah declared,

But as for you, Bethlehem Ephrathah,
Too little to be among the clans of Judah,
From you One will go forth for Me to be ruler in Israel.
His goings forth are from long ago,
From the days of eternity (Micah 5:2).

The child who was born in a Bethlehem stable was the Son who existed from all eternity complete and self-sufficient. And we can find our completeness in Him. How foolish we are to scrape, claw, fret, stew, cry, flatter, and manipulate a thousand different ways to get other people to meet our needs when the God who dwells within us in the person of His Son is all that we need. We are complete in Him.

Well, there He is—our eternal God without beginning or end, free from the succession of events, and sufficient in Himself. The eternal life He possesses is far more than an endless extension of life in time as we know it. It is a different quality of life, boundless life, all-encompassing life, life marked by infinite richness, completeness, and satisfaction. And it is ours to enjoy, now and forever, through the person of His Son. "And the witness is this, that God has given us eternal life, and this life is in His Son. He who has the Son has the life; he who does not have the Son of God does not have the life" (1 John 5:11-12).

Does God's Son live in us? It is a matter of admitting our sin and placing our trust in Jesus Christ as the only one who can pay sin's penalty. If we have done that, then we know an etrenal God and we possess eternal life. We have something far bigger and better to live for than the temporal things in this world. We can live in the light of eternity's values.

Mankind is striving for immortality. Politicians want to etch their names in the history books, athletes want to memo-rialize their feats in the record books, and businessmen want to build a financial empire that will endure for generations. But it seldom works that way. Politicians are forgotten, records are broken, and money has a strange way of evaporating. It is futile to live for the things of earth. Only what we build into people's souls, our own and others, will endure for eternity.

Some people have higher ideals and nobler goals than mere fame or fortune. They want to make the world a better place in which to live, to improve the quality of life on earth. That is commendable. But God has warned us that this entire world will eventually be consumed by fire (cf. 2 Peter 3:10). It seems futile to live for the things of earth when someday they will all be destroyed. It bears repeating: only what we build into people's souls, our own and others, will endure for eternity. If God is eternal then no endeavor on earth has higher priority than knowing Him, loving Him, worshiping Him, serving Him, and sharing Him with others. That would be the most profitable way to spend our fleeting moments on earth. That has eternal value.

Action To Take:

Sit down right now, while it is fresh on your mind, and write out some goals for your life that reflect your knowledge of God's eternality.

6

I CHANGE NOT

CHANGE is one of the most threatening things many of us face in life, and yet we encounter it every day. The universe itself is changing. Scientists tell us that all observed systems are continually changing from order to disorder, and that every transformation of energy is accompanied by a loss in the availability of energy for future use. In other words, our universe is running down.

Besides that, the world we live in is changing. Highly sophisticated technical developments have radically altered our lifestyle, and now they threaten our very existence. Ideological developments have changed the balance of world power and threaten our freedom as a nation. Governments are toppled and new ones established overnight, and sometimes it seems as though revolutions are as common as eating and sleeping. Every day the news reports focus on some new changes occurring in our world.

People change. One day we may be in a good mood, the next day in an ugly mood. And it is disconcerting if we never know what to expect from our wives, our husbands, our parents, or our bosses. Nice people sometimes get irritable and touchy. Fortunately, grouchy people sometimes get nicer. But we all change. That is the nature of creaturehood, and that is the nature of life. We find it unpleasant and intimidating at times. We would rather keep things the way they always were because the old and the familiar are more secure and comfortable, like an old shoe. But shoes wear out and need to be replaced, as does most everything else in life. So we struggle to adjust to change.

We grow and we strive to better ourselves, and that is change. Sometimes our sense of well-being collapses around us; we lose our health, our loved ones, our money, or our material possessions, and that is change. Our bodies begin to wear out; we can no longer do the things we used to do, and that is change. It is all unsettling and unnerving, but it is inevitable. What can we do about it? Is there anything unchanging that we can hold on to in a world where everything is so tenuous and transitory?

The Revelation of God's Immutability

An unnamed psalmist asked that question in a moment of great trial. The inspired title of Psalm 102 says, "A Prayer of the Afflicted, when he is faint, and pours out his complaint before the LORD." This man is in trouble. He is facing some devastating changes in his life. Listen to his lament.

> Do not hide Thy face from me in the day of my distress;
> Incline Thine ear to me;
> In the day when I call answer me quickly.
> For my days have been consumed in smoke,
> And my bones have been scorched like a hearth.
> My heart has been smitten like grass and withered away,
> Indeed, I forget to eat my bread.
> Because of the loudness of my groaning
> My bones cling to my flesh (verses 2-5).
>
> My enemies have reproached me all day long;
> Those who deride me have used my name as a curse
> (verse 8).
>
> My days are like a lengthened shadow;
> And I wither away like grass (verse 11).

Is there some kind of life preserver a person can hang on to when, like this psalmist, he feels as though he is about to go under? Is there something solid, stable, and unchanging? There is, and he is going to tell us about it.

> But Thou, O LORD, dost abide forever;
> And Thy name to all generations (verse 12).

There is a God who will never cease to exist. But He is more than eternal. He is absolutely unchanging.

> Of old Thou didst found the earth;
> And the heavens are the work of Thy hands.
> Even they will perish, but Thou dost endure;
> And all of them will wear out like a garment;
> Like clothing Thou wilt change them, and they will
> be changed.
> But Thou art the same,
> And Thy years will not come to an end (verses 25-27).

This is one of the first great Biblical statements of God's *immutability.* Simply stated, that means God is unchangeable. He is neither capable of nor susceptible to change. And that makes sense. Any change would probably be for the better or for the worse. God cannot change for the better because He is already perfect. And He cannot change for the worse, for then He would be imperfect and would therefore no longer be God. Created things change; they run down or wear out. It is part of their constitutional nature. But God has no beginning or end. Therefore He cannot change.

People sometimes think He changes, especially when they experience trying circumstances. The people of Israel felt that way. Their prophets warned them that God would chasten them for their rebelliousness and sin, and they assumed that such discipline would indicate that He was changing, that He was getting more harsh and less fair. For example, Malachi predicted that Messiah would come suddenly like a refiner's fire and a purifier of silver and judge the sinners among them (Malachi 3:1-5). The people were probably wondering when God began to develop such a concern about their sin. Malachi reminded them that He always has been concerned. That is His nature. He is unchangeably holy and righteous and just. God Himself declared, "For I, the LORD, do not change" (verse 6).

God's immutability not only brought Israel discipline. It also guaranteed her continued national existence. After establishing His immutability God goes on to say, "Therefore you, O sons of Jacob, are not consumed" (verse 6). He is unchangeably holy and righteous but He is also unchangeably merciful and faithful. He promised Abraham that his seed would endure forever (Genesis 13:15), and He cannot go back on His Word because He is immutable. The existence of the nation Israel to this day is a testimony to God's immutability.

We may begin to think God has changed when trials invade our lives. We say to ourselves, "God used to be good to me, but this surely doesn't seem very good." The Apostle James had some penetrating observations for a group of persecuted people who were beginning to think like that. Listen to James encourage them: "Do not be deceived, my beloved brethren. Every good thing bestowed and every perfect gift is from above, coming down from the Father of lights, with whom there is no variation, or shifting shadow" (James 1:16-17).

The "Father of lights" is the God who created the heavenly bodies. They move and turn and cast shadows on the earth and on each other. They are created things, so they change. But the God who made them does not change. There is absolutely no variation with Him, no eclipse of His lovingkindness and care. His gifts always turn out to be good, even when, for the present, we cannot figure out how. He will give nothing but what is best. We can count on that. It is the promise of an unchanging God.

If Jesus Christ is God in flesh, then we would expect Him likewise to be unchanging. That truth was revealed to another group of people who were suffering for their faith. The writer to the Hebrews said, "Remember those who led you, who spoke the word of God to you; and considering the result of their conduct, imitate their faith. Jesus Christ is the same yesterday and today, yes and forever" (Hebrews 13:7-8). He wanted them to know that the unchanging Saviour who was at work in the lives of the men who taught them the Word of God could do a supernatural work in their lives as well. He is the same Saviour that He always was, and what He has done for others He can do for you.

Some will protest, "But He seems to do more for my Christian friends than He does for me. They seem to be so spiritually stable, and I'm so up and down, so hot and cold. You say God is consistent. I say He's different in the way He deals with me." Things may never be any better for us until we believe that He truly is unchangeable, and acknowledge that the problem lies with us rather than with Him. That is why the writer to the Hebrews exhorted us to imitate the *faith* of our spiritual leaders. As we learn to *believe* that God is what He claims to be, we shall begin to enjoy the stability and steadiness which His immutability can minister to our lives. Most of us find it easier to be calm and steady in turbulent circumstances when we believe that those around us, particularly those in charge, are calm and steady. Well, God is in charge; He has complete control of every situation, and His hand never gets shaky. Trust Him, and enjoy a consistency and a constancy you may not have known before.

The Ramifications of God's Immutability

We have seen the doctrine clearly revealed, but what does it involve? Obviously, it includes everything about God of which we can possibly conceive. All that God ever was, He always will be. But look at a few Biblical examples:

The Word of God Is Unchanging. "Forever, O LORD, Thy word is settled in heaven" (Psalm 119:89). That is not true of our word. We often change our minds about things and find that we can no longer honor what we said in the past. Sometimes we say things we do not mean or we say things which later prove to be wrong and which must be retracted. But when God speaks it is always true. He never speaks in error. He never changes His mind. He never said anything He was sorry for or had to take back. His Word is settled and un-changing.

> The grass withers, the flower fades,
> But the word of our God stands forever (Isaiah 40:8).

The Plans of God are Unchanging. "But the plans of the LORD stand firm forever, the purposes of His heart through all generations" (Psalm 33:11 NIV). God's plans are firm. His purposes will always be carried out. Our plans and purposes change. Sometimes they are not very realistic and we must alter them. On other occasions somebody frustrates them. But God's plans are perfect and nobody can thwart them. So there is no reason to change them.

The writer to the Hebrews had something to say about this aspect of God's immutability: "In the same way God, desiring even more to show to the heirs of the promise the unchange-ableness of His purpose, interposed with an oath, in order that by two unchangeable things, in which it is impossible for God to lie, we may have strong encouragement, we who have fled for refuge in laying hold of the hope set before us" (Hebrews 6:17-18). God's purpose and His oath are both un-changeable. It is comforting to know that God's plan for this world will never change, and that He will carry it out right on schedule according to His own good pleasure. As He said through Isaiah,

Remember the former things long past,
For I am God, and there is no other;
I am God, and there is no one like Me,
Declaring the end from the beginning
And from ancient times things which have not
    been done,
Saying, "My purpose will be established,
And I will accomplish all My good pleasure"
    (Isaiah 46:9-10).

What God established before the foundation of the earth as the goal of human history will inevitably come to pass. What a comforting thing it is to know that no amount of satanic opposition can change that!

The Knowledge of God Is Unchanging. There are other applications of God's immutability in Scripture, but look at one more: "Known unto God are all His works from the beginning of the world" (Acts 15:18 KJV). We could have figured that out even if the Apostle James had not said it at the Jerusalem council. If God is unchanging and nothing about Him varies, then obviously His knowledge never increases or decreases. He knows everything and always has known everything. Anything less would make Him less than God. For example, if there ever was a time when God did not know what I would write on this page of this book, then He was not complete at that time and, therefore, He was not God. But you can be sure He did know. His knowledge is unchanging.

That is surely different from my knowledge. It has grown (hopefully). Yet I still know only a minute fraction of what there is to know. Quite frankly, I have forgotten more than I have remembered. So my knowledge also decreases. But it is a consolation to know a God who possesses complete and unchanging knowledge of everything. He can never lose anything. He will never forget to do anything He wants to do. And He has our lives in His unchanging care.

The Resistance To God's Immutability

Not everybody believes what you are reading right now.
They point to Scriptures that tell us God repents and they say,
"You see, God is mutable. He does change His mind. Therefore, He may not keep His Word. He may not carry out His
purposes. He may not know everything." We need not read
more than a few pages in our Bibles before coming to a
passage that raises that question. "Then the LORD saw that the
wickedness of man was great on the earth, and that every
intent of the thoughts of his heart was only evil continually.
And the LORD was sorry that He had made man on the earth,
and He was grieved in His heart" (Genesis 6:5-6).

But there are other passages, however, assuring us that
God will not change His mind:

> God is not a man, that He should lie,
> Nor a son of man, that He should repent;
> Has He said, and will He not do it?
> Or has He spoken, and will He not
>   make it good? (Numbers 23:19)

"And also the Glory of Israel will not lie or change His
mind; for He is not a man that He should change His mind"
(1 Samuel 15:29). Is that a contradiction in the Bible? I do not
think so.

We need to understand that, while God's character never
changes, His methods of dealing with men and administering
His program on earth may vary. Whatever He does will be
consistent with His eternal nature and will have been known
to Him from eternity past. But He does do things differently
at different times. The same writer who reminded us of God's
immutable counsel and oath (Hebrews 6:17-18) also told us
that God changed the priesthood and the law (Hebrews 7:12),
and that He took the old covenant away that He might establish the new (Hebrews 10:9).

God sometimes acts on the basis of what man does, and Scripture may picture that as God changing His mind in order to help us understand what is happening. But man's actions did not take God by surprise. He knew what man would do from eternity past, and He knew how He would respond. His actions, which appear to be a change of mind and are so described for our help, are fully consistent with His unchanging nature (Genesis 6:6; 1 Samuel 15:11). Sometimes Scripture portrays God as changing His mind when He threatens some punishment in order to demonstrate how strongly He feels about sin, then withholds that punishment as an act of mercy (Exodus 32:14; Jonah 3:10). Sometimes He reduces His sentence because His good purposes have been accomplished (2 Samuel 24:16). That hardly destroys the doctrine of immutability. God's immutability simply requires that He always act in accord with His eternal nature.

The Rewards of God's Immutability

The obvious question is, "So God is immutable. What does that mean to me?" If we really want to know Him, then it means everything, for a God who changes would not be worth knowing. We would not be able to trust Him. Do you trust a friend who changes his attitudes or actions toward you from one day to the next? Of course not. You are not going to open your heart to him, share your feelings with him, or tell him your weaknesses and your needs. If he is sympathetic and helpful on some occasions but disinterested or judgmental on others, you probably will not take the chance. If he keeps your intimate secrets to himself sometimes but spreads them around on other occasions, you are not going to confide in him anymore. Human friends sometimes act that way but God never changes. We can trust Him.

And He is never in a bad mood. That is different from us. We get disagreeable periodically. We growl at our spouses, snap at our children, criticize our fellow workers. Not God!

His mood never changes. What a pleasure to know that when-ever we approach Him through the merits of His Son He receives us warmly and lovingly.

That is one thing that makes prayer such a pleasure. We know that He is always open to our requests. He never gets tired of our coming to Him. In fact, He keeps inviting us to come. "Call to Me, and I will answer you, and I will tell you great and mighty things, which you do not know" (Jeremiah 33:3). "Ask, and it shall be given to you; seek, and you shall find; knock, and it shall be opened to you" (Matthew 7:7). "Until now you have asked for nothing in My name; ask, and you will receive that your joy may be made full" (John 16:24). "Be anxious for nothing, but in everything by prayer and supplication with thanksgiving let your requests be made known to God" (Philippians 4:6).

We would have little interest in praying to a God who might be listening, but who, on the other hand, might be out for a walk or taking a nap. Elijah taunted the prophets of Baal with the possibility that their god might be doing one of those very things (1 Kings 18:27). But we have the assurance that the Lord's ear is always open to our prayers.

> The eyes of the LORD are toward the righteous,
> And His ears are open to their cry (Psalm 34:15).

Some will object, "What sense is there in praying to an unchangeable God? Hasn't He already made up His mind what He is going to do? How can our prayers change any-thing?" We know that prayer changes things because God told us that it does. He decided in eternity past that He would take certain actions, provide certain benefits, and bestow certain blessings when we come to Him in prayer. So we come because He asked us to come and we make our requests known because He promised us that it would make a difference. We have the assurance that if we ask anything according to His will He hears and answers us (1 John 5:14-15). We can count on Him to be faithful to His promise.

Maybe we can understand what difference prayer makes by visualizing a mother caring for her sick child. Before she tucks him in bed for the night she gives him his medicine and quietly reassures him of her presence. She knows he will cry out to her during the night, and when the cry comes it does not change her mind about anything. She responds exactly as she planned to respond and does precisely what she knew would be best for him. But her help comes in answer to his request. That is the way she planned it. God has some good things prepared for us, but His plan is to give them to us in answer to our prayers. So ask and you will receive.

Since God is immutable we can always count on Him. We cannot consistently count on our human friends. They let us down at times. Their actions are sometimes affected by how they feel or how we have treated them. Their love is conditioned on our performance. But not God's. His love is everlasting and therefore unchanging (Jeremiah 31:3). He always acts on the basis of love. Likewise, His kindness is everlasting and therefore unchanging (Isaiah 54:10). He always acts on the basis of kindness. We can count on it. The better we know Him as the immutable God, the more we shall be able to trust Him and hold on to Him for stability and strength when everything around us is changing.

This is a great doctrine, and it would be beneficial for us to keep it in mind. But unfortunately one of our most glaring defects as mortal human beings is our inability to remember what we have learned about God when we need it most. Did you know that God has given us a visible sign to help us remember His immutability? It is the rainbow. When Noah and his family emerged from the ark God promised them that He would never again destroy the whole earth with a flood. He said, "I set My bow in the cloud, and it shall be for a sign of a covenant between Me and the earth" (Genesis 9:13). He has not destroyed the whole earth by water again. He is a God of His Word. He always does what He says He will do. He never changes.

Action To Take:

Every time you see a rainbow remind yourself that you know the immutable God. And remind yourself that a God who is unchanging in His love and kindness to you deserves your unchanging love, loyalty, devotion, and service.

7

GOD IS ABLE

WE LIVE IN AN AGE of unprecedented power. Mighty engines power race cars hundreds of miles per hour, pull freight trains that are literally miles in length, lift mammoth airplanes off the ground carrying hundreds of passengers with all their cargo, and hurtle tons of sophisticated scientific equipment into space. By harnessing the power of the atom we have created enough energy to light entire cities and enough weaponry to annihilate them many times over. Power is something we are just beginning to understand.

Throughout human history mankind has stood in awe before the mighty power of the natural elements—light so powerful it can blind us, water so powerful it can wash away whole civilizations, wind so powerful it can topple brick and steel buildings, fire so powerful it can melt rock. We know what power is.

Athletes are power conscious. Baseball has its power hitters, football its power runners, basketball its power forwards. Weight lifters may be billed as the most powerful men in the world. Athletes in nearly every sport are striving for greater power to establish new world records. Power is something with which we are all familiar. We can grasp its significance.

At least we think we can, until we come to God. Then suddenly our minds are boggled. He claims to be all-powerful, and that defies our imagination. Add the power of the world's greatest athletes to the power of the world's natural elements to the incredible power man has developed through science and technology, and the total does not even begin to approach God's power. In fact He himself is the source of all power, not only in the physical realm about which we have been talking, but in the spiritual realm as well, where the true nature and extent of power eludes our understanding. God is omnipotent! What does that mean? It means that God possesses infinite, complete, and perfect power. He can do anything He wants to do, absolutely anything. None of us can make that claim. Our capabilities are limited. But God is able to do everything He wills.

We sometimes use the term *power* to refer to God's authority or His prerogative to do what He pleases. But that is more accurately His sovereignty. Power refers to His strength to act, His ability to perform, and that is the kind of power in God's omnipotence. He is able to do anything He wants to do.

Meet the God Who Is Able

One of God's names tells us that He is able to do whatever He pleases, a name He first revealed to Abraham. He had promised to make Abraham the father of a great nation, and naturally Abraham needed a son in order for that promise to come true. He thought Hagar's child, Ishmael, was to be that son, but God told him that Sarah would bear a son named Isaac through whom the promise would be fulfilled. The whole idea was preposterous. Abraham was ninety-nine years old and Sarah was ninety, and humanly speaking there was no possible way they could have a son. But God helped them to believe it by the way He introduced Himself that day. "Now when Abram was ninety-nine years old, the LORD appeared to Abram and said to him, 'I am God Almighty; Walk before Me, and be blameless' " (Genesis 17:1).

El Shaddai is God Almighty, the God who can do anything

He wants to do, even rejuvenate dead wombs and give babies to couples in their nineties! He is almighty, all-powerful. That name is used forty-seven more times in the Old Testament and never of anyone but God. It has a New Testament equivalent, used ten times, which means literally "to hold all things in one's power." Scripture is punctuated with references to God's omnipotence from beginning to end. He is the Lord strong and mighty (Psalm 24:8). Power belongs to Him (Psalm 62:11). "Great is our Lord, and abundant in strength" (Psalm 147:5). He wants us to know Him as the God who is able to do anything.

It is interesting to watch Biblical characters discover Him in that light. Abraham was one of the first who did. Sometime after that initial revelation of Himself as the Almighty, God again promised Abraham a son, this time in Sarah's hearing, and she laughed to herself (Genesis 18:12). "Why did Sarah laugh?" God asked with convicting insight. Then He added, "Is anything too difficult for the LORD?" (Genesis 18:14) When Abraham and Sarah learned the answer to that question they would be able to believe that God would keep His Word. And they finally did, "being fully assured that what He had promised, He was able also to perform" (Romans 4:21). In other words, they grasped the truth of God's omnipotence.

Most of us have had disillusioning experiences with people who have promised more than they have been able to deliver, and we have a tendency to transfer our skepticism to God. Does He really care? Is He really in control? Does He really have the power to bring good out of adversity? Our doubts do nothing but raise our anxiety level and cause us grief. Believe it, Christian, just as Abraham and Sarah finally believed it. God is able to do whatever needs to be done in your life. No other being is all-powerful. No problem is all-powerful. Only God is all-powerful, and He is on our side. His omnipotence is pitted against our problem. The odds in our favor are infinite.

Jeremiah was another great saint who learned this lesson.

God had been telling him that Judah would be invaded by the Babylonians and taken into captivity, but then He directed him to go out and buy his cousin's field. That made no sense at all to Jeremiah. Why own a field if the Babylonians are going to destroy everything and take everybody into captivity? Could it be that God would bring them back from captivity? That was almost too good to believe. But he wanted to believe it and he was trying to believe it when he prayed, "Ah Lord GOD! Behold, Thou hast made the heavens and the earth by Thy great power and by Thine outstretched arm! Nothing is too difficult for Thee" (Jeremiah 32:17).

Jeremiah was acknowledging that God's power is displayed nowhere more dramatically than in creation. Everything *we* make requires existing materials but God made the worlds out of nothing. He merely spoke and it was done (Psalm 33:6,9). That is power! The writer to the Hebrews assures us that He continues to sustain all things by the word of His power (Hebrews 1:3). A God who is able to create everything out of nothing by a word, then continues to hold it all together by a word, is certainly able to do anything else He wants to do, including restore the nation Israel to her land. As if to strengthen Jeremiah's struggling faith God Himself speaks: "Behold, I am the LORD, the God of all flesh; is anything too difficult for Me?" (Jeremiah 32:27) No, Lord. Absolutely nothing! Jeremiah saw it. God is able to do anything.

The virgin Mary questioned God's spectacular revelation to her. How could she possibly bear a son when she had never had relations with a man? It would be by the very same means her elderly cousin Elizabeth would bear a son when she was past the age of child-bearing, by the supernatural power of God. "For nothing will be impossible with God" (Luke 1:37). That verse literally says, "For no word from God shall be without power." That puts the whole matter right where it belongs, in the realm of God's omnipotence. He has the power to do whatever He says He is going to do. If He wants to plant a child in the womb of a virgin He can do it. And He did do it, giving the world a divine Saviour.

The disciples were disturbed when Jesus told them how difficult it would be for a rich man to enter the kingdom of Heaven. "Then who can be saved?" they asked rather hopelessly. That was when they got a decisive lesson on God's omnipotence. "Looking upon them, Jesus said, With men it is impossible, but not with God; for all things are possible with God" (Mark 10:27). He is able to do anything He pleases, and He longs for us to know Him as the omnipotent God.

Know What He Is Able To Do

If we really want to know the omnipotent God intimately and experientially, we ought to think through some of the things He is able to do. The New Testament word "to be able" means essentially "to have power" (*dunamai,* the verb form of that familiar Greek noun, *dunamis*). When we read that God is able to do something it means He has the *power* to do it. It is a concept related to His omnipotence. The Old Testament word has somewhat the same connotation. While we know God can do anything He wants to do, look at a few of the specific things the Bible says He is able to do.

He Is Able to Save Us Completely. "Hence, also, He is able to save forever those who draw near to God through Him, since He always lives to make intercession for them" (Hebrews 7:25). The writer to the Hebrews is assuring us that God is able to save us perfectly for all time and eternity. Once we have trusted Christ as Saviour from sin and been born again, we never need to fear for our eternal destiny. Our omnipotent God has the power to keep us. Peter put it in those very words. He said we are "kept by the power of God" (1 Peter 1:5 KJV). And it is a good thing that we are. None of us would feel very secure if our salvation depended on our power.

He Is Able to Keep Us from Sin. "Now to Him who is able to keep you from stumbling, and to make you stand in the presence of His glory blameless with great joy" (Jude 24).

That great benediction assures us that God has the power to keep us from falling into sin. We know how He does it: "For since He Himself was tempted in that which He has suffered, He is able to come to the aid of those who are tempted" (Hebrews 2:18). Our omnipotent Saviour has conquered temptation Himself, and now He is right there for us to lean on when we are tempted. When we learn to lay hold of His power we will conquer those stubborn sins that disrupt our lives.

He Is Able to Supply Our Needs. "And God is able to make all grace abound to you, that always having all sufficiency in everything, you may have an abundance for every good deed" (2 Corinthians 9:8). That promise was addressed to faithful and cheerful givers. They can count on God to take care of everything they need, in every circumstance of life, all the time. Only an omnipotent God could make a promise like that. My wife and I have experienced that power. There were days, early in our marriage, when we acted as though God could not really take care of our needs, as though providing for a seminary student with a wife and child were more than He could handle. Sometimes we got anxious and irritable over finances. But we tried to be faithful in sharing our meager resources with Him, and He kept showing us, sometimes in miraculous ways, that He was able to supply our needs.

He Is Able to Heal Our Diseases. Jesus taught this lesson to two blind men right after He emerged from the house where He had raised Jairus's daughter from the dead, the supreme demonstration of His power. The two men cried out, "Have mercy on us, Son of David!" (Matthew 9:27) Jesus turned and asked, "Do you believe that I am able to do this?" (Matthew 9:28) When they answered, "Yes, Lord," Jesus touched their eyes and made them to see. He may be asking you the same question: "Do you believe I have the power to heal you?" He does not always heal, because He knows that sickness is sometimes the best way to accomplish His perfect purposes in our lives. But He is able, and He wants us to believe that.

Believing it could be the very thing that starts us on the road to recovery.

He Is Able to Deliver Us from Death. Daniel's three friends taught us this lesson when they were standing beside the door of a blazing fiery furnace heated seven times hotter than normal. They boldly declared to King Nebuchadnezzar, "our God whom we serve is able to deliver us from the furnace of blazing fire" (Daniel 3:17). He does not always deliver us from death. Many have laid down their lives for their faith through the centuries. But He is able to deliver us if He so chooses.

Jesus knew that. The writer to the Hebrews said, "He offered up both prayers and supplications with loud crying and tears to the One able to save Him from death" (Hebrews 5:7). As He prayed in the garden to His Father, He said, "All things are possible for Thee; remove this cup from Me; yet not what I will, but what Thou wilt" (Mark 14:36). While all things were possible, He submitted to His Father's will and trusted Him to do what was best. That is exactly what He wants us to do. It has been said that we are invincible and immortal until God's time to take us home. There is no reason for the child of God ever to fear, for God is able to deliver him from any danger.

After Daniel had spent an entire night in a den of lions, King Darius hurried to the den in the morning and called out to him, "Daniel, servant of the living God, has your God, whom you constantly serve, been able to deliver you from the lions?" (Daniel 6:20) That kind of question would be asked only by someone who does not know God. He most certainly was able to deliver him. Hungry lions are no more of a problem to an omnipotent God than fiery furnaces, or terminal illnesses, or scary noises in the dark, or barking dogs, or poisonous snakes, or earthquakes, or floods, or anything else. He has power over creation, power over nature, power over animals, power over the nations, power over rulers, and power over demons. And He is able to deliver us.

There are other references in Scripture to what God is able

to do, but none more exciting than the one in Ephesians 3:20:
"Now to Him who is able to do exceeding abundantly beyond all that we ask or think, according to the power that
works within us." That is real power, the very same power
that raised Christ from the dead and is operating in us right
now (Ephesians 1:19-21). The Holy Spirit of God, the Omnipotent One Himself, actually lives in us and makes His power
available to us. He is willing to give strength to all (1 Chronicles 29:12). Whoever you are and whatever your need, God's
strength is available to help you. From the little crisis, like a
stubborn jar lid you cannot unscrew when there is no one
there to help, to the major crisis like an extended illness of
a loved one that has put superhuman demands on you physically, God's strength is available to help.

With the promise of that kind of power at our disposal why
do we feel so weak, fearful, and powerless so much of the
time? Maybe we have not yet learned to appropriate God's
power.

Learn How To Enjoy His Power

The secret of releasing God's power lies in three basic
principles. The first was revealed to King Asa of Judah during
a time when he was displeasing the Lord by relying on human
treaties rather than on the power of the living God. A prophet
said to him, "For the eyes of the LORD run to and fro throughout the whole earth, to show Himself strong in the behalf of
them whose heart is perfect toward Him" (2 Chronicles 16:9
KJV). God is actually looking for people He can help, people
for whom and through whom He can release His power. But
there is a condition: *He wants our hearts to be wholly His,* our
allegiance to Him to be undivided. In other words, He wants
us to be yielded to Him, to desire His will more than our own
will. If he is going to supply us with His power, He wants to
be sure we will use it for His glory. Some of us may be so
weak and fearful and powerless because God cannot trust us

with His power. We would take the credit for ourselves. When we yield our wills to Him we are ready to experience His power.

The second key to enjoying God's power was revealed by the prophet Isaiah to a nation that desperately needed it. Israel was a midget surrounded by giants who were ready to pounce on her. Isaiah sought to encourage the nation by devoting an entire chapter of his book to the greatness of God in contrast to the weakness of men (Isaiah 40). But the nation was saying, just as we often say, "If God is so great and powerful, why doesn't He help us?" That is exactly what He wants to do.

> Do you not know? Have you not heard?
> The Everlasting God, the LORD, the Creator
>   of the ends of the earth
> Does not become weary or tired.
> His understanding is inscrutable.
> He gives strength to the weary,
> And to him who lacks might He increases
>   power (Isaiah 40:28-29).

Well then, how can we get His power? Isaiah is careful to tell us.

> Though youths grow weary and tired,
> And vigorous young men stumble badly,
> Yet those who wait for the LORD
> Will gain new strength;
> They will mount up with wings like eagles,
> They will run and not get tired,
> They will walk and not become weary (Isaiah 40:30-31).

To wait for God is to keep on prayerfully and patiently looking to Him. Some of us may be so weak and fearful and powerless because we are not consistently looking to God for His power. We connive, scheme, pull strings, and manipulate people to work out our problems and meet our needs rather than look to the Lord. He says, "I want to use my omnipotence on your behalf. Just ask Me, just look to Me rather than to yourself or to others." When we focus our attention on the Lord, rather than on our circumstances or on human solutions, we are ready to experience His power.

But there is a third key. *God's power is always released on our behalf through faith,* an unmistakable principle found throughout Scripture. There is little hope of enjoying God's power when we do not expect Him to release it, or if we are not sure that He can or will release it, or if we are not trusting Him to release it.

A needy man in Jesus' day had to learn that lesson. His son was hopelessly possessed by a vile demon which had nearly destroyed him. He brought the boy to Jesus' disciples to be delivered, but it turned out to be another frustrating dead-end for him. He was about to give up when Jesus arrived on the scene. This was his last ray of hope. He pleaded, "But if You can do anything, take pity on us and help us!" Listen to Jesus' answer; it is the pivotal issue to enjoying God's power: "If You can! All things are possible to him who believes" (Mark 9:23). The man cried out, "I do believe; help my unbelief" (verse 24). It was an honest admission that his faith was weak but a sincere request for the Saviour to strengthen it. That was all Christ asked. He spoke a word and the omnipotence of God was released, delivering the boy from demonic power.

God is able! There is no deficiency in His power. The deficiency may be in our faith. Believe that He can do what needs to be done in your life. Expect Him to answer, then watch for Him to do it. He may work in totally unexpected ways, but He will work with supernatural power. At this very moment He is looking for people through whom He can demonstrate that power. Why not let it be you?

Action To Take:

List some problems in your life that seem to be impossible to solve. Now meet the conditions for enjoying God's power: Yield your will fully to Him; Commit the problems to Him in prayer regularly; Believe that He will solve them in His own perfect way.

8

PERFECT IN KNOWLEDGE

FREQUENTLY in our years of married life, my wife has turned to me and asked, "What are you thinking?" Quite frankly, there have been times when I did not want to tell her, and I even resented her asking. My thoughts may have been selfish and sinful and I didn't want to admit them, or I may have been enjoying my own private fantasy and I was too embarrassed to tell her about it. Can you imagine the pressure you would feel if you lived with someone who knew everything you were thinking all the time?

Suppose you had an acquaintance who knew the future with perfect accuracy. He would know what the stock market is going to do tomorrow, what food prices will be next week, what crisis you are going to face in the near future. Can you imagine what a disadvantage that would put you under and how he could capitalize on his knowledge at your expense?

Did you ever have a friend who thought he knew everything? Whatever subject was being discussed, he could give you the straight scoop on it. It made you feel pretty dumb, didn't it? He probably did not know nearly as much as he thought he knew, but can you imagine the frustration you would feel if you lived with someone who really did know everything?

There is such a person. He knows what we are thinking; He knows what our future holds; in fact, He knows everything about everything. And surprise of all surprises, when we get to know Him, we find that it does not put pressure on us or make us feel frustrated, stupid, or taken advantage of. Instead it brings confidence and consolation to our lives. Let's meet Him—the God who knows everything.

The Reality of God's Omniscience

The Apostle Paul tells us about God's knowledge: "Little children, let us not love with word or with tongue, but in deed and truth. We shall know by this that we are of the truth, and shall assure our heart before Him, in whatever our heart condemns us; for God is greater than our heart, and *knows all things*" (1 John 3:18-20). All of us have moments when our hearts condemn us, but God knows that we belong to Him even when we are having doubts about it due to guilt feelings. He knows it, John assures us, because He knows everything. That is the doctrine of omniscience, which simply means "all-knowing" (omni—all; science—knowledge). God has perfect knowledge of everything—past, present, and future—both of what is actual and what is possible. As a godly woman named Hannah said in a famous Old Testament prayer, "For the LORD is a God of knowledge" (1 Samuel 2:3).

We already understand a few things about God's knowledge from our study of other attributes. For instance, because God is *eternal* He must know everything immediately and simultaneously. He never learns anything new by observing the succession of events that occur in time. Because He is *immutable* His knowledge never varies. It does not increase or decrease. God never has to say, as I have often said, "I remember studying that once, but it has slipped my mind. Let me check my notes." God's knowledge is constant and unchanging.

But it would be good for us to grasp a few more facts about God's knowledge. For one thing, it is *perfect* and *complete*. The Psalmist said, "His understanding is infinite" (Psalm 147:5). That was a lesson Job learned in the course of his suffering.

His misery was so intense that he was beginning to wonder whether God really knew all the details of what was going on in his life. We can understand that. We would be wondering the same thing if we had the trouble he experienced. But Elihu helped him see it by asking, "Do you know about . . . the one perfect in knowledge?" (Job 37:16) God's knowledge is perfect—comprehensive and all-encompassing. There is nothing that lies outside its scope. Nothing can possibly happen to us that God does not already know and has not known eternally. And that includes every trial we face in the course of a lifetime.

The Bible is filled with details of God's knowledge. For example, He knows the number and names of all the stars (Psalm 147:4). He knows every sparrow (Matthew 10:29). He knows every bird of the mountains and every wild beast in the fields (Psalm 50:11). But most important of all, He knows us and everything about us.

The classic passage on that subject is Psalm 139. David assured us that God knows when we sit down and when we stand up (verse 2). He knows our thoughts before we think them, while they are far away from us (verse 2; cf. also Ezekiel 11:5). He knows all our *ways* (Psalm 139:3), a word referring to the whole course and conduct of our lives. In other words, He knows everything that we do (cf. also Job 23:10; Proverbs 5:21; Jeremiah 16:7). He knows every word we speak while it is still on our tongues, before it ever comes out of our mouths (Psalm 139:4). In absolute awe David exclaimed,

> Such knowledge is too wonderful for me;
> It is too high. I cannot attain to it (verse 6).

Jesus told us that the Father even knows how many hairs we have on our head (Matthew 10:30). We don't know that. Even the fellow who has very few hairs left, who would desperately like to know that they are all still there, has no way of keeping track of how many he has. But the Father knows. He doesn't need to count them. He just knows.

As you can well imagine, it would be impossible to give God a surprise party. There is no way that we can possibly keep any secrets from Him (Psalm 44:21). We can keep secrets from other people. We may succeed in living a whole lifetime without exposing some of our hidden thoughts to anybody. But God knows everything that goes on in our hearts and minds.

He gave us a demonstration of his mind-reading, heart-searching techniques one day in Bethlehem. The prophet Samuel had arrived in town to choose Israel's future king. One by one Jesse paraded seven of his sons before Samuel, but God rejected them all. He was looking at something Samuel could not see. As he explained it to Samuel, "God sees not as man sees, for man looks at the outward appearance, but the LORD looks at the heart" (1 Samuel 16:7). God wanted a man whose heart was wholly His, one with a desire to do His will. He knows whether or not we have that desire. We can make others believe that we do when in reality we want our own will. But God knows.

God knew that there was something missing from the lives of those seven sons of Jesse. But when the youngest was brought in from keeping his father's sheep, God's spiritual X-ray vision perceived a heart that dearly loved Him and longed to please Him. "Arise, anoint him; for this is he" (1 Samuel 16:12). David had his moments of spiritual failure, as we all do, but few people in Scripture could rival his wholehearted devotion to God. God saw that devotion while David was still a youth.

One of the last things David did before he died was to give this charge to his son Solomon: "As for you, my son Solomon, know the God of your father, and serve Him with a whole heart and a willing mind; for the LORD searches all hearts, and understands every intent of the thoughts" (1 Chronicles 28:9). It was a reminder of a truth David knew well, that God knows the secrets of the heart, a good reason to serve Him willingly and keep our thought lives pure and pleasing to Him.

Since there are no secrets with God we might as well face the fact that there is no such thing as a secret sin. We like to think there are some things in our lives that nobody else knows about, but Moses exploded that misconception:

> Thou hast placed our iniquities before Thee,
> Our secret sins in the light of Thy presence (Psalm 90:8).

The writer to the Hebrews agreed with him. "And there is no creature hidden from His sight, but all things are open and laid bare to the eyes of Him with whom we have to do" (Hebrews 4:13). We play little games to keep other people from knowing what we are really like on the inside, and we get pretty good at it. We learn how to fool most of the people most of the time. We even begin to fool ourselves. But God is not susceptible to our games. He never gets fooled. He knows everything about us.

If God knows everything then *He obviously knows our future,* and Scripture bears that out. He knows "what is to come" (John 16:13), and "the things which must shortly take place" (Revelation 1:1). He knows "the end from the beginning" (Isaiah 46:10), that is, He has known how things will turn out since before time began. That includes a personal knowledge of our lives. For instance, He knew before Jeremiah was formed in his mother's womb that he would be a prophet to the nations (Jeremiah 1:5). He knew before Paul was born that he would preach Christ among the Gentiles (Galatians 1:15-16).

That poses a problem to some. If God knows all of our future actions then it would seem as though they are fixed, settled, and unalterable. If nothing can happen apart from God's knowledge then the very fact that He knows it will happen makes it certain to happen. Where then is human freedom? For example, if God knows that I am going to cut my grass tomorrow then I am certainly going to cut it, am

I not? But suppose I don't want to cut my grass tomorrow! Do I have a choice?

The Bible teaches that God created us with volition. We make choices every day. We even have the privilege of choosing to obey God or disobey Him (cf. Deuteronomy 30:19; Joshua 24:15). So we certainly have the ability to act contrary to what God knows we will do. But we won't, because if we did, then that new act would have been the one known from eternity past. He knows everything because everything that happens is part of His perfect plan (Ephesians 1:11). He has included in that plan from eternity past all the choices He knew we would make of our own volition.

There is one more thing we should know about God's knowledge before we explore its application to our lives. It is *innate* and *inherent*. Nobody taught God what He knows. He never had to go to school to learn. He knows simply because of who He is.

> Who has directed the Spirit of the LORD,
> Or as His counselor has informed Him?
> With whom did He consult and who gave Him
>   understanding?
> And who taught Him in the path of justice
>   and taught Him knowledge,
> And informed Him of the way of understanding?
>   (Isaiah 40:13-14)

The obvious answer to those questions is "no one!" He knows everything by the very essence of His being. An infinite God must possess infinite knowledge as a necessary part of His nature. When Paul thought about that, it caused him to exclaim, "Oh, the depth of the riches both of the wisdom and knowledge of God! How unsearchable are His judgments and unfathomable His ways! FOR WHO HAS KNOWN THE MIND OF THE LORD, OR WHO BECAME HIS COUNSELOR?" (Romans 11:33-34) What a magnificent God we know!

The Relevance of God's Omniscience

Are you agreed that the fact is indisputably established in the Bible? God really does know everything! Unbelievers do not like that one bit.

> They mock, and wickedly speak of oppression;
> They speak from on high.
> They have set their mouth against the heavens,
> And their tongue parades through the earth.
>
> And they say, "How does God know?
> And is there knowledge with the Most High?"
> (Psalm 73:8-9,11)

It bothers them to think that there is a God who knows what goes on in their minds. At first they will try to hide their thoughts and deeds from Him and pretend that He doesn't really know (Isaiah 29:15). But when they realize how futile that is they usually deny that there is a God (Psalm 14:1). That is the only way they can rid themselves of the pressure and frustration of a God who knows everything.

The growing Christian does not view God's omniscience as a threat, however. It does provide him with a challenge to grow, just as my wife's question about what I am thinking motivates me to grow. I want to be able to share my mind with her freely and without embarrassment. The more I mature in my relationship with her and with the Lord, the more comfortable I am about telling her what I am thinking, and the more comfortable I am with the realization that God knows what I am thinking. So the challenge is there. But the omniscience of God is more than a challenge. It is also the source of great encouragement. We can discover some rea-sons why that should be true, particularly from the life of our Lord Jesus, the omniscient God in human flesh.

It was two days after John the Baptist had identified Him

as the Messiah that Jesus called Philip to be His disciple, and Philip in turn found his friend Nathanael. The first time Jesus laid eyes on Nathanael He said, "Behold, an Israelite indeed, in whom is no guile!" (John 1:47) Jesus saw into his innermost being before He had even met him, and He perceived a man whose motives were pure, one who was honest, trustworthy, and free from deceit. It did not matter what anyone else thought. The Lord knew Nathanael's heart.

Have people ever accused you of being crafty, underhanded, devious, or mercenary when you knew your intentions were pure? As hard as you tried to explain they refused to believe you. Have they made other unjust judgments about your character and your motives? What an encouragement it is to realize that God knows our hearts and that He evaluates us on the basis of what is actually there. All of us are subject to unfair and unkind criticism at times. There is no reason to become defensive. God knows the truth about us and that is all that really matters.

Shortly after Christ's earthly ministry began He was teaching and healing in a crowded house in Capernaum when, suddenly, He was interrupted by four men tearing the tiles off the roof and lowering a paralytic friend into His presence. When He saw their faith He said, "My son, your sins are forgiven" (Mark 2:5). The scribes and Pharisees did not appreciate Jesus' assuming that He could forgive sins, a prerogative of deity, and they were fuming on the inside. "And immediately Jesus, aware in His spirit that they were reasoning that way within themselves, said to them, 'Why are you reasoning about these things in your hearts?' " (Mark 2:8) He knew the thoughts of those critical unbelievers and He went on to handle the situation beautifully, demonstrating conclusively that He had the power to forgive sins.

We sometimes encounter people who, like the scribes and Pharisees, are rigidly opposed to the person and word of Christ. We do not know what they are thinking nor are we sure what we should say to them or how we should deal with them. But God knows what is going on in their minds and He knows exactly how to approach the situation. He can give us the right words to say, or He can deal with them through somebody else at some later time if He so chooses. But whatever He does, we can be assured that He knows what is in the heart of man, and He has every situation in perfect control.

Not long ago a man came to tell me about his salvation. "You said something that really got me thinking," he related. Naturally I asked him what it was so I could use it again in dealing with other unbelievers. But when he told me what I had said, it didn't sound very impressive to me at all. In fact, I didn't even remember saying it. Quite frankly, I can't remember now what it was I said. But God knew what that man needed to hear at that precise moment and *He* obviously led me to say it. He knows the heart of every person and He knows what they need to hear.

Jesus made a rather startling observation about God's knowledge when He predicted judgment on the Israelite cities where He had performed most of His miracles. "Woe to you, Chorazin! Woe to you, Bethsaida! For if the miracles had occurred in Tyre and Sidon which occurred in you, they would have repented long ago in sackcloth and ashes" (Matthew 11:21). "And you, Capernaum, will not be exalted to heaven, will you? You shall descend to Hades; for if the miracles had occurred in Sodom which occurred in you, it would have remained to this day" (verse 23).

He knew what the people of Tyre, Sidon, and Sodom would have done if they had enjoyed the same spiritual benefits which those Israelite cities received. God's omniscience includes the potentialities and possibilities as well as the actualities. God knows the "what-ifs" and the "what-might-have-beens," and His judgment will be based on those facts as well. It will be less severe on those who had less advantages when God knows they would have responded with more (verses 22,24). The reason why He did not give them more is locked in the stronghold of His sovereign and unsearchable wisdom.

But one thing we know for sure—His evaluation will be based on absolute and perfect knowledge.

God knows what we could have been if we had enjoyed the same spiritual advantages which others have had. That can be a source of great encouragement, particularly to people who have been saved late in life, who never had the benefit of a Christian home or Sunday school training. There is no need to compare ourselves with others. God merely wants us to use what we are now and what we have now for His glory.

There are other indications of omniscience in the life of our Lord Jesus, for instance, in Jerusalem during the last week of His ministry on earth. He was eating with His disciples in a second-story room when He said, "But behold, the hand of the one betraying Me is with Me on the table. For indeed, the Son of Man is going as it has been determined; but woe to that man by whom He is betrayed!" (Luke 22:21-22) Some theologians insist that God does not know what we are going to do until we do it. That is hardly the case here. Jesus had just informed His disciples that He knew which one of them would betray Him.

But that is not all He knew on that occasion. A little later He said, "Simon, Simon, behold, Satan has demanded permission to sift you like wheat; but I have prayed for you, that your faith may not fail; and you, when once you have turned again, strengthen your brothers" (Luke 22:31-32). When Peter affirmed his faithfulness, Jesus said, "I say to you, Peter, the cock will not crow today until you have denied three times that you know Me" (Luke 22:34). Jesus knew that Satan was going to tempt Peter, that Peter's faith would falter but not fail, that later he would repent and come back stronger than he was before, able to strengthen his brethren. Although He knew all that, it did not diminish His love for Peter at all. He promised to use His power of intercessory prayer to sustain Peter through the entire ordeal.

What a wonderful application of our Lord's omniscience! He knows all of our faults and failures. Not one shortcoming will ever surface unexpectedly to disillusion Him. He sees the whole of our lives, including the temptations we shall face and the sins we shall commit, yet He never stops loving us (Jeremiah 31:3) and He never stops interceding for us (Hebrews 7:25). Somebody asked, "Isn't it odd that a being like God, though He sees the facade, still loves the clod that He made out of sod? Isn't it odd?" It's not only odd; it's absolutely incredible! He knows me yet He still loves me.

Look at the sequel to the story. It was after Christ's death and resurrection and He was with His disciples again, this time by the Sea of Galilee. "So when they had finished breakfast, Jesus said to Simon Peter, 'Simon, son of John, do you love Me more than these?' He said to Him, 'Yes, Lord; You know that I love You.' He said to him, 'Tend My lambs.' He said to him again a second time, 'Simon, son of John, do you love Me?' He said to Him, 'Yes, Lord; You know that I love You.' He said to him, 'Shepherd My sheep.' He said to him the third time, 'Simon, son of John, do you love Me?' Peter was grieved because He said to him the third time, 'Do you love Me?' And he said to Him, 'Lord, You know all things; You know that I love You.' Jesus said to him, 'Tend My sheep' " (John 21:15-17).

Why did Jesus ask Peter those questions if He knew everything? We must conclude that He was not seeking information. He knew that Peter loved Him. Peter himself attested to that when he said, "Lord, You know all things; You know that I love you." That is another clear statement of divine omniscience. Jesus did not ask those questions in order to find out whether Peter loved Him; He asked them for Peter's sake. Peter had recently denied His Lord and did not understand why he had done it. He probably doubted his own love for Christ and wondered whether he could ever again be used effectively. But the Lord lovingly drew him out, helped him understand his own heart, helped him reaffirm his love, then reassured him of future usefulness. The Lord understood him when he did not understand himself, and He had just the right words of encouragement for the occasion.

The same thing is true of us. God understands us better than we understand ourselves and He is right there to minister to us with the appropriate encouragement and the perfect provision. He does that today through His Word. Do you have a need that you yourself may not fully understand? Turn to the Scriptures and allow the omniscient Lord who inspired them and who revealed Himself through them to minister to your need just as He did to Peter's.

There is only one thing that God blots out of His knowledge, and that is our sins. He said, "for I will forgive their iniquity, and their sin I will remember no more" (Jeremiah 31:34). That is a blessed promise for every true child of God. God knows whether or not we are truly His children. On several occasions the Lord Jesus demonstrated His penetrating knowledge of people who had professed to believe on Him but whose commitment was not sincere (John 2:23-25; 6:64). He knows the same thing about us. If you have never genuinely acknowledged your sin and trusted Him for forgiveness, do it now. He will blot every sin you ever committed forever from His memory.

Action To Take:

List some of the things you are glad that God knows about you that other people may not know. Try to remember that He knows them when you are feeling misunderstood or falsely judged.

List some of the things you wish God did not know about. Determine now that by His grace you are going to change them.

9

THE LORD IS WITH US

AVE YOU EVER FELT as if you wanted to run away from God? Maybe you thought the responsibilities of the Christian life were too heavy for you, or you just could not be the person you were supposed to be and do the things God was asking you to do. If you could just get away, things would be better. Or maybe the model of a Christian husband or wife was too overwhelming and you could not live up to it. Or you knew how a Christian parent was supposed to treat his children but you seemed to fall short several times a day. Or you knew you ought to talk to those unsaved neighbors about Christ but you could not bring yourself to do it, and now they are gone and you are embarrassed and ashamed. Maybe you committed yourself to teach a class of children for a year but you just did not want to face them another Sunday. Or you knew God expected you to flee temptation but you could not seem to resist it, and now you feel as though God is on your back. If you could just get away from Him for awhile, go someplace where He could not see you, then everything would be all right.

That is exactly what the prophet Jonah thought. God told him to go to the city of Nineveh and preach against its wicked-ness, but that was the last thing in the world Jonah wanted to do. Nineveh was the capital of a proud and powerful nation, and he was sure the people there would reject him, maybe even try to kill him for pointing out their sin. If they did repent God would probably hold back the punishment He had predicted and Jonah would become the laughingstock of the whole city. As far as he was concerned there was no way he would ever go to Nineveh.

"But Jonah rose up to flee to Tarshish from the presence of the LORD. So he went down to Joppa, found a ship which was going to Tarshish, paid the fare, and went down into it to go with them to Tarshish from the presence of the LORD" (Jonah 1:3). It is mentioned twice in that verse that Jonah wanted to get away form God's presence. Somehow he had developed the ridiculous notion that God did not live in Tarshish (a city which some scholars believe was located on the Atlantic coast of Spain). Do you share his sentiments? Do you think there might be some place on this earth where you can hide from God?

The Explanation of God's Omnipresence

Jonah should have known better. As a prophet in Israel he was certainly familiar with the inspired Psalms of Israel's greatest king. David had written a powerful message about trying to run away from God's presence:

> Where can I go from Thy Spirit?
> Or where can I flee from Thy presence?
> If I ascend to heaven, Thou art there;
> If I make my bed in Sheol, behold, Thou art there.
> If I take the wings of the dawn,
> If I dwell in the remotest part of the sea,
> Even there Thy hand will lead me,
> And Thy right hand will lay hold of me.
> If I say, "Surely the darkness will overwhelm me,
> And the light around me will be night,"
> Even the darkness is not dark to Thee,
> And the night is as bright as the day.
> Darkness and light are alike to Thee (Psalm 139:7-12).

If God is an infinite spirit then He is not only free from the limitations of time, but He is free also from the limitations of space. He is omnipresent, that is, present everywhere all the time. No other living being has that attribute. Every other being is restricted to a particular place at a particular time. I cannot be in Los Angeles and New York City at the same time. Angels cannot even do that. Satan cannot do it. But God is wholly present in every part of His domain at the same instant. He is not partly present in one place and partly present in another, but He is as fully present in every particular place as if He were in no other place. God cannot be split into little pieces. Wherever He is, He is in the fullness of His being.

This attribute of God is one of the most difficult for us to grasp with our finite minds. We can understand to some degree that God has infinite power and that He knows everything. But how can He be everywhere at once? The inability of the human mind to comprehend this doctrine may be one reason why so many people choose to worship some lesser being. They suspect that to be everywhere may really mean He is nowhere, and they want to worship a god who is somewhere, so they turn to a finite being or to an idol.

While I do not fully understand it, there is no question but that God claims omnipresence for Himself in His Word. David assured us that there was absolutely no place he could go to escape the presence of God, even if he wanted to. Not even pitch-blackness could screen him from God's presence, because God sees in the dark as well as in the light. Daniel confirmed that:

> It is He who reveals the profound and hidden things;
> He knows what is in the darkness,
> And the light dwells with Him (Daniel 2:22).

Jeremiah proclaimed the same truth to the people of his day. The land was filled with dishonesty, profanity, and immorality, and the false prophets of the day were not only condoning it but actually participating in it (Jeremiah 23:11,14). They assured the people that God would not judge them for their sin (verse 17). That is when God spoke through Jeremiah:

> Am I a God who is near, declares the LORD,
> And not a God far off? (verse 23)

Those false prophets thought God did not know what they were doing and saying, that He was limited to one place at a time, that if He were near somebody else He could not be near them. Not so!

> Can a man hide himself in hiding places,
> So I do not see him? declares the LORD.
> Do I not fill the heavens and the earth?
>   declares the LORD (verse 24).

He fills Heaven and earth, just as fully present in one place as another. There is no conceivable place where God is not completely present in the totality of His essence. If there were any place where God was not present He could hardly have said that he fills Heaven and earth. But He said it and He meant it. Just as light, or air, or sound, or odor fill a room so God fills His universe. Through Isaiah He said, "Heaven is My throne, and the earth is My footstool" (Isaiah 66:1). There is no place to hide from His presence.

Solomon mentioned God's omnipresence on the day that the temple was dedicated. It was a beautiful building where God would place His name, where He would personally dwell, and where He would meet with His people. But in Solomon's majestic prayer of dedication he revealed a truth that we still misunderstand today. "But will God indeed dwell on the earth? Behold, heaven and the highest heaven cannot contain Thee, how much less this house which I have built!" (1 Kings

8:27) God would dwell in that temple but He would not be restricted to it. We cannot limit God to a building. We cannot even limit Him to a universe. God is everywhere.

He is immanent, that is, right here, inhabiting and pervading His universe. But at the same time He is transcendent, that is, rising above and exalted supreme over His universe. Many people would rather not hear that. They would prefer to lock God in a building where they can visit Him when it suits them and get away from Him the rest of the time.

The Jewish religious leaders in Jerusalem didn't like it. They killed Stephen for quoting Solomon and Isaiah on this subject, along with a few other thoughts from the Old Testament Scriptures (Acts 7:48-49). The Athenian intelligentsia ridiculed Paul on Mars Hill for daring to suggest the same thing. He had said, "The God who made the world and all things in it, since He is Lord of heaven and earth, does not dwell in temples made with hands" (Acts 17:24). He cannot be locked in a building. Since He is everywhere, He is not far from any one of us (verse 27). In fact, we live and move and exist in Him (verse 28). Incredible! Just as a bird lives in the air and a fish lives in the water, so we actually live in God. Each of us, believer and unbeliever alike, lives in God's sphere and in God's presence every minute.

Philosophers since Paul's day have not liked this doctrine any more than those on Mars Hill. They have devised interesting ways to pervert the truth. The *pantheists* have overemphasized God's immanence. To them God is merely the impersonal forces and laws of nature. He is to be identified with the material universe, and consequently ends up being the trees, mountains, rivers, and sky rather than a personal, omnipresent being. The *deists* on the other hand, overemphasize God's transcendence. For them, God is present in His creation only by His power, not in His being and nature. While He made the world He is not actively involved in governing it. He has left it to itself. English literature is filled with both distortions. The truth is that God is both immanent and transcendent. He is distinct from His creation yet present in every part of it, both in His power and in His essential being. God is everywhere!

Yet the Bible will not let us suppose that God is present in exactly the same sense everywhere. For example, He does not dwell on earth in the same sense that He dwells in Heaven (Matthew 6:9). He did not dwell in Gentile nations in the same sense He dwelled with His ancient people Israel (Exodus 25:8; 40:34). He did not dwell with the Old Testament Jew in the same sense that He dwells with the New Testament Christian (John 14:17). He does not dwell with the unbeliever in the same sense He dwells with the believer (John 14:23). And He does not dwell with the believer now in the same sense He will dwell with him in eternity (Revelation 21:3).

I am not sure how God can dwell with different people in different ways at different times, yet be fully present everywhere in His total being. Maybe He simply makes His presence known in a different measure. But He does claim to be everywhere and I, for one, believe it. I read somewhere about a little boy who believed it too:

> He was just a little lad, and on a fine Lord's day,
> > was wandering home from Sunday School and
> > > dawdling on the way.
> He scuffed his shoes into the grass; he found a caterpillar;
> > he found a fluffy milkweed pod and blew out
> > > all the filler.
> A bird's nest in the tree o'erhead, so wisely placed and high,
> > was just another wonder that caught his eager eye.
> A neighbor watched his zigzag course and hailed him
> > from the lawn,
> > > asked him where he'd been that day, and what
> > > > was going on.
> "Oh, I've been to Sunday school," (he carefully
> > turned the sod,
> > > and found a snail beneath it.) "I've learned a lot
> > > > 'bout God."

"M'm, a very fine way," the neighbor said, "for a boy to
    spend his time.
If you'll tell me where God is, I'll give you a
    brand-new dime."
Quick as a flash his answer came, nor were his accents faint,
    "I'll give you a dollar, Mister, if you'll tell me
    where God ain't."

The Application of God's Omnipresence

Jonah soon found out that David, the psalmist, was right all along. God is everywhere, and there is no way that we can hide from His presence. He went down into the hold of the ship, and God was there. He was thrown into the raging sea, and God was there. He was swallowed by a great fish, and he discovered that along with the tangled seaweed, stifling heat, and burning acids, God was there. Then he was vomited out on dry land and found that God was there. He finally decided that the smartest thing would be to obey a God who was everywhere. He would have saved himself a great deal of grief had he remembered that truth from the very beginning.

That seems to be one of our great weaknesses too. We hear these truths and believe them, but we tend to forget them when we need them. We become oblivious to God's presence and begin to live our lives as though He were nowhere around. Jacob had that problem. He was running from his brother's wrath when he stopped for a night's rest at Bethel. During the night he had a dream about a ladder. The Lord stood above it and said, "And behold, I am with you, and will keep you wherever you go, and will bring you back to this land; for I will not leave you until I have done what I promised you" (Genesis 28:15). God was with Jacob and would not leave him, but he did not realize it. The record states, "Then Jacob awoke from his sleep and said, 'Surely the LORD is in this place, and I did not know it' " (verse 16).

Isn't that just like us? The eternal, changeless, all-powerful, all-knowing, sovereign God of the universe is with us and we are not even aware of it. We ignore Him. I doubt that He is very happy about that—probably no happier than a wife whose husband pays no attention to her. So many lonely, grieving wives have sat in counselors' offices and moaned, "He acts as if I weren't even there." God must feel that same grief.

Let's remind ourselves of some of the places God specifically promised to go with us, then begin to acknowledge His presence in those situations, and learn to share them with Him. He will be pleased, and at the same time things will go better for us.

He Is With Us in Temptation. The Apostle Paul taught us that our bodies are the temples of the Holy Spirit. God the Holy Spirit lives within us and goes everywhere we go. That should provide an added incentive for us to flee from sin. As Paul put it, "Flee immorality. Every other sin that a man commits is outside the body, but the immoral man sins against his own body. Or do you not know that your body is a temple of the Holy Spirit who is in you, whom you have from God, and that you are not your own?" (1 Corinthians 6:18-19) The believer's body is a mini-temple, a sacred dwelling place for the omnipresent God, and we must treat it as such. Sexual relations outside of marriage defile the temple of God. They dirty up God's dwelling place. To be conscious of God's presence is to guard the purity of His home.

But respect for God's home is not the only deterring power of this doctrine. If we love our Lord and want to please Him, the knowledge that He is with us is going to have an influence on where we take Him and what we do in His presence. We usually try not to offend someone we truly love. While we may be tempted to do something of which they disapprove when we are separated from their watchful eye, we seldom entertain the thought of doing it when they are standing right there looking at us. The next time you are tempted to disobey

God's Word and disregard His will, visualize Him standing there watching the whole scene. He is there, you know, so we might as well think about it. Sometimes we act like ostriches with our heads in the sand. We think that because we cannot see God, He cannot see us. But He does.

> The eyes of the LORD are in every place,
> Watching the evil and the good (Proverbs 15:3).

He Is With Us in Need. The writer to the Hebrews had something to say about God's presence. Some of the folks to whom he was writing had lost their jobs because of their faith in Jesus Christ, and they were facing desperate needs. They were probably worrying about how their needs would be met and, worse still, they were envying people who had every-thing they needed. They would benefit from this pertinent exhortation: "Let your character be free from the love of money, being content with what you have; for He Himself has said, 'I WILL NEVER DESERT YOU, NOR WILL I EVER FORSAKE YOU' " (Hebrews 13:5).

We may not have everything in life we want, but we do have the Lord. He is right there with us all the time. He sees all our needs and He will meet every one of them in His own time and in His own way. Some may be saying, like those Hebrew Christians of old, "But I have this bill due tomorrow that I can't pay." That situation could be God's way of en-couraging you to reevaluate your lifestyle. He wants us to be diligent, to work hard, to seek His wisdom about every penny we spend, and to stay out of debt. Unpaid bills sometimes reveal that we have been overly enthusiastic about gratifying our desires rather than merely meeting our needs. The next time you are tempted to spend money on something you do not need, remember that the omnipresent Lord of the uni-verse is right there with you. Ask His advice before you move ahead. Then trust Him faithfully to supply every need. That is what He promised to do (Philippians 4:19).

He Is With Us in Loneliness. I want you to meet a lonely woman. Hagar was a slave, uprooted from her home in Egypt and taken to be the handmaid of Abraham's wife, Sarah. She had gotten pregnant by Abraham at Sarah's suggestion, and the resultant situation had brought such tension and turmoil to their household that she finally ran away to the wilderness—unloved, unwanted, pregnant, and absolutely alone in a strange land, the victim of someone else's sin.

That was when the Lord appeared to her with tender words of encouragement and advice, and she called His name El Roi, the God who sees (Genesis 16:13). She had come to the comforting realization that God was right there with her, that He saw her in her loneliness, and that He cared. Ezekiel called Him Jehovah-Shammah, the Lord who is there (Ezekiel 48:35).

He is the same God today. He sees us in our loneliness and offers us words of encouragement and advice. He is the God who is there, and He still cares. Most of us prefer a warm body near us when we are lonely, a hand we can touch, and a voice we can hear. God may provide that for us in His perfect time. But meanwhile, He is with us, and the very fact that we are physically alone can make His presence more precious than it would be if there were people around us. To believe that He is with us can help to dispel the aching loneliness.

He Is With Us Through Difficult Service. Many godly people in Scripture faced tasks which they believed were beyond them, but the confidence to carry on came through the assurance of God's presence. For example, when Moses was called by God to return to Egypt and deliver the people from bondage, he shuddered at the enormity of the task. When he tried to beg off, God said, "Certainly I will be with you" (Exodus 3:12). That was just the encouragement he needed to go on.

Again, after the nation's sin with the golden calf, God told Moses to lead the people on to their promised land. But he was afraid to go until the promise was reaffirmed. Finally it was: "My presence shall go with you, and I will give you rest" (Exodus 33:14). The promise of God's presence was the inspiration he needed to do the job he was called to do.

When Joshua took over the leadership of the nation after Moses' death, he struggled with the same lack of confidence. But God was right there to encourage him: "No man will be able to stand before you all the days of your life. Just as I have been with Moses, *I will be with you*; I will not fail you or forsake you" (Joshua 1:5). "Have I not commanded you? Be strong and courageous! Do not tremble or be dismayed, for *the LORD your God is with you* wherever you go" (verse 9). If God would be with him, he could conquer the land against insuperable odds.

When our Lord's disciples heard His commission to make disciples of all nations, they must have trembled at the vastness of what they were being asked to do until the Lord added, "And lo, I am with you always, even to the end of the age" (Matthew 28:20). That would make all the difference in the world.

I can testify to you quite honestly that I would not be in the Lord's service today were it not for the promise of God's presence. The job is too big, the responsibilities too great, and my abilities much too weak and inadequate. But I have that promise—God is with me. And you have it too. God never asks us to do anything by ourselves. When he gives us a job to do He promises to be with us as we do it. Whether it is teaching a class, witnessing to a friend, sharing our testimony with a group of unbelievers, lovingly confronting another Christian with his sin, or anything else He might want us to do, He is right there with us, directing, assisting, and enabling us as we do His will.

He Is With Us in Danger. The Apostle Paul faced many dangerous situations in the course of his apostolic ministry, one of which was in Corinth. The Jews there were disturbed at the great numbers of people turning to Christ and the situation seemed to be as potentially explosive as a barrel of

TNT beside a campfire. Paul seriously considered leaving. "And the Lord said to Paul in the night by a vision, 'Do not be afraid any longer, but go on speaking and do not be silent; for *I am with you,* and no man will attack you in order to harm you, for I have many people in this city' " (Acts 18:9-10). The key to Paul's courage was in those words, "I am with you."

God said much the same thing to the tiny nation Israel when she was surrounded by giant world powers which threatened to destroy her.

> Do not fear, for *I am with you;*
> Do not anxiously look about you, for I am your God.
> I will strengthen you, surely I will help you,
> Surely I will uphold you with My righteous
>   right hand (Isaiah 41:10).

That is also His promise to us. There is nothing to fear for the child of God. He is present in all the places people sometimes fear. He is on that airplane, in that elevator, in that cramped room, on those high places, in that wild animal infested jungle, in that new and strange situation with people we do not know, in that operating room during delicate surgery, in the recovery room where the pain and discomfort are fierce. He was even in the fiery furnace with Shadrach, Meshach, and Abednego. King Nebuchadnezzar was astonished to see four people in the furnace instead of only the three he had cast in (Daniel 3:24-25). It was a fulfillment of God's promise to His people.

> When you pass through the waters, *I will be with you;*
> And through the rivers, they will not overflow you.
> When you walk through the fire, you will not be scorched,
> Nor will the flame burn you (Isaiah 43:2).

Why should we fear anything when God is there? The Psalmist put it so beautifully.

God is our refuge and strength,
A very present help in trouble.
Therefore we will not fear, though the earth
    should change,
And though the mountains slip into the heart
    of the sea (Psalm 46:1-2).

The LORD *of hosts is with us;*
The God of Jacob is our strong hold (verse 7).

He Is With Us in Death. Death is the ultimate source of fear and anxiety for many people. But again, God is right there with us.

Even though I walk through the valley of the shadow
    of death,
 I fear no evil; for *Thou art with me;*
Thy rod and Thy staff, they comfort me (Psalm 23:4).

When we face the death of a loved one, this thought brings greater consolation than all the well-intentioned words of our human friends put together: God is with us. And when we face our own departure from this earthly scene there is no reason for alarm. God will accompany us right into Heaven's glory.

Sometime ago someone handed me this interesting account:

I dreamed I was walking along the beach with the Lord and across the sky flashed scenes from my life. For each scene, I noticed two sets of footprints in the sand, one belonging to me, the other to the Lord. When the last scene of my life flashed before me, I looked back at the footprints in the sand. I noticed that many times along the path of my life there was only one set of footprints. I also noticed that it happened at the very lowest and saddest times in my life.

I questioned the Lord about it. "Lord, You said that once I decided to follow You, You would walk with me all the way. But

I have noticed that during the most troublesome times in my life, there is only one set of footprints. I don't understand why in times when I needed You most, You would leave." The Lord replied, "My precious child, I would never leave you during your times of trial and suffering. When you see only one set of footprints, it was then I carried you."

What more can we ask? Wherever we go, whatever we face, our omnipresent Lord is with us. Ignore Him no longer. Let Him be part of every situation and circumstance. The awareness of His presence will add an exciting new dimension to the quality of your life and to the confidence you enjoy in living.

Action To Take:

Begin to cultivate a consciousness of God's presence. Greet Him at the beginning of each new day. Remember often through the day that He is right there with you. At bedtime rehearse the events of the day and think about how you could have allowed Him to be more a part of them, and what difference it would have made if you had. Say "goodnight" to Him before you drop off to sleep, remembering that He will be with you all night long.

10

THE MOST HIGH RULES

THE BABYLONIAN EMPIRE was the greatest power in the world of its day, and its king, Nebuchadnezzar, had no equal. But the great king had not been sleeping well. Whenever he tried to go to sleep troubling thoughts from a recent dream flooded his mind and he was terrified. He tried to get help from his magicians, astrologers, and diviners, but to no avail.

Finally he turned to Daniel, remembering that it was Daniel who had helped him with a frightening dream earlier in his reign. He carefully described his nightmare. It was about a huge tree that grew to the sky and continued to provide food and shelter for all until suddenly a holy messenger from Heaven declared that the tree would be cut down. The messenger added,

> This sentence is by the decree of the angelic watchers,
> And the decision is a command of the holy ones,
> In order that the living may know
> That the Most High is ruler over the realm of mankind,
> And bestows it on whom He wishes,
> And sets over it the lowliest men (Daniel 4:17).

Whatever dramatic event that dream anticipated, its purpose would be to convince the inhabitants of the earth that the Most High God rules the affairs of men. We call that great

truth the sovereignty of God. It was essential that Nebuchadnezzar understand it, so important, in fact, that God let him
lose his mind, grovel in the fields like an animal, and eat grass
like an ox until he was willing to admit it. And he finally did.
After recuperating from his ordeal, he praised and honored
the Most High God who lives forever, and said:

> For His dominion is an everlasting dominion,
> And His kingdom endures from generation to generation.
> And all the inhabitants of the earth are accounted as nothing,
> But He does according to His will in the host of heaven
> And among the inhabitants of earth;
> And no one can ward off His hand
> Or say to Him, What hast Thou done? (Daniel 4:34-35)

That is one of the clearest statements of God's sovereignty
found anywhere in the Bible. Nebuchadnezzar learned the
doctrine well and it is just as important for us to understand it.

The Meaning of God's Sovereignty

The dictionaries tell us that *sovereign* means chief or highest,
supreme in power, superior in position, independent of and
unlimited by anyone else. Some theologians insist that sovereignty is not technically an attribute of God, but rather a
prerogative that issues from the perfections of His nature.
That makes little difference. We still need to know Him as the
sovereign God, and there is probably no more comforting
truth about Him that we will ever learn. To know the sovereign God is to find peace in the problems and pressures of
daily living.

God is truly and perfectly sovereign. That means He is the
highest and greatest being there is, He controls everything,
His will is absolute, and He does whatever He pleases. When
we hear that stated, we can understand it reasonably well,

and we can usually handle it until God allows something that we do not like. Then our normal reaction is to resist the doctrine of His sovereignty. Rather than finding comfort in it, we find that it gets us upset with God. If He can do whatever He pleases, why does He allow us to suffer? Our problem is a misunderstanding of the doctrine and an inadequate knowledge of God. If we can explore what sovereignty involves, then we can truly get to know our sovereign God.

It should not be any problem for us to admit that God is the highest and greatest being there is. If He is the eternal, self-existent, self-sufficient, unchanging Spirit, all-powerful, all-knowing, and everywhere, it is obvious that He stands alone, above all. No one can equal Him. If anyone existed before Him or is more powerful than He is or knows more than He knows, if He needs anyone else to complete Him, then that one would be God rather than the One we know as God. But that idea is ridiculous. There is only one true and living God, and in order for Him to be God He must be the highest and greatest. The very name by which he revealed Himself to Nebuchadnezzar shows that He is. He called Himself the Most High God, that is, the exalted One, lifted far above all gods and men.

Other passages concur. Isaiah said:

> Thus says the LORD, the King of Israel
> And his Redeemer, the LORD of hosts:
> "I am the first and I am the last,
> And there is no God besides Me" (Isaiah 44:6)

The writer to the Hebrews put it succinctly: "For when God made the promise to Abraham, since He could swear by no one greater, He swore by Himself" (Hebrews 6:13). Who else could He call on to establish that solemn oath? He is the greatest and highest being there is (cf. also Exodus 18:11; Deuteronomy 4:39; Psalm 95:3; 135:5; Isaiah 40:12-15,18, 22,25; 45:5; 1 Timothy 6:15).

This still may not convince us that God can do anything He pleases. We then need to go back to the beginning of God's creative activity. If God made everything and sustains everything by His power, then He obviously owns everything and has a right to rule what is His and do what He pleases with it. Did He make everything? There is no question about that. Speaking of God the Son, Paul said, "For by Him all things were created, both in the heavens and on earth, visible and invisible, whether thrones or dominions or rulers or authorities—all things have been created by Him and for Him" (Colossians 1:16). Not only did He create all things, but He created them for Himself, for His own glory. Solomon went so far as to say, "The LORD hath made all things for Himself: yea, even the wicked for the day of evil" (Proverbs 16:4 KJV). That sounds rather shocking at first. But we need to realize that He did not cause them to be wicked. He made them, they subsequently practiced evil of their own volition, yet somehow He is going to use them to fulfill His own eternal purposes.

Furthermore, what He made for Himself He is presently holding together. Paul went on to say, "And He is before all things, and in Him all things hold together" (Colossians 1:17). God the Son keeps the particles of the universe from flying apart. All things cohere in Him.

If God created everything and now takes the necessary steps to make it all stick together, He must consider it all to be His. That is exactly what Scripture teaches. In a great prayer of thanksgiving King David declared, "Yours, O LORD, is the greatness and the power and the glory and the majesty and the splendor, for everything in heaven and earth is yours" (1 Chronicles 29:11 NIV). To this, all Scripture agrees. For example, "The earth is the LORD's, and the fulness thereof; the world, and they that dwell therein" (Psalm 24:1 KJV; cf. also Genesis 14:19; Deuteronomy 10:14; Psalm 50:10-12).

If God made everything and owns everything, then He has the right to rule everything. That is what He taught Nebuchadnezzar during his harrowing experience (Daniel 4:17,25,34-35). Actually, David had said it years before. In that same prayer of thanksgiving he went on to declare, "Thou dost rule over all" (1 Chronicles 29:12). Passages in both the Old and New Testaments verify this truth. For example, "The LORD has established His throne in heaven, and His kingdom rules over all" (Psalm 103:19 NIV). "He rules by His might forever" (Psalm 66:7). "Alleluia: for the Lord God omnipotent reigneth" (Revelation 19:6 KJV). His omnipotence provides the strength to do what His sovereignty gives Him the right to do. Nothing is outside the scope of His sovereignty—absolutely nothing.

A godly king named Jehoshaphat found great encouragement in knowing the sovereign God of the universe who rules everything, when he faced a fearsome coalition of invading enemy armies. "Then Jehoshaphat stood in the assembly of Judah and Jerusalem, in the house of the LORD before the new court, and he said, 'O LORD, the God of our fathers, art Thou not God in the heavens? And art Thou not ruler over all the kingdoms of the nations? Power and might are in Thy hand so that no one can stand against Thee' " (2 Chronicles 20:5-6). God proved that He ruled the nations by giving Jehoshaphat and his people a miraculous victory that day. When trials invade our lives, we too can find great comfort in knowing the God who rules everything. He loves to give His people victory (cf. also Psalm 47:2-3,7-8; Psalm 93:1-2; Proverbs 21:1; Matthew 28:18; Acts 17:26; Revelation 19:6).

Since God is infinite, His sovereignty must be absolute. His rule must involve total control of everything in His domain—every circumstance, every situation, every event. God claims responsibility for establishing and removing human rulers, however acceptable or unacceptable we may consider them to be (Daniel 2:20-21). The Psalmist said that God controls the weather (Psalm 147:16-18; 148:8). Sometimes we don't like it, but we learn to accept it from the One who rules everything.

He even holds the life of every creature in His hand (Job

12:10). Everyone in my family is convinced that God led a collie named Levi to our door. His name was engraved on the tag hanging around his neck when he arrived. Can you imagine a dog named Levi finding the Strauss house? Our youngest son had been praying for a dog for nearly three years, but we had laid down some stringent requirements. He had to be housebroken. He had to be obedient. And he had to be a gentle, people-dog in order to live in a pastor's home where visitors come and go regularly.

When my wife returned the dog to its owner, whose address was also engraved on the tag, she said kiddingly, "If you ever want to get rid of this dog, please let us know." The surprising reply was, "I do. I'm looking for a good home for him right now." My wife asked if we could think about it overnight. To our delight, Levi got out of his house and found his way to our residence again the next morning. This time we decided he could stay. When the owner brought us his papers, we learned that he had been conceived at the approximate time our son began to pray for a dog, that he was born on my wife's birthday, and that he was an honor graduate of obedience school. No one will ever convince us that Levi's coming was anything other than the gracious work of our sovereign God. Incidently, he did meet the other requirements as well.

God's sovereignty means that He either directly causes or consciously permits *everything* that happens in human history. Paul said to the Romans, "For from Him and through Him and to Him are all things" (Romans 11:36). He taught the Ephesians that God works "all things after the counsel of His will" (Ephesians 1:11).

We may be shocked to learn that God even admits to causing adversity and calamity.

> The One forming light and creating darkness,
> Causing well-being and creating calamity;
> I am the LORD who does all these (Isaiah 45:7).

Think of that. God may on occasion purposely build problems into our lives, little problems like the flat tire on a
deserted road, or big problems like the undiagnosed illness
that lingers on interminably and disrupts our lives. While
on other occasions He may merely allow events to take
their normal course, it is obvious that He controls every
circumstance in our lives (Proverbs 16:33; Lamentations
3:37-38).

It looks as though we have reached the summit of God's
sovereignty. *He has the right to do anything He pleases.* Through
the prophet Isaiah, He boldly declared:

> Remember the former things long past,
> For I am God, and there is no other;
> I am God, and there is no one like Me,
> Declaring the end from the beginning
> And from ancient times things which have not
>   been done,
> Saying, "My purpose will be established,
> And I will accomplish all My good pleasure"
>   (Isaiah 46:9-10).

The Psalmist agreed.

> But our God is in the heavens;
> He does whatever He pleases (Psalm 115:3).

> Whatever the LORD pleases, He does,
> In heaven and in earth, in the seas
>   and in all deeps (Psalm 135:6).

That was the lesson Nebuchadnezzar learned the hard way,
as did a suffering believer named Job. He was sitting on an
ash heap feeling sorry for himself, bearing excruciating pain,
enduring intense grief over the loss of his family and all his
material goods, blaming God for being unfair, when God

began to reveal Himself in His sovereign power and glory.
Getting to know a sovereign God caused Job's problems to
pale by comparison. He was able to relax when he finally
concluded,

> I know that Thou canst do all things,
> And that no purpose of Thine can be
>   thwarted (Job 42:2).

Jesus taught the same lesson to His disciples by means of
a parable, the story of the laborers in the vineyard. Some
were hired very early in the morning, others at various times
throughout the day. When evening came, the owner of the
vineyard instructed his foreman to call them together and
pay them all the same amount. Those who had worked through
the heat of the day grumbled because they received only the
same as those who were hired shortly before quitting time.
The landowner replied, "Is it not lawful for me to do what
I wish with what is my own?" (Matthew 20:15) That landowner pictures God. He has a right to do as He pleases with what
is His, without asking permission from anyone. Isaiah warned
years before, "Woe to the one who quarrels with his Maker"
(Isaiah 45:9).

The Apostle Paul took up the same theme: "So then He has
mercy on whom He desires, and He hardens whom He desires. You will say to me then, 'Why does He still find fault?
For who resists His will?' On the contrary, who are you, O
man, who answers back to God? The thing molded will not
say to the molder, 'Why did you make me like this,' will it?
Or does not the potter have a right over the clay, to make
from the same lump one vessel for honorable use, and another for common use?" (Romans 9:18-21) If God is sovereign,
then we have no right to argue with Him about what He
allows to happen to us (cf. also Job 23:13; 33:12-13; Jeremiah
27:5).

The Message of God's Sovereignty

By this time some are probably saying, "Where is the comfort in all of this? If God controls everything, why does He allow human tragedy and pain? It is important to under-stand that, while God controls everything, He does not ma-nipulate people like puppets on a string or program them like computerized robots. He gives them the freedom to make decisions and He holds them responsible for their choices. All human suffering is ultimately linked in some way to man's volition. But just as God's omniscience assures us that He knew what man's choices would be, so His sovereignty as-sures us that He consciously allowed those choices as the best possible means of displaying His own glory, that He has complete control of them at every moment, and that He will overrule them to accomplish His own perfect purposes. The Psalmist made that last point clear when he said, "For the wrath of man shall praise Thee" (Psalm 76:10). He can even use man's belligerent opposition against Him to bring praise to Himself.

The Bible is filled with illustrations. For example, God overruled the evil designs of Joseph's brothers when they sold him into slavery. He used that painful experience in Joseph's life to keep Jacob's family alive through a devastating famine so that the line through which the Messiah was to come could be preserved. When Joseph was reunited with his brothers many years later, he said, "And as for you, you meant evil against me but God meant it for good in order to bring about this present result, to preserve many people alive" (Genesis 50:20).

God also overruled the murderous designs of the Jewish religious leaders who plotted the death of His Son, by laying on Him the guilt and penalty of the world's sins and so providing forgiveness for the human race. He overruled the persecution suffered by the early Church in Jerusalem and used it to spread the gospel to places it might never have gone otherwise (Acts 8:1-4). He causes man's actions to serve His own purposes.

His purposes are always perfect. David assured us that God never makes mistakes. "As for God, His way is perfect" (Psalm 18:30 KJV). Jeremiah, through a letter to the discouraged Jewish captives in Babylon, revealed that God has our well-being at heart in all His aims and goals. "For I know the plans that I have for you, declares the LORD, plans for welfare and not for calamity to give you a future and a hope" (Jeremiah 29:11). We cannot always understand how His actions will work out perfectly for our welfare, but He does not expect us to understand. He just wants us to trust Him. What seems like calamity will work for the best.

Abraham did not always understand God's purposes, yet he trusted Him. When God told him He was about to destroy the city of Sodom, Abraham feared for the lives of his nephew Lot and family, so he pleaded with God to spare the city. But behind his request was a settled assurance that God would do what was best: "Shall not the Judge of all the earth do right?" (Genesis 18:25 KJV) He trusted God to do what was best.

Yes, God does have the right to do with us anything He pleases because we belong to Him, and we have no right to argue. He controls *all* our circumstances, and as bleak as they may appear to us, He is already at work to use every one of them for the accomplishment of His good ends. No circumstance is excepted. David said, "My times are in Thy hand" (Psalm 31:15). He was referring to all the situations and circumstances of daily living. They are all of God's appointment.

> The steps of a man are established by the LORD;
> And He delights in his way (Psalm 37:23).

The course of life, all that befalls a believer, is established, fixed, and settled by the Lord. Things may be out of our control, but God has them in His total control at every moment (cf. also Proverbs 20:24; Ecclesiastes 9:1). And He always does what is best. "Trust Me," He says. "There is no reason to worry, fret, complain, or argue. Just trust Me to accomplish My own perfect purposes."

One of His purposes is to teach us important lessons that He wants us to learn. He allows trials as tools to bring us to maturity and completeness in Him (cf. James 1:2-4). Rather than asking, "Lord, why did this have to happen to me?" it might be advantageous to ask, "Lord, what Christlike quality of spiritual maturity do you want to build into my life through this experience?"

There is something to be learned in every situation. For example, when someone is unloving to us we can learn what it means to love unselfishly and unconditionally. When someone hurts us deeply we can learn to forgive. When we are experiencing conflict with someone in authority over us we can learn to cultivate a submissive spirit. When we face financial difficulties we can learn to be good stewards. When temptations entice us we can learn to claim God's power to overcome them. When we become bored and discouraged with our lot in life we can learn to be faithful. When we suffer an extended illness we can learn to rejoice in the Lord. When we lose a precious loved one we can learn to find our satisfaction in the Lord alone.

God may be allowing some tragedy to invade your life right now. As an omniscient God, He knows about it. As an omnipotent God, He could have stepped in supernaturally and changed that circumstance and so protected you from it. But He did not do that. Instead, He allowed it to remain. So we must conclude that He wants it to be there and that He has some perfect purpose to accomplish through it. Trust Him to fulfill that purpose.

A godly woman in my first pastorate taught me the application of God's sovereignty to human experience. She was in the hospital dying of cancer, suffering great pain, but still mustering the strength to read her Bible every day. She was eagerly anticipating my visit one particular day because she wanted to tell me what God had shown her that morning. She asked me to open my Bible to Psalm 119 and to read verses 67 and 68. I read aloud,

> Before I was afflicted I went astray,
> But now I keep Thy word.
> Thou art good and doest good;
> Teach me Thy statutes.

"Now read verse 71," she said. So I read again,

> It is good for me that I was afflicted,
> That I may learn Thy statutes.

"And one more," she added. "Read verse 75." I continued,

> I know, O LORD, that Thy judgments are righteous,
> And that in faithfulness Thou hast afflicted me.

When I finished, she looked up at me and smiled.

"You know, I wouldn't trade this experience for anything in the world," she said. "I'm right where God wants me to be, and it's good."

That is the doctrine of God's sovereignty put into practice. The bottom line is yieldedness to His sovereign will. He has a right to do with us as He pleases. He can allow our best-laid vacation plans to fall through at the last minute if He so chooses. He can let the boss blame us for somebody else's mistake if He so chooses. He can let the bride get the measles on the day before the wedding if He so chooses. He can let our whole world fall apart around us if He so chooses. We can react in one of two ways. We can resist Him, grumble, complain, accuse Him of being unfair or unkind, and end up with a tension headache, a knot in the pit of the stomach, and possibly an ulcer or a heart attack. Or we can believe that He will use our circumstances to fulfill His perfect purposes, then willingly yield to His sovereign will and find inner peace and rest. The choice is ours.

Action To Take:

Think of something in your life at the present time that disturbs you deeply, over which you have no control. Now consciously bow to God's sovereignty in that area of your life and ask Him what Christlike qualities He wants to build into your life through that situation.

11

THE HOLY ONE

THERE IS SOMETHING about holiness that scares us, and something about a person who claims to be holy that threatens us. People like that make us feel uncomfortable, inferior, unworthy, guilty, and condemned. The less holy we think we are, the farther away from them we want to run.

That is the way some people feel about God. The thought of His holiness makes them want to hide. That is an understandable response for the unbeliever. He has good reason to hide from an infinitely holy God who must punish sin. But sometimes people whose sins have been forgiven, and who have been clothed with divine righteousness, also draw back from Him and that is probably due to a faulty understanding of His holiness. Satan enjoys perverting this doctrine and using it to drive a wedge between believers and their Lord.

Holiness is clearly out of style in our day, and the opinions of the day have a definite influence on the Christian's mind. The prevailing viewpoint seems to be that nice guys finish last, that honest people never get ahead, and that clean-living people never have any fun. We have been conditioned to accept a lack of holiness as the normal pattern of life. We expect people to be immoral, dishonest, selfish, and greedy. Books are available that teach people how to get rich by cheating others. That's the way life is, and some of us have decided that we might as well get our share. So we accept the philosophy of the world and begin doing unto others before they do unto us. We may even consider anybody who wants to be genuinely holy as being out of touch with reality.

One professing Christian challenged me to name anybody who had succeeded in business after consecrating his life to Jesus Christ. I was able to name some, but his challenge was revealing. If our highest priority in life is to succeed in business, and we do not think we can be successful as committed Christians, we will never desire to be holy or ever yield our lives to Jesus Christ. We may even ridicule anybody who wants to be holy, and we will certainly not want to hear anything about God's holiness. If, on the other hand, our highest priority in life is to do God's will and to bring glory to Him, then we will have much to gain from an understanding of His holiness. Assuming that this is our desire, let's meet the Holy One.

The Meaning of God's Holiness

King Sennacherib of Assyria had no time for the God of Israel. He laughed at the suggestion that Jehovah could protect the Jews against his mighty military machine, and he instructed his personal representative to stand before the walls of Jerusalem and shout blasphemies against Him. When he sent a personal letter to King Hezekiah defying the Lord, Hezekiah took that letter to the temple, spread it out before the Lord, and prayed. God assured him through the prophet Isaiah that Sennacherib had gone too far with his blasphemy.

> Whom have you reproached and blasphemed?
> And against whom have you raised your voice,
> And haughtily lifted up your eyes?
> Against the Holy One of Israel! (2 Kings 19:22)

He had insulted the Holy One and had to learn that there was no God like Him. Because of his impudence and audacity, his armies were defeated and he lost his life by an assassin's sword.

That encouraging message from Isaiah to King Hezekiah introduces us to a name—the Holy One. It is one of the most glorious names of our great God. The basic idea in both the Old and New Testament words for *holy* is "separation." God is the separated One. But separate from what? There are two basic answers to that question. First, God is separate from His creatures. He is exalted high above them in infinite glory and transcendent majesty. Isaiah emphasized this aspect of God's holiness when he declared,

> For thus says the high and exalted One
> Who lives forever, whose name is Holy,
> "I dwell on a high and holy place" (Isaiah 57:15).

His holiness is associated with His elevated position. It sets Him apart, above all His creation (cf. also Exodus 15:11 and 1 Samuel 2:2).

Holiness has an ethical connotation as well, a sense in which God is separated from all evil. He cannot sin, He will not tempt anyone else to sin, and He can have no association with sin of any kind. He is untainted with the slightest trace of iniquity.

As Elihu put it to Job,

> Far be it from God to do wickedness,
> And from the Almighty to do wrong (Job 34:10).

The prophet Habakkuk insisted that God is so pure, He will not even look at sin (Habakkuk 1:13). The Psalmist assured us that no evil dwells with Him (Psalm 5:4). Other passages affirm that He hates sin (e.g., Proverbs 6:16-19; Hebrews 1:9). Our holy God is totally separated from sin.

The Apostle John described God's holiness as light: "God is light, and in Him there is no darkness at all" (1 John 1:5). There is not much in this world that is pure enough to illus-trate the intensity of God's holiness, but John chose one of the purest things we know—light. There is not even a hint of anything sinful in God, no darkness at all, no shadow of sin. He is morally perfect.

When Isaiah saw a vision of the glory of the Lord, the seraphim were magnifying Him by saying, "Holy, Holy, Holy, is the LORD of hosts" (Isaiah 6:3). This is the only attribute of God that is ever repeated three times in succession. It empha-sizes the absoluteness and completeness of His holiness. Our God is infinitely holy.

As a matter of fact, there are probably more references to God's holiness in Scripture than to any other attribute. If there is one thing God wants us to know about Himself, above all else, it is that He is infinitely holy. We may find it to be one of the most difficult of all His attributes to accept, but for some reason He finds it one of the most important for us to comprehend. He wants us to know Him as the infinitely Holy One.

This same holiness was seen in the earthly life of God the Son. Peter said that He committed no sin (1 Peter 2:22). John said that there was no sin in Him (1 John 3:5). Paul said that He knew no sin (2 Corinthians 5:21). The writer to the He-brews said He was "holy, innocent, undefiled, separated from sinners" (Hebrews 7:26). We are not surprised to hear Peter refer to Him in his sermon at the gate of the temple as the Holy One, the very same exalted name applied to the Father (Acts 3:14).

Jesus Christ was truly holy. That is one reason why the self-seeking, self-righteous religious rulers of the day hated Him and wanted to destroy Him. They stood condemned in His presence. That is why demons trembled before Him and feared for their very existence. In the synagogue at Caperna-um, one of them cried out, "What do we have to do with You, Jesus of Nazareth? Have You come to destroy us? I know who You are—the Holy One of God!" (Mark 1:24) The Holy One of God! Sinful men feared Him and fallen angels fled from His presence. His holiness is awesome.

The Beauty of God's Holiness

While it repulses the unbeliever, threatens the carnal Christian, and inspires awe in everyone who acknowledges it, there
is something in God's holiness that attracts the person who
loves Him. The godly king, Jehoshaphat, revealed what attracts us when he organized his armies and appointed a choir
to lead them into battle. They were to sing unto the Lord and
"praise the beauty of holiness" (2 Chronicles 20:21 KJV).
There are few things uglier than self-righteousness and hypocritical holiness, but true holiness is beautiful to behold.

That should be easy to understand. We seldom consider
soiled things to be beautiful. A beauty contest winner is never
in a soiled, wrinkled dress. When "grease monkeys" climb
out of the pits under cars, or coal miners emerge from the
mines, nobody raves about their beauty. Beauty is usually
associated with what is clean and pure, not what is dirty and
defiled. A babbling brook loses some of its beauty when we
learn that its water is polluted. A beautiful woman loses some
of her attractiveness when we learn of her immoral involve-
ments. But the perfect purity of our holy God is beautiful.

We have seen that God is light, and light is also a thing of
beauty. I doubt that anyone ever praised the beauty of a
totally dark room. The beauty of the night is seen in the
sparkling lights that God has placed in the sky. The beauty
of the sunrise is the splash of colorful light painted on the
canvas of the heavens by the sun. In the physical realm,
beauty is associated with light, not darkness. The radiantly
pure light of our holy God is beautiful.

David longed to behold the beauty of the Lord (Psalm 27:4).
He wanted to understand and appreciate God's perfect purity, His infinite holiness, His absolute freedom from anything
sinful. We cannot even imagine God being soiled or spotted
or lurking in dark shadows. He is brilliant, beautiful, unblem-
ished light. He is lovely to contemplate right now, and He will
be exciting to behold in glory.

That is one of the reasons why we are so attracted to the
Lord Jesus. He is without blemish and without spot (1 Peter
1:19)—perfectly pure. The unbeliever finds no beauty in Him
and has no desire for Him (Isaiah 53:2-3). But His face, even
marred by thorns and twisted with pain, is beautiful to us
who believe, because it is the face of God's sinless Son who
gave Himself for our eternal salvation. The Psalmist was
looking through the corridors of time to Him when he said,

> Thou art fairer than the sons of men;
> Grace is poured upon Thy lips;
> Therefore God has blessed Thee forever (Psalm 45:2).

It is so easy for us to be affected by the world's values and
develop a distorted view of beauty. We actually begin to think
that beauty has to do solely with the outer layer of skin or
what is pleasing to the eye. God wants us to get to know Him,
and then we shall understand that genuine beauty is found
in a holy life.

The Challenge of God's Holiness

This challenge was first issued to God's ancient people
Israel, then repeated to the Church of Jesus Christ. Look at
it first in the Old Testament. The Lord had just delivered His
people from their Egyptian bondage and was directing them
to their promised land. Along the way He paused to give
them some laws, and He advised them that it would be to
their benefit to obey them. Then He issued the challenge:
"For I am the LORD your God. Consecrate yourselves therefore, and be holy; for I am holy. And you shall not make
yourselves unclean with any of the swarming things that
swarm on the earth. For I am the LORD, who brought you up
from the land of Egypt, to be your God; thus you shall be holy
for I am holy" (Leviticus 11:44-45). Since God is holy, the
people who are rightly related to Him must also be holy. A
holy God requires a holy people.

The Apostle Peter took up the same theme when he encouraged believers not to be conformed to the sinful desires they had before they met Christ: "But just as He who called you is holy, so be holy in all you do; for it is written: Be holy, because I am holy" (1 Peter 1:15-16 NIV). Here is where some Christians begin to back away. "If God wants me to be as holy as He is, I'm in big trouble. There's no way that I can ever live up to that." So some decide they will not even try. It seems to be more tolerable to live with the guilt of ignoring God than the guilt of trying to be holy but consistently failing.

But they misunderstand this exhortation completely. God never told us to be as holy as He is. That is impossible, and God knows it better than we do. He told us to be holy *because* He is holy, and there is a difference. Our holiness at best looks pathetic next to His. But we can grow in holiness, and He has made available to us everything we need to accomplish that. We can be separated from sin and set apart to God for His use and for His glory. Because He is holy and offers us all the assistance we need to be holy, He has a right to expect us to be holy. Some of us probably will admit that we are so far from any significant degree of holiness that we do not even know where to begin.

Maybe Isaiah can help us. Let's go back to his experience. It began when he got a glimpse of God's absolute and complete holiness. And that is where we must begin. That is why we need to study this attribute. There is little hope for us to be holy until we contemplate the Holy One Himself—infinitely holy, perfectly pure, totally separate from sin. We must see Him as the seraphim described Him: "Holy, Holy, Holy, is the LORD of hosts" (Isaiah 6:3).

Don't miss what happened to Isaiah when he grasped the reality of God's holiness.

> Then I said,
> "Woe is me, for I am ruined!
> Because I am a man of unclean lips,

And I live among a people of unclean lips;
For my eyes have seen the King,
     the LORD of hosts" (Isaiah 6:5).

Isaiah's understanding of God's holiness brought an over-whelming sense of his own uncleanness, his own guilt and shame. That is when most of us want to run. It's unpleasant. It strikes at the very heart of our self-esteem and self-worth. We feel threatened, insecure, rejected, and condemned. So in a desperate attempt to protect our fragile egos, we cry out, "Don't tell me any more about God's holiness. I don't want to hear it." Then we settle back into a comfortable substitute for real Christian living. We go through the forms, use the right language, and do the bare minimum of what we think is expected of us. We talk about God's love, which is vital to an understanding of His person. But we seldom ever mention His holiness or think about what it means for us to be holy.

Isaiah did not try to run and hide from God's holiness. It exposed his sin and that was not very pleasant, but he did not turn away. Neither did he try to excuse himself by blaming his parents or his spouse or his poor circumstances in life. He admitted it and accepted the responsibility for it. The only way he could ever be holy was to see himself as God saw him, acknowledge his sin, and admit that he deserved divine judg-ment. "Woe is me!" he cried.

If that were the end of the story, we would be destined to live our lives under a continuous cloud of guilt. "Then one of the seraphim flew to me, with a burning coal in his hand which he had taken from the altar with tongs. And he touched my mouth with it and said, 'Behold, this has touched your lips; and your iniquity is taken away, and your sin is forgiven' " (Isaiah 6:6-7). That does not sound any more pleas-ant than facing up to his sin, but remember, this occurred in a vision. Nobody actually scorched Isaiah's lips with a hot coal. The action of the angel in the vision was symbolic of purging. God took the initiative and cleansed Isaiah's sins. Nothing brings greater relief or more joyous freedom than the assurance that God has forgiven and cleansed us. The pressing burden of guilt is gone.

God's provision for our cleansing is the cross of Jesus Christ. He does not put hot coals on our lips. Instead, He placed the judgment for our sin on His own sinless Son.

> But He was pierced through for our transgressions,
> He was crushed for our iniquities;
> The chastening for our well-being fell upon Him,
> And by His scourging we are healed.
> All of us like sheep have gone astray,
> Each of us has turned to his own way;
> But the LORD has caused the iniquity of us all
> To fall on Him (Isaiah 53:5-6).

When we confront God's holiness, it does expose our sinfulness. But the solution is not to run and hide, nor is it to ridicule the whole idea of holiness. It is to acknowledge our sin and to accept the forgiveness He has offered us in His Son. Then God shares His own holiness with us in the person of His Son. He washes away every sinful stain, then actually allows Jesus Christ to become our holiness (1 Corinthians 1:30)[1], accepting us because of our relationship to Him. That is real worth. Confronting God's holiness does not destroy our self-worth if we respond properly. It enhances it. To know we are children of the living God, sinful though we are, is to possess an inestimable sense of real worth.

But that is not the end of the matter. Christians still sin, and their sin often lays on them a new sense of guilt, makes them hesitant to enter the presence of God, or offer themselves to serve Him. But the same sacrifice that provided for our initial cleansing also provides for our daily cleansing. The blood of Jesus Christ keeps on cleansing us from all sin (1 John 1:7).

---

[1]The word *sanctification* is the same Greek word elsewhere translated "holiness."

We still have an obligation, however, and that again is to acknowledge our sin. "If we confess our sins, He is faithful and righteous to forgive us our sins and to cleanse us from all unrighteousness" (1 John 1:9). When we see ourselves as God sees us and admit our sin, it brings us a fresh realization of cleansing. That is what happened to Isaiah, and it was that cleansing which qualified him for fruitful service. "Then I heard the voice of the Lord, saying, 'Whom shall I send, and who will go for Us?' Then I said, 'Here am I. Send me!' " (Isaiah 6:8) Nothing can bring us more satisfaction, more fulfillment, or a greater sense of personal worth than the assurance that God can use us.

In the normal Christian life this process just keeps going on and on. We learn a little more about God's holiness and consequently a little more about our own sinfulness. Then we acknowledge the sin, enjoy a renewed sense of God's cleansing, yield that area of our lives to His control, and so grow a little more in His holy likeness. This is what Paul was referring to when he encouraged the Corinthians to move on and perfect holiness out of reverence for God (2 Corinthians 7:1). As we grow in His image we become progressively set apart unto Him.

Sometimes our heavenly Father helps us along through discipline. That is what most earthly fathers try to do, but some usually do it rather poorly. "For they disciplined us for a short time as seemed best to them, but He disciplines us for our good, that we may share His holiness" (Hebrews 12:10). His loving discipline helps us partake more fully of His holiness, which will in turn make our lives more productive and satisfying.

Christian, don't run from God's holiness. Explore it more deeply. Get to know God as the Holy One. There are few things we could ever possibly do to bring greater joy and blessedness to living.

Action To Take:

Have you trusted Jesus Christ as your own personal Saviour from the guilt and penalty of sin? If so, thank God for cleansing you and imparting to you Christ's holiness.

Are there still sins in your daily life as a Christian? Confess them to God and trust His power for victory over them. Be in your daily practice what you are by virtue of your eternal position in Christ.

12

JUSTICE FOR ALL

"ONE NATION UNDER GOD, indivisible, with liberty and justice for all." The pledge of allegiance to the flag claims that ours is a nation where every human being, regardless of race, color, creed, sex, or social standing, receives fair and equal treatment. One of the purposes for the United States Constitution, as stated in its preamble is to "establish *justice*"; that is, to provide every individual with equal rights before the law, without partiality or favoritism.

Some people in this country feel that we have failed to achieve that goal. They point to blatant instances of inequity, such as people with money, power, or position securing more favored treatment under the law than the poor, the friend-less, or the obscure. They enumerate examples of discrimination against minorities or against women which demonstrate to their satisfaction that injustice persists in our society.

Most of us believe that we have been treated unfairly at some time or other. We have been blamed for things we have not done, denied things we feel we deserve, overlooked when we should have been recognized, treated in an inferior manner, or have otherwise suffered without just cause. Some have lost their jobs, their savings, their homes, their friends, their spouses, and even their lives unjustly. Some have languished in prisons for crimes they never committed. Others have endured the poverty, squalor, and disease of slums through no fault of their own. Where is the justice in all of that?

We believe in a sovereign God who controls all things. On one occasion He said, "There is no God else beside Me; a just God and a Saviour" (Isaiah 45:21 KJV). How can a just God allow injustices to exist? We learn from the Bible that people who have not trusted Christ as Saviour from sin are condemned to eternal separation from God, even if they have never heard the message of salvation. Some may protest rather indignantly, "How can a just God allow that?" Maybe we need to find out what God's justice involves.

The Meaning of God's Justice

While the most common Old Testament word for *just* means "straight," and the New Testament word means "equal," in a moral sense they both mean "right." When we say that God is just, we are saying that He always does what is right, what should be done, and that He does it consistently, without partiality or prejudice. The word *just* and the word *righteous* are identical in both the Old Testament and the New Testament. Sometimes the translators render the original word "just" and other times "righteous" with no apparent reason (cf. Nehemiah 9:8 and 9:33 where the same word is used). But whichever word they use, it means essentially the same thing. It has to do with God's *actions*. They are always right and fair.

God's righteousness (or justice) is the natural expression of His holiness. If He is infinitely pure, then He must be opposed to all sin, and that opposition to sin must be demonstrated in His treatment of His creatures. When we read that God is righteous or just, we are being assured that His actions toward us are in perfect agreement with His holy nature.

Because God is righteous and just, He has established moral government in the world, laid down principles which are holy and good, then added consequences which are just and fair for violating those principles. Furthermore, He is totally impartial in administering His government. He does not condemn innocent people or let guilty people go free. Peter says

He is a God "who impartially judges according to each man's work" (1 Peter 1:17). His treatment is never harsher than the crime demands.

For example, when Ezra the scribe returned to Israel after the Babylonian captivity, he was distressed to find that the people had intermarried with the unbelieving inhabitants of the land. He was appalled at their sin and proceeded to lead them in á prayer of confession in which he enumerated the discipline they had experienced. He concluded his prayer with these words: "O LORD God of Israel, Thou art righteous, for we have been left an escaped remnant, as it is this day; behold, we are before Thee in our guilt, for no one can stand before Thee because of this" (Ezra 9:15). God is fair. His discipline is never more severe than our sin deserves. He allowed those disobedient Jews to remain as an escaped remnant in spite of their sin and guilt.

Daniel ministered during Israel's exile in Babylon. He knew from Jeremiah's prophecy (25:11) that the captivity was to last seventy years, but he was concerned lest the nation's disobedience prolong it. He, like Ezra, offered a great prayer of confession to God, and in it he made this statement: "Therefore, the LORD has kept the calamity in store and brought it on us; for the LORD our God is righteous with respect to all His deeds which He has done, but we have not obeyed His voice" (Daniel 9:14). Their captivity was the perfectly just discipline for their sin. All calamity is not necessarily discipline for sin, but we can be sure that if it is, it will be uniquely tailored to our particular situation by an infinitely wise God to teach us the lessons we need to learn. It will be perfectly fair. What God does is always right. As the psalmist put it,

> The LORD is righteous in all His ways,
> And kind in all His deeds (Psalm 145:17).

We can never accuse Him of injustice. Everything He does is fair.

The Requirements of God's Justice

If God is truly just and always acts in harmony with His holy nature, then He must show His displeasure with sin by opposing it and punishing it wherever it exists. He cannot enact a holy law, threaten a penalty, then take no action when His law is broken. Scripture makes that quite clear. God "will by no means leave the guilty unpunished" (Exodus 34:7). "The soul who sins will die" (Ezekiel 18:4). "For the wages of sin is death" (Romans 6:23). "There will be tribulation and distress for every soul of man who does evil" (Romans 2:9). Since the violation of God's infinitely holy nature demands an infinite punishment, eternal condemnation can be the only just penalty for sin. Jesus said, "And these will go away into eternal punishment" (Matthew 25:46).

God takes no pleasure in punishing the wicked (Ezekiel 33:11). But it is the only response which is consistent with His holy nature. However, God loves sinners and since He finds no delight in punishing them, He has devised a plan by which they can be delivered from the just penalty of their sin.

Justice allows for one person to substitute for another, so long as no injustice is done to the rights of any person involved. So God provided a substitute. When His Son voluntarily offered Himself to die in our place, our sin was punished and God's justice was forever satisfied. The Apostle Paul explained how God publicly displayed Jesus Christ as a propitiation and thus demonstrated His righteousness (Romans 3:25). A propitiation is a sacrifice that satisfies a justly pronounced sentence. Christ's death on the cross completely satisfied God's just judgment against our sin. The penalty has been paid. Now God can forgive the sins of those who will accept His payment, and still maintain His own justice. He can at the same time be both "just and the justifier of the one who has faith in Jesus" (Romans 3:26).

Justice also demands that when the penalty has been paid by one, it never needs to be paid by another who has accepted that payment. There can never be any condemnation for the person who has trusted Jesus Christ as Saviour from sin (Romans 8:1).

My children used to listen to a recorded story about a wise and just king who ruled over a nation of wicked people. In order to curtail their wickedness, the king decided that anyone breaking the law of the land would have his eyes put out. A young man was apprehended for violating the law, and when he was brought in the king was dismayed to discover that the lawbreaker was his own son. What could he do? If he were merely a just king, he could exact the punishment and forget about the incident. If he were merely a loving father, he could overlook the crime and let his son go free. But he was both a just king and a loving father. So he said, "You have broken the law, and the punishment is the forfeiture of two eyes. That is what it shall be—one of yours and one of mine." From that day on, the appearance of both the king and his son reminded the people of the king's justice and his love.

That is essentially what God did. However, instead of making us pay part of the penalty, He paid it all. The death of His sinless Son was sufficient to pay for the sins of the whole world (1 John 2:2). Now those who accept His payment can go free. Who then can accuse God of injustice for condemning people to hell? He would be just if He assigned everyone to hell. Yet He satisfied His own justice and provided forgiveness for all. Those who refuse His forgiveness choose His wrath of their own volition. They have expressed their desire to live apart from God and He simply confirms them in their choice. That hardly can be labeled injustice.

What about those who have never heard? The Apostle Paul assured us that God has not left Himself without a witness in the world (Acts 14:17), and that lost men have willfully rejected His witness (Romans 1:18-32). But whether or not we can explain every problem and answer every objection, we accept God's revelation of Himself as a just God, and we believe Him when He says He will not act wickedly or pervert justice (Job 34:12).

The Expression of God's Justice

It should be obvious by now that God's justice has little relationship to the suffering we observe in the world around us. That suffering is the natural consequence of the sin which Satan introduced into God's creation. In a sinful world, where sinful men have the will to choose their own sinful ways, injustices are going to exist.

There is coming a day when the infinitely just Son of God will physically return to the earth and will rule it with a rod of iron. No sin will be tolerated in that day. Zechariah predicted that the King will be just (Zechariah 9:9). Jeremiah assured us that He will execute justice on the earth (Jeremiah 23:5). We can expect no injustices to exist in that day (cf. Isaiah 11:3-5). But for now we can count on many inequities to exist. However, God wants us to do what we can to reduce them. He shows a concern for social justice throughout Scripture—fair treatment of the poor, the orphans, the widows, the hungry, the needy, foreigners, and underprivileged of all kinds. He encourages us to share His concern. The needs of other people should move our hearts to compassion and motivate us to make some personal sacrifices for their good. That is a major evidence of true faith in Christ (cf. 1 John 3:17-19). But try as we will, we are not going to eliminate all injustice from the earth. It is the natural by-product of living in a sinful world.

God's justice relates not so much to the suffering in the world as to His attitude toward and treatment of the sin that causes suffering. He will deal with all sin with perfect justice, without a trace of partiality or favoritism. He says that He "will render to every man according to his deeds" (Romans 2:6). That almost sounds like salvation by works, although actually it has nothing to do with salvation. It establishes again the principle of God's justice. Entrance into Heaven is dependent solely upon faith in Christ's sacrifice at Calvary. But God is going to treat every person in accord with the quality of his life—believers and unbelievers alike. Unbelievers will be punished in hell on the basis of their works and believers will be rewarded in Heaven on the basis of their works.

Scripture clearly teaches degrees of punishment for unbelievers: "Woe to you, Chorazin! Woe to you, Bethsaida! For if the miracles had occurred in Tyre and Sidon which occurred in you, they would have repented long ago in sackcloth and ashes. Nevertheless I say to you, it shall be more tolerable for Tyre and Sidon in the day of judgment, than for you" (Matthew 11:21-24). If it will be more tolerable, more bearable, or more endurable for some than for others, then there are obviously degrees of suffering. The issue on which they are judged seems to be the light they received. Those who saw the greater demonstration of God's power and rejected it will experience greater punishment than those who saw less of God's power and rejected it.

Some of our Lord's most scathing denunciations were reserved for the scribes and Pharisees, men who enjoyed some of the greatest spiritual privileges yet exhibited some of the least of God's love. They "devour widows' houses, and for appearance's sake offer long prayers; these will receive greater condemnation" (Mark 12:40). Greater condemnation can mean nothing less than degrees of punishment.

To illustrate this truth, Jesus told a story in which he contrasted two servants—one who knew his master's will and did not do it, and one who did not know it. "And that slave who knew his master's will and did not get ready or act in accord with his will, shall receive many lashes, but the one who did not know it, and committed deeds worthy of flogging, will receive but few. And from everyone who has been given much shall much be required; and to whom they entrusted much, of him they will ask all the more" (Luke 12:47-48).

Again, we have a clear reference to degrees of punishment—many stripes and few stripes. And again, the issue is their response to the knowledge they had.

A native in the jungle who has never heard the gospel does not have the same degree of responsibility as an American who can hear the gospel any day of the week. Therefore that native will not receive the same degree of punishment. A person who was raised in a secular home and taught to be nonreligious may not have the same degree of responsibility as a person who was raised in a Christian home and taught the truth of God's Word yet rejected it. That less privileged person will not receive the same degree of punishment (cf. also 2 Peter 2:20-21).

When unbelievers stand before the great white throne, they will be consigned to the lake of fire because their names are missing from the book of life. But at the same time they will be judged "according to their deeds" (Revelation 20:12-13). That makes very little sense unless those works make some difference in the degree of their punishment. We do not know what the difference will be, but the justice of God will be expressed by different levels of punishment. There finally will be justice for all.

On the other hand, believers will be rewarded in Heaven on the basis of their works. Works will have nothing to do with their entrance into Heaven. That is based solely on their acceptance of the merits of Jesus Christ and His provision of eternal life. But believers' works will be tested by fire at the judgment seat of Christ to determine their quality. "For no man can lay a foundation other than the one which is laid, which is Jesus Christ. Now if any man builds upon the foundation with gold, silver, precious stones, wood, hay, straw, each man's work will become evident; for the day will show it, because it is to be revealed with fire; and the fire itself will test the quality of each man's work. If any man's work which he has built upon it remains, he shall receive a reward. If any man's work is burned up, he shall suffer loss; but he himself shall be saved, yet so as through fire" (1 Corinthians 3:11-15).

Everybody knows the difference externally between gold and hay, but the fire reveals something the eye cannot see—motivation and enablement. Were the works performed for the glory of God or to fulfill some personal ambition? Were they performed by the power of the Holy Spirit or in the energy of the flesh? Those done for the glory of the Lord and by the power of the Holy Spirit will become the basis for reward. So it seems likely that everyone's reward will be different.

We are not told here what the rewards will be, but several things are mentioned in other passages. The New Testament speaks of crowns that are cast before the throne of God (Revelation 4:10), a probable reference to our capacity to glorify Him (cf. 1 Corinthians 9:25; 1 Thessalonians 2:19; 2 Timothy 4:8; James 1:12; 1 Peter 5:4; Revelation 2:10). Nothing will bring us greater satisfaction in eternity than our ability to exalt the Lord Jesus.

In addition to crowns, Biblical writers refer to the ability to shine (cf. Matthew 13:43; Daniel 12:3), a probable reference to our capacity to reflect the glory and radiance of our Lord, another source of great pleasure in eternity. Some have likened it to a great chandelier containing some twenty-five-watt bulbs, some fifty, some seventy-five, and some one hundred, each shining to the peak of his ability, but all magnifying the Lord.

Jesus told a parable that implied different levels of governmental authority in God's kingdom. A nobleman leaving for a far country entrusted the same amount of money to each of ten servants, and they were to invest it for his benefit. When he returned he called them into account. The first gained ten times the original amount and was commended by his master: "because you have been faithful in a very little thing, be in authority over ten cities" (Luke 19:17). The second gained five times the original amount and was likewise commended by his master: "And you are to be over five cities" (Luke 19:19). Our rewards will not be trophies to put on a shelf, but greater responsibilities and greater authority.

There will be no jealousy between us, but clearly there will be differences—a different number of crowns, a different capacity to shine, a different level of authority. God's justice does not require Him to reward us. Everything worthwhile we ever accomplish is by His power and through His grace, so at best we deserve nothing, and He does not owe us anything. The rewards He gives us will be out of His storehouse of grace. But since He has decided to reward us, He will do it with perfect justice in accord with our works—not just what shows on the outside, but what is in our hearts! Not just what we did, but how and why we did it! There will be justice for all.

Action To Take:

Are you engaged in some Christian service? Honestly and prayerfully examine your *motives*. Could there be some desire to be seen by others or to have power over others or to be well thought of in the Christian community? Ask God to help you purify your motives so that you serve Him for His glory alone.

Now examine the *power* by which you serve Him. Do you rely predominately upon your own natural abilities and personality? Ask Him to help you rely on Him alone.

13

GOD IS LOVE

ONE OF OUR GREATEST NEEDS as human beings is to be loved. We all need love. We need to know that we are important to somebody, that somebody truly cares about us, wants us, and accepts us unconditionally. When we doubt that we are loved, we may develop unacceptable behavior patterns to compensate for it.

For example, we may act irresponsibly in a desperate attempt to get attention. Attention is a poor substitute for love but it seems better than nothing at all. We may develop physical symptoms that bring us sympathy and concern. The symptoms cause us genuine pain, but the pain of sickness is more bearable than the pain of admitting that nobody cares. We may angrily lash out at those whom we think should care or we may try to run away from them and hide, but in either case, we are trying to protect ourselves from the hurt they are causing us by their lack of concern. We all need to know that somebody loves us.

The good news from God's Word is that somebody does. To know Him is to find release from the crippling effects of feeling unloved. Twice the Apostle John categorically stated that God is love (1 John 4:8,16). *Love* is one of the warmest words in the English language, and that God is love is one of the most sublime, uplifting, and reassuring truths known to mankind. Love is His nature. It is not merely a friendly attitude He projects. It is the essence of His being. He is

149

always going to act toward us in love because He cannot do otherwise. Love is the way He is.

No one attribute of God is any more important than any other, and all His attributes are expressed in conjunction with each other. Yet some believe that love may be the most powerful motivating force in all of God's being. It deeply affects everything else God is and all that He does. Knowing God's love could well be the believer's key to a well-balanced, satisfying life of peace, productivity, and power. It would be rather presumptuous to assume that we can exhaust the subject of God's love in one brief chapter, but let us try to scratch the surface and begin to explore this fathomless truth. Here are eight characteristics of God's love.

God's Love Is Self-Giving

Love involves action. It is expressed in the giving of oneself for the good of another, so it always demands an object. Whenever we talk about love we are suggesting that there is more than one person involved. There must be at least two— the one who loves and the one who is loved. If God has always been love and love demands an object, we may wonder how God demonstrated His love before He created angels or men. Jesus answered that question. He revealed that there was a love relationship between the persons of the triune Godhead from eternity past, when He said to His Father, "Thou didst love Me before the foundation of the world" (John 17:24). We have seen that God is complete and sufficient in and of Himself. He has no needs which must be met by others outside Himself. He did not need to create other beings in order to express His love. It was perfectly expressed between the persons of the Trinity from all eternity.

Yet He did create. Why? He wanted so much to manifest His love that He first created the angelic hosts and later the human race so that he might communicate Himself to them, give of Himself for them, and bestow His very best on them for their benefit and blessing. Our love is often selfish and demanding. God's love is pure. Because He is love, He loves to give. Jesus said He gives good things to those who ask Him (Matthew 7:11). James went so far as to say that every good gift finds its source in Him (James 1:17). Since God is love, we can expect Him to give of Himself.

Knowing the God of love can help to make us more loving and giving persons. Not only will getting to know Him more intimately cause us to become more like Him, but resting secure in the assurance that He loves us will keep us from making demands of others and free us to reach out unselfishly and minister to them for their benefit alone. It is vitally important that we understand how much God loves us.

God's Love Is Sacrificial

Not only does God's love motivate Him to give, but it motivates Him to give when it costs Him dearly. That too is different from our love. We hesitate to do anything for others that will cost us too much or inconvenience us too greatly. But God's love cost Him the very best that He had—His only Son. That is the message of the greatest love text in the Bible: "For God so loved the world, that He gave His only begotten Son, that whoever believes in Him should not perish, but have eternal life" (John 3:16). God's giving His Son involved more than merely allowing Him to leave Heaven's glory and enter earth's history. It meant allowing Him to die in our place and pay the awful debt of our sins. God proved His love conclusively and irrefutably by sending His Son to the cross as an atoning sacrifice for our sins (Romans 5:8; 1 John 4:9· 10). That is sacrificial love.

It was no less of a sacrifice for God the Son than it was for God the Father. His willingness to offer Himself was the summit of sacrificial love. Paul called Him "the Son of God, who loved me, and delivered Himself up for me" (Galatians 2:20). When the same apostle outlined God's principles for harmonious marital relationships, he said, "Husbands, love your wives, just as Christ also loved the church and gave Himself up for her" (Ephesians 5:25). Jesus Christ made the supreme sacrifice for us when He died in our place. He was falsely accused, beaten, spit on, crowned with thorns, nailed to a cross, and left to die the most excruciating death known to man. The infinite curse of sin's penalty, the Father's just punishment for the whole world's guilt, was laid on Him as He hung on that cross. He possessed the power to walk away from it unscathed, yet He voluntarily stayed there and bore that suffering for us. There simply is no greater love (John 15:13).

Whenever we are tempted to think that nobody loves us, we need to think of the cross. Jesus bore that shame and suffering because He loves us. He values us so highly that He was willing to make the ultimate sacrifice to secure for us eternal joy. That is the epitome of love. Knowing Him intimately will motivate us to make some sacrifices for the good of others—for our spouses, our children, and other members of the body of Christ. It will help us give up what we want in order to minister to their needs.

God's Love Is Unconditional

One of the most amazing things about God's love is that it is extended to us when we do not deserve it and continues steadfast and strong even when we do not respond to it. In other words, His love is unconditional. That certainly is different from our love. We have a tendency to show more love to the people who obviously love us and less love to the ones who do not. We express our love to our spouses and our children when they perform to our expectations and we withhold it from them when they displease us. We shower affection on the lovable children and avoid the belligerent little rascals who look as if they might want to kick us in the shins. I find it easy to express my love to my wife when she tells me what a wonderful husband I am, but not quite so easy when she scolds me for not taking out the trash. I find it easier to be loving toward my children when they are obeying me willingly, but not quite so easy when they are resisting me.

God is not like that. The best-loved verse in the Bible says, "For God so loved *the world*," that is, the whole world. That does not refer to the materials out of which our planet is constructed, but to the world of people. It does not mean the whole mass of humanity generally; it refers to each individual sinful person. The Bible categorizes all of them as God's enemies, people who have willfully set themselves against Him (cf. Romans 5:10; Colossians 1:21). God even loves His enemies—all of them.

There is not one good thing in any of us that merits God's love. He does not love us because we are so lovable or because we can somehow make ourselves worthy of His love. We are totally unworthy, yet He prizes us highly and showers His very best on us. It is His love for us that gives us our worth. God finds great delight and receives great glory when we respond to His love, enter His fellowship, and do His will. In fact, He made us for that purpose. But whether or not we ever return His love, He keeps on extending it to us. There is nothing we can do to make Him love us any more, and nothing we ever do will cause Him to love us any less. He loves us perfectly and completely regardless of how we perform. His love is unconditional.

So many of us are performance oriented. We have felt approved and accepted when we have performed to someone else's satisfaction, and disapproved and rejected when we have failed to live up to their standards. Consequently, we treat others the same way. If they please us, we treat them kindly and considerately. If they displease us, we feel justified in treating them unkindly and unlovingly. Knowing God intimately will help us express love to others when they do not perform to our expectations.

There is a great Biblical illustration of God's unconditional love in His relationship with the nation Israel. "The LORD did not set His love on you nor choose you because you were more in number than any of the peoples, for you were the fewest of all peoples, but because the LORD loved you and kept the oath which He swore to your forefathers, the LORD brought you out by a mighty hand, and redeemed you from the house of slavery, from the hand of Pharaoh king of Egypt" (Deuteronomy 7:7-8). Can we see what He is implying? There is no human reason for His love for Israel. They were a rebellious, stiff-necked people. But He loved them simply because He loved them.

That is how it is with you and me. He loves us just because He loves us. Nothing we ever did made Him love us, so nothing we ever do will make Him stop loving us. He loves us when we're grouchy just as much as when we're glad. He loves us when we sin just as much as when we don't. He loves us when we open our mouths and say things we know we shouldn't have said. He loves us when our wives or husbands or parents or children are not treating us as though they love us. He loves us when we're feeling as though nobody in the whole world loves us. He loves us even when we don't like ourselves. He never stops loving us.

God's Love Is Eternal

This message also was given originally to the nation Israel, but its application is for every true child of God. "The LORD appeared to him from afar, saying,

> I have loved you with an everlasting love;
> Therefore I have drawn you with lovingkindness
> (Jeremiah 31:3).

That everlasting love reaches into eternity past. He knew us and loved us before He made us, when we were but a thought in His mind. And He will love us for eternity to come, for, as Paul assured us, nothing shall be able to separate us from the love of God (Romans 8:39). The love of an eternal God must be an eternal love.

If anybody ever deserved to forfeit the love of Christ it was His earthly disciples. They were men of inestimable spiritual privileges, yet they displayed an amazingly small degree of spiritual insight. Witness their behavior on the evening of the last Passover. The impending ordeal of bearing the world's sins was weighing heavily on the Lord's heart and He longed for their prayerful support. But Luke informs us that they were more interested in arguing about which one of them was the greatest (Luke 22:24).

None of them even extended the common social courtesy of the day by washing the others' feet when they entered the room for dinner. They probably were too busy competing for the seats of honor near the Lord. Later three of them fell asleep when they were supposed to be praying, all of them deserted the Lord when He was taken captive, one of them denied Him, and another one later doubted Him. Notice how this upper room episode began: "Now before the Feast of the Passover, Jesus knowing that His hour had come that He should depart out of this world to the Father, having loved His own who were in the world, He loved them to the end" (John 13:1). To the end of what? Who can really say? He will love us to the end of our waywardness and wanderings. He will love us to the end of our deepest need. He will love us to the end of our lives, to the end of time, to the farthest extremity of eternity. He will love us forever. His love is eternal.

God's Love Is Infinite

How can we ever exhaust the love of God! The love of an infinite God must be infinite love. Paul called it a love that "surpasses knowledge" (Ephesians 3:19), far greater than our finite minds can grasp. He also called it a "great love"

(Ephesians 2:4). He referred to its breadth, its length, its depth, and its height (Ephesians 3:18), but it is obvious that he was speaking of dimensions that defy measurement: breadth and length which encompass the whole world, a depth which reaches to the lowest sinner, a height which exalts us to the loftiest Heaven. God's love has no limit. It is described in F. M. Lehman's gospel song:

> Could we with ink the ocean fill,
>> And were the skies of parchment made;
> Were every stalk on earth a quill,
>> And every man a scribe by trade;
> To write the love of God above
>> Would drain the ocean dry;
> Nor could the scroll contain the whole,
>> Tho' stretched from sky to sky.

I read somewhere that those words were penciled on the wall of a narrow room in an asylum by a man who supposedly was demented, and they were discovered after his death. He was not demented at all. He had learned one of the most precious truths of all time, that God's love is infinite. We can no more exhaust it than we can empty the ocean with a bucket. And we are invited to keep drawing from His inexhaustible supply. To do so will enable us to keep extending love to those around us even when our love is not returned.

God's Love Is Holy

When some people hear that God's love is self-giving, sacrificial, unconditional, eternal, and infinite, they get the idea that it is merely soft, sloppy sentimentality, that God is an indulgent Father who gives us everything we want and conveniently turns His head the other way when we sin. But that is not the case. Everything God does is done in the totality of His being, so His love must always be consistent with His other attributes. Since God is holy, then His love must be a holy love that encourages holiness in those loved.

The evidence is overwhelming! For example, in the same context in which Paul explains that we in love were predestined unto the adoption of sons, he states God's purpose for choosing us. It is "that we should be holy and without blame before Him" (Ephesians 1:4). Love and obedience consistently go together in Scripture: "For this is the love of God, that we keep His commandments; and His commandments are not burdensome" (1 John 5:3; cf. also John 14:15; 15:10).

God will use every loving means at His disposal to encourage our obedience. He does that because He loves us. We discussed discipline when we studied God's holiness, but we cannot overlook it here. The writer to the Hebrews encouraged us not to regard God's discipline lightly. It is the evidence of His love for us (Hebrews 12:5-6). He knows that obedience to His Word will be for our greatest happiness, so He takes steps to help us want to obey Him. If he did not love us, He would not care about our happiness.

What kind of loving parents would we be if we let our children do anything they pleased, such as put their hands in the fire, ride their tricycles on the freeway, or play superman on the roof of the house? The authorities would probably declare us to be unfit parents. Our love constrains us to discipline in order to insure the kind of behavior that will bring our children future happiness. And that is exactly what our loving heavenly Father does.

He does not enjoy inflicting pain any more than we do. Before my father spanked me as a child, he used to say, "This is going to hurt me more than it hurts you." That was difficult for me to believe at the time, and I never understood it until I became a parent myself. Then it became all too clear. It wasn't my hand that hurt; it was my heart. God says the same thing. Concerning His people Israel we read, "In all their affliction He was afflicted" (Isaiah 63:9). He feels our pain because He loves us. Don't chafe under His disciplinary hand. He knows best what we need, and He always administers it in love for our best interests. We can respond to His holy love by bringing our lives into conformity to His Word.

God's Love Is Comforting

Some children would give everything they have for some-one who loves them and cares enough for them to set limits on their behavior and administer loving discipline when they violate those limits. That would mean more to them than all the material things in the world because it is the evidence of true love, and true love brings security and comfort. They know that someone who loves them enough to endure the unpleasantness of administering discipline will do everything in his power to take care of them, and that brings them genuine consolation. When we grasp the reality of God's love, we will no longer seek our security in jobs, bank accounts, investments, houses, husbands, wives, friends, or health. We will rest in the Lord, free from all fear, secure in the assurance that He is going to provide all that we need and protect us from everything that will not be for our good.

Listen to the Apostle John again: "There is no fear in love; but perfect love casts out fear, because fear involves punish-ment, and the one who fears is not perfected in love" (1 John 4:18). God never *punishes* His children. He laid all the punish-ment for our sins on His Son. He *disciplines* us in love for our benefit, but even that is nothing to be afraid of. Understand-ing God's love eliminates all fear—fear of God's discipline, fear of what tomorrow holds, fear of losing a loved one, fear of losing a job, fear of natural catastrophies, fear of global war, fear of suffering, fear of death, fear of being alone, fear of rejection. God loves us! There is nothing to fear. His love is comforting.

God's Love is Life-Changing

Most of us long to be loving people, able to give love to our spouses, our children, our fellow believers, our unsaved acquaintances, and, most of all, to the Lord Himself. But we find it so difficult. It is nearly impossible for us to love others unless we are genuinely convinced that we ourselves are loved. Some of us are hard, calloused, insensitive, and unloving people because we are not convinced we are really loved. We are saying unconsciously, "Why should I be loving to others when nobody shows me any love?" God's love can change that. We can find all the acceptance and affection we crave in Him; then with the confidence that we ourselves are loved, we can extend love to others. "We love," said the Apostle John, "because He first loved us" (1 John 4:19).

It really is true—God loves us. Jesus said it plainly: "For the Father Himself loves you" (John 16:27). It is to our advantage to know and believe the love that He has for us (1 John 4:16). We may never be able to grasp it fully with our human understanding alone, but God is ready to make it real to us if our hearts are open and receptive to His Word. Then, secure in His love, we shall be able to reach out in love to others, unselfishly, sacrificially, unconditionally, and inexhaustibly. It will profoundly influence our relationships with those around us.

A world-renowned theologian was asked by a student what he considered to be the most significant theological truth he ever learned. His answer was, "Jesus loves me. This I know; for the Bible tells me so." Believe it, Christian. God loves you!

Action To Take:

Look for evidences of God's love for you all throughout the day, and remind yourself often that you are the object of His endless love.

Tell several others during the day that God loves them.

14

THE GOD OF ALL GRACE

MOSES was a man who truly longed to know God. We have heard him cry out to God earnestly, "I pray Thee, show me Thy glory!" (Exodus 33:18) That heart-felt longing led to an exciting encounter with the Lord. It was early the next morning when he cut two new tablets of stone to replace the ones he had broken in anger; then, tablets in hand and all alone, he climbed Mount Sinai and waited.

Scripture says, "And the LORD descended in the cloud and stood there with him as he called upon the name of the LORD. Then the LORD passed by in front of him and proclaimed, 'The LORD, the LORD God, compassionate and gracious, slow to anger, and abounding in lovingkindness and truth' " (Exodus 34:5-6). Moses did not see God's face on that occasion, but God did assume some visible form which allowed His seeking servant a limited glimpse of His radiant glory, a privilege afforded very few people in all of human history. What God revealed about Himself on such an extraordinary occasion is extremely important. The second thing He claimed about Himself in that list of His attributes was that He is *gracious.*

What do you think about when you hear the word *gracious?* Maybe you conjure up the mental image of a charming hostess with good taste and a pleasant personality, gliding around the room with a tray of hors d'oeuvres. Or possibly you think of a person who is kind and courteous, agreeable, easy to get along with. Or you may envision somebody who has great tact and diplomacy in dealing with other people. *Gracious* could mean any of those things when applied to human beings. But how do you picture *God* who says He is gracious? What do you think came to Moses' mind when God made that statement on Mount Sinai that day?

Grace Is the Essence of God's Being

God was explaining to Moses exactly what He is like, the essence of His being, and He used a word derived from a root which means "to bend or stoop." It expresses His willingness to reach down with affection to people who can never deserve it, and to do good things freely and unconditionally for people who can make no claim to His favor. He is even willing to forgive guilty people their sins and deliver them from the punishment they deserve when they are totally unworthy of such kindness. He mentions that specific aspect of His graciousness in the next verse: "who forgives iniquity, transgression, and sin" (Exodus 34:7). More amazing still is that He loves to give these rich benefits to undeserving people without demanding any compensation in return. True grace is both unearnable and unrepayable.

The New Testament establishes the same truth about God. Peter called Him "the God of all grace" (1 Peter 5:10). All grace! That means He has an inexhaustible supply of good gifts which are adequate for every conceivable need and which are available to all who will receive them, regardless of their performance. The New Testament word for grace originally referred to something attractive and charming that brings delight and pleasure, but it soon came to have the same connotation as its Old Testament equivalent, that of showing kindness and goodwill to the undeserving. Our God loves to give. He gives freely, without obligation and without ulterior motives. He does not need to give. He does not give to get something in return. He is totally self-sufficient so He does not need anything from anybody. He gives simply for the joy and happiness of the ones who receive His benefits.

Grace is a difficult concept for us to understand because it is so unlike the way we human beings operate. Our most magnanimous acts are often colored by some selfish motive. Several years ago my wife cracked a bone in her wrist and was required to wear a cast to protect it. Naturally I volunteered to do some of the household chores for her. As I prepared to wash the dishes one evening, she nudged me away from the sink and said, "I'll do them tonight. I just bought a large rubber glove to fit over my cast so I won't get it wet." When I protested, she said, "But there's no reason for you to wash them now." My reply was, "I don't need a reason. I just want to wash them for you because I love you."

Had my motives been absolutely pure, that would have been a great illustration of grace, but I'm afraid they were not entirely untainted. For one thing, I was looking for an illustration of grace to use in the following Sunday's sermon and I thought my answer would be just the thing. Secondly, I didn't want to put up with the taunts of my friends: "You let your wife wash the dishes with a broken arm!?" Very seldom are our gracious deeds perfectly pure. If it is nothing more than to project our image as a gracious person, which image may be very important to us, we usually have some additional intent in mind.

God made us to glorify Himself, so He is pleased when we fulfill His purpose for our creation. Furthermore, He wants the whole universe to see the glory of His grace. Yet His aim in giving us good things is not to get anything for Himself. He gives because we desperately need what He has to offer. Our external well-being depends on it.

One of the first things we learn about the eternal Word who became flesh and dwelled among us is that He is full of grace (John 1:14). His ministry was marked by favor freely extended to guilty and undeserving people, to people whose best efforts were still not enough to make them worthy of His kindness. We could expect nothing less from a God who is full to overflowing with an innate fondness for giving, for showing kindness to those who have no merit in themselves. That is the way He is.

Grace Is the Basis of God's Actions

The way God is always affects the way He acts, so His grace causes Him to seek undeserving subjects to whom He can give and toward whom He can act graciously. He does not have to look very far to find them. His world is filled with sinful rebels who have turned their backs on Him, resisted His will, defied His authority, and deserve nothing from Him but eternal punishment.

The nation Israel was among them. But Moses understood the implications of God's grace: "And Moses made haste to bow low toward the earth and worship. And he said, 'If now I have found favor [literally, grace] in Thy sight, O Lord, I pray, let the Lord go along in our midst, even though the people are so obstinate; and do Thou pardon our iniquity and our sin, and take us as Thine own possession' " (Exodus 34:8-9). He is saying, "God, if you really are a God of grace, then be with us even though we are a stubborn and sinful people. Let us be your own special possession even though we deserve to be cast off and destroyed." He was asking his gracious God to act in a gracious manner. And He did.

How can He afford to do that? How can a holy God freely forgive people who deserve to be condemned? We need to remember that none of God's attributes operates in isolation. All are beautifully interwoven and intertwined so that He acts in the totality of His being. His holiness does not operate apart from His love. When the unconditional love of a holy God is expressed toward worthless, undeserving sinners, that is grace. Grace is the bridge between God's holiness and His love. It allows a holy God to act in loving ways toward guilty people.

God's grace is expressed in numerous ways, foremost of which is in securing our *salvation*. It was grace that allowed Him to relinquish Heaven's riches and enter earth's history in poverty to provide hopeless sinners with the riches of eternal salvation. "For you know the grace of our Lord Jesus Christ, that though He was rich, yet for your sake He became poor, that you through His poverty might become rich" (2 Corinthians 8:9). It was grace that led Him to Calvary, where He offered Himself as a sacrifice in our place and where He shed His life's blood so that we might be forgiven of sin's guilt and delivered from sin's penalty. "In Him we have redemption through His blood, the forgiveness of our trespasses, according to the riches of His grace" (Ephesians 1:7).

It is God's grace that makes salvation available to every sinful person: "For the grace of God has appeared, bringing salvation to all men" (Titus 2:11). It is His grace that applies salvation to the hearts and lives of those who believe. "For by grace you have been saved through faith; and that not of yourselves, it is the gift of God; not as a result of works, that no one should boast" (Ephesians 2:8-9). It is His grace which will someday usher us into glory: "Through whom also we have obtained our introduction by faith into this grace in which we stand; and we exult in hope of the glory of God" (Romans 5:2). It is all of His unmerited favor.

These concepts are not very popular among most people today, if indeed they are even understood. In order to grasp the reality of God's grace we must first understand the reality of our own sinfulness. If we are convinced that in spite of the little vices which we all have, we are basically good people deserving of God's favor, then we shall see no need for His grace. If we believe that God is obligated to let us enter Heaven because we have tried to keep His laws and done the best we can, then grace is totally unnecessary. The whole concept will appear absurd. But if we accept God's as-sessment of our lives—that we are unrighteous, deceitful, desperately wicked, guilty, condemned sinners, incapable of measuring up to God's standard and unworthy of His acceptance—then a deep appreciation for His grace will begin to dawn on our sin-dulled minds. We will get to know the God of all grace.

We learn a valuable lesson about grace from observing God's gracious actions toward us in salvation. Just as the root meaning of the New Testament word involves joy and pleasantness, so we notice that God's grace has an uncanny way of transforming the unpleasant into the pleasant. He takes an unbeliever, chained to his wretchedness and sin and bound for the bitterness of an eternal hell, freely gives him the lovely garments of Christ's righteousness, then assures him of Heaven's glory and beauty. What a transformation! That is God's grace for salvation.

Then He continues to act toward us in grace. Not only does He bring delight to our drab existence by giving us the gift of eternal life, but He keeps on giving us good things to meet our needs and brighten our lives. For example, He gives us the resources to build us up and set us apart more fully to Himself, progressively replacing the ugliness of our daily sin with the attractiveness of holy living. That was Paul's message to the Ephesian elders: "And now I commend you to God and to the word of His grace, which is able to build you up and to give you the inheritance among all those who are sanctified" (Acts 20:32). That is grace for *sanctification.*

Sanctification is not slavishly submitting in the energy of the flesh to somebody's man-made list of do's and don'ts in order to enhance our own reputation or earn points with God. It is laying hold of God's gracious assistance to become more like Christ for His glory and praise. Grace delivers us from bondage to laws and frees us to enjoy God in an enriching and satisfying relationship. We will be motivated to please Him from within rather than pressured from without. We delight in pleasing someone who never stops giving good things to us.

God also provides grace for Christian *service*. We have a tendency to get carried away with our own abilities, and we begin to think that God is rather fortunate to have us on His team to do His work. We may feel that He is obligated to prosper us when we do serve Him. Those attitudes often lead to failure. The Apostle Paul admitted without shame that he was unworthy to serve Christ: "I was made a minister, according to the gift of God's grace which was given to me according to the working of His power" (Ephesians 3:7; cf. also 2 Corinthians 8:1-2).

We do not deserve to have the pleasure of serving the eternal God, but He has bestowed that privilege on us by His grace. We serve Him not to obtain His favor, but because we already have it. Any success we may enjoy will be the gift of His grace. He freely gives us the abilities and strength we need to serve Him. He transforms our feeble, bungling, embarrassing, unpleasant efforts into an effective, satisfying, and rewarding ministry that brings glory to Him. It is all part of His gracious actions toward us.

Then there is also grace for *suffering*. Most of our suffering is simply the result of living in a sinful world. Some of it is the result of our own foolish and sinful choices. In either case, God certainly has no obligation to help us through it. But He does. When the Apostle Paul faced a painful, physical disability, the God of all grace was there to meet him. "And He has said to me, 'My grace is sufficient for you, for power is perfected in weakness.' Most gladly, therefore, I will rather boast about my weaknesses, that the power of Christ may dwell in me" (2 Corinthians 12:9). God's grace can transform the unpleasantness of suffering into the pleasantness of knowing Christ's power.

His grace is available for every need. Peter described it as "manifold grace" (1 Peter 4:10). The word "manifold" was used in secular Greek to mean "many-colored." That is an interesting concept to consider. For every shade of human need God has a matching shade of divine grace. If we are blue with despondency, God's grace is sufficient to cheer us. If we are yellow with fear, God's grace is sufficient to encourage us. Whether we are enjoying the golden joys of good health and success, or encountering the blackness of pain or failure, God's grace is sufficient to sustain us. When temptations assail us, such as the tendency to be red with anger or green with envy, God's grace is sufficient to resist them. His many-colored grace is sufficient for every color of need.

So He invites us to come boldly to His throne of grace, the reservoir of His never-ending supply, and there find grace to help, whatever our need might be (Hebrews 4:16). His grace is available for the taking. As the Apostle John put it, "For of His fulness we have all received, and grace upon grace" (John 1:16). He just keeps pouring it on, filling the believer's life with grace, piling one gracious provision on top of another, transforming one unpleasant circumstance after another into joy and delight.

Grace Is the Aim of God's Children

Getting to know the God of all grace and becoming the receptacles into which He keeps pouring His grace will obviously have an effect on our lives. We are going to become more like Him, more gracious, giving people, people with true *charisma*. We are all familiar with that term. It comes from the Greek word for grace. When we hear it we usually visualize someone with the personal magnetism of leadership, someone who excites loyalty and enthusiasm. But we misunderstand charisma as God views it.

We may be like the little boy in the cartoon who was surrounded by a group of admiring girls. Off to the side, two jealous little friends were evaluating the situation. One said to the other, "He hasn't got charisma. He's just got a bag of jelly beans." The world has a poor imitation of the real thing, a mere bag of jelly beans. True charisma is *grace,* and only the believer who is enjoying the reality of God's grace in his

life can exemplify it. We gain true charisma as God transforms us from the unpleasant people we were into the pleasing image of His Son. And that will affect some surprising
areas of our lives.

For one thing, it will put a *song* in our hearts: "Let the word
of Christ richly dwell within you, with all wisdom teaching
and admonishing one another with psalms and hymns and
spiritual songs, singing with thankfulness [literally, grace] in
your hearts to God" (Colossians 3:16). To know that our
eternal salvation depends not on us, but on the grace of God,
keeps us singing all day long. To have divine assistance for
sanctification, service, and suffering keeps us singing when
others have long since stopped. To believe that our gracious
God is working every detail of our lives together for good can
keep us singing in the darkest hour of affliction.

Paul and Silas knew about that. They sat in a Philippian jail
cell, beaten and bleeding, wracked with pain, and locked
firmly in stocks, yet they were singing praises to God (Acts
16:25). Incredible? Not for someone who has gotten to know
the God of all grace. His grace can transform the most miserable of circumstances into an opportunity for rejoicing. I talked
recently to a man who was defrauded in a business investment. He faced the possibility of losing everything he owned
including his home—a total of nearly two million dollars in
assets. He said, "I have more peace and more joy than I've
ever known. Those material things for which I once lived
don't own me anymore. God's grace really is sufficient." The
experience of God's grace in our hearts gives us true joy.

God's grace will also affect our *speech*. "Let your speech
always be with grace, seasoned, as it were, with salt, so that
you may know how you should respond to each person"
(Colossians 4:6). The word grace is rich with meaning, and in
this context most all of it seems to be applicable. It is easy to
let harsh, cutting, critical, complaining, and gossiping words
come tumbling out of our mouths. But God wants our words
to be saturated with grace, not sugarcoated and sickeningly

sweet, but genuinely attractive, kind, considerate, pleasing, favorable, beneficial, and thankful. All of that is involved in grace. That is true charisma.

God wants His grace to govern our speech *always*. Do not miss that! Courtesy and kindness are especially important when speaking to unbelievers (cf. Colossians 4:5), but a good dose of God's grace will affect everything we say to everyone in our lives—our wives, our husbands, our children, our parents, our friends, even those who do not seem to like us very much. It may even help us bridge the gulf that may exist between us.

Many of us are quick to speak brusquely to people who displease us or offend us. We usually feel justified in accusing them, blaming them, criticizing them, or expressing anger toward them. Knowing the God of all grace, whose attitude toward us is never affected by our performance, will help us act kindly and speak graciously even to people who have wronged us. God's grace operating through us will minister grace to them (Ephesians 4:29), and will transform the un-pleasantness of tension and friction into the pleasantness of harmony and fellowship.

God's grace also will help us know when not to talk. Peter writes, "For this finds favor [literally, for this is grace], if for the sake of conscience toward God a man bears up under sorrows when suffering unjustly" (1 Peter 2:19). It is an evidence of God's grace in our lives when we are willing to suffer for doing what is right without arguing or retaliating. "For what credit is there if, when you sin and are harshly treated, you endure it with patience? But if when you do what is right and suffer for it you patiently endure it, this finds favor with God" [again, literally, this is grace with God] (1 Peter 2:20). God's grace at work in us allows us to control our tongues, to return good for evil, and so it can transform an explosive situation into one that gives glory to God.

Most of us would be willing to admit that we could use a great deal more of God's grace. We understand that there is

a never-ending supply and that it is available for the taking.
We know that receiving it does not depend on how well we
have performed or whether we deserve it. But some of us are
still not sure how to get it. Solomon made an interesting
comment in Proverbs that both Peter and James quoted in
their Epistles: "But He gives a greater grace. Therefore it says,
'GOD IS OPPOSED TO THE PROUD, BUT GIVES GRACE TO THE HUMBLE' "
(James 4:6). The humble are those who see themselves as God
sees them and are willing to admit their needs. If we do not
see any need for change in our lives, then obviously we will
not be open to receiving God's grace. The flow of grace
begins when we admit our weaknesses, our shortcomings,
our failures, and our sins—when we acknowledge our needs.

But there is a second step. We hear much in ecclesiastical
circles about the means of grace, that is, the way God ministers grace to our lives. Scripture clearly defines only one
means, and that is *faith.* We see it in several passages. "For
by grace you have been saved through faith" (Ephesians 2:8).
"We have obtained our introduction by faith into this grace
in which we stand" (Romans 5:2).

Enough Grace

Whether it is grace for salvation, grace for sanctification,
grace for service, grace for suffering, grace to keep us singing,
grace to govern our speech, or grace for any other need, we
experience it by believing God, believing that we need His
grace, that He has enough available to help us, that He is
willing to share it with us, and that it will be adequate to
transform our burdens into blessings. When we truly believe,
all that remains is to open our hearts to the God of all grace
and receive what He has to offer. "Let us therefore draw near
with confidence to the throne of grace, that we may receive
mercy and may find grace to help in time of need" (Hebrews
4:16).

Action To Take:

List some of the evidences of God's grace in your life, some of the things He has done for you which you know you did not deserve, and thank Him for them.

Now list some of the areas of your life where you need to lay hold of His grace, some areas in need of change, and ask Him in faith to help you make those changes.

15

RICH IN MERCY

NEARLY ALL OF US are familiar with "Murphy's law," and some of us may even believe it: "Nothing is as easy as it looks. Everything takes longer than you expect. And if anything can go wrong, it will ... at the worst possible moment." Murphy seems to have suggested some corollaries to his law. One is that everything you decide to do costs more than first estimated. Another is that if you improve or tinker with something long enough, eventually it will break. Still another—the light at the end of the tunnel will probably turn out to be the headlamp of an approaching freight train. If you were to boil down the essence of Murphy's law and all its corollaries into one terse statement it would probably be this: "Life is miserable and nothing is going to turn out right."

Joseph L. Felix wrote a humorous exposition of Murphy's law from a spiritual perspective and called it, *Lord, Have Murphy!*[1] The title is appropriate because it makes us think about a cry heard from the lips of miserable people all through the gospel records, "Lord, have mercy!" Mercy has a direct relationship to misery. Nobody seems to know exactly who Murphy was, but whoever he was, he did not seem to know much about God's mercy.

Murphy is not alone. Few people understand mercy. What is it? I have asked that question of a number of people and

---

[1] Nashville: Thomas Nelson, Inc., 1978.

the most common response I get is a blank stare. The word is used literally hundreds of times in the Bible, and most of us have read it over and over again. But it is one of those concepts that we find difficult to put into words. The Psalmist said, "Our God is merciful" (Psalm 116:5 KJV). What did He mean? What is God's mercy?

His Relief for the Miserable

Nowhere is the essence of mercy unveiled for us any more clearly than in our Lord's parable of the good Samaritan. The victim in that story was miserable. He had been beaten, robbed, and left for dead. The priest and the Levite in the story showed no concern for him whatsoever. "But a certain Samaritan, who was on a journey, came upon him; and when he saw him, he felt compassion" (Luke 10:33). The word most often translated "mercy" in the King James Version conveys strong feelings of pity, sympathy, compassion, and affection. The Old Testament word is sometimes translated "loving-kindness" in the King James, and nearly always so in the New American Standard, and that describes one important aspect of mercy. When God looks at suffering people, He feels love, tenderness, and kindness toward them in their need.

When we read that God is merciful or that He has mercy, we may be assured that He is feeling our misery just as intensely as we are. As the writer to the Hebrews taught us, the reason we can come boldly to the throne of grace to receive mercy and find grace to help in time of need is because the occupant of that throne is a merciful high priest who is touched with the feeling of our infirmities, who sympathizes with us in our weaknesses (Hebrews 4:15-16). Those feelings are the foundation of His mercy.

But mercy does not stop with tender feelings. It acts to relieve the misery. In our Lord's parable, the Samaritan "came to [the victim], and bandaged up his wounds, pouring oil and wine on them; and he put him on his own beast, and brought him to an inn, and took care of him. And on the next day he took out two denarii and gave them to the innkeeper and said, 'Take care of him; and whatever more you spend, when I return, I will repay you' " (Luke 10:34-35). The Samaritan's compassionate feelings led him to a practical demonstration of kindness, concrete actions which were intended to relieve the man's misery and distress.[2] When Jesus asked which one of the three passersby was the true neighbor to the victim, the lawyer to whom He was speaking answered immediately, "The one who showed mercy toward him" (verse 37). He used that term mercy to sum up those feelings of steadfast love which were followed by helpful acts of kindness.

Because God is full of mercy, He acts to relieve our distress. Psalm 136 is a good place to see some of the merciful things He does. The whole psalm magnifies God's mercy. Every one of its twenty-six verses tells us something about God, then concludes, "for His mercy endureth for ever" (KJV). First His goodness is mentioned, then His acts of creation, then His relationship with His people Israel. He delivered them from their Egyptian oppressors (verses 10-12). He took them safely through the Red Sea (verses 13-15). He led them through the wilderness (verse 16). He gave them victory over powerful kings who threatened to destroy them (verses 17-20). He brought them at last into their promised land (verses 21-22). But the Psalmist gets to the heart of God's mercy in the next two verses. God remembered them in their low estate, in their miserable and humiliating condition, and He delivered them (verses 23-24). Mercy is God's tender compassion toward us in our distress that causes Him to act on our behalf and relieve our suffering, at the time and in the manner which He knows will be best.

It might be profitable for us to compare grace and mercy since they are such closely related terms. Both offer us help,

---

[2]Sometimes the Old Testament word *chesed* is also translated "goodness" (e.g. Exodus 34:6; Psalm 107:8,15,21,31 KJV), emphasizing this aspect of mercy.

but grace emphasizes assistance for the undeserving while mercy emphasizes relief for the unfortuante. Grace describes God's attitude toward guilty lawbreakers and rebels, while mercy describes His attitude toward those who are suffering and distressed. The first letter of each word helps us re- member the distinction: grace for the guilty, mercy for the miserable.

The same sins that make us guilty, however, also cause us most of our misery. So God must deal with our sin problem before He can relieve our distress. That is why we find both His grace and His mercy involved in providing our salvation: "But God, being rich in mercy, because of His great love with which He loved us, even when we were dead in our transgres- sions, made us alive together with Christ (by grace you have been saved)" (Ephesians 2:4-5). Mercy comes first in the mind of God. He loved us so much and cared about us so intensely in our miserable condition that in grace He sent His Son to die in our place. Mercy motivates His actions. But in the application of salvation to our lives the order is reversed. Only after we receive God's gracious gift of salvation does He begin to alleviate the misery which our sin has caused us. We receive His grace, then we enjoy His mercy. That explains why grace precedes mercy in every one of the apostolic salu- tations where both words appear (cf. 1 Timothy 1:2; 2 Timo- thy 1:2; Titus 1:4; 2 John 3).

One reason we can enjoy forgiveness of sins and the gift of eternal life is because our God is rich in mercy. The Apostle Paul put it, "He saved us, not on the basis of deeds which we have done in righteousness, but according to His mercy" (Titus 3:5). We are called vessels of mercy (Romans 9:23), containers into which God has poured His mercy. And now that God has saved us, He continues to extend to us His mercy. Jeremiah said His mercies are new every morning (Lamentations 3:22-23). Even better than waking up to the delectable aroma of fresh pastries hot out of the oven, accom- panied by the tantalizing smell of fresh coffee brewing, we

wake up to a fresh supply of God's mercy when we open our
eyes to greet each new day. He is there to meet us and to help
us through our difficult times.

Unfortunately we do not always recognize God's mercies.
Somehow it seems easier to focus on our misery and misfor-
tune than on God's mercy. The people of Israel had that
problem. God had promised David in a solemn covenant that
His mercy would never depart from David's family (2 Samuel
7:12-16). Solomon referred to that promise shortly after he
became king (1 Kings 3:6; 2 Chronicles 1:8), and again in his
prayer dedicating the temple (2 Chronicles 6:42). The promise
is the subject of Psalm 89, where mercy is mentioned seven
times. In the last mention of the word, the Psalmist asks,

> Where are Thy former lovingkindnesses, O Lord,
> Which Thou didst swear to David
> in Thy faithfulness? (Psalm 89:49)

We all feel that way at times: "Lord, where are all the mercies
You promised me? All I can see are the problems." I must
admit, there are weeks when I am personally convinced that
Murphy was right after all, nothing is going to turn out right.
When we feel like that, we need to turn to a passage like
Psalm 103 and begin to count our blessings.

> Bless the LORD, O my soul;
> And all that is within me, bless His holy name.
> Bless the LORD, O my soul,
> And forget none of His benefits;
> Who pardons all your iniquities;
> Who heals all your diseases;
> Who redeems your life from the pit;
> Who crowns you with lovingkindness and compassion;
> Who satisfies your years with good things,
> So that your youth is renewed like the eagle.
> The LORD performs righteous deeds,
> And judgments for all who are oppressed.

> He made known His ways to Moses,
> His acts to the sons of Israel (Psalm 103:1-7).

These multiplied benefits are the evidences of God's loving-kindness (verse 4), that is, His mercy. If we cannot relate to anything else in the psalm, we can certainly appreciate the aspect of God's mercy which the Psalmist describes in the next few verses.

His Restraint Toward the Blameworthy

It has been said that God's grace gives us the favor that we do not deserve, while His mercy holds back the judgment that we do deserve. That may not be the major difference between the two terms, but there does seem to be an element of truth in it.

> The LORD is compassionate and gracious,
> Slow to anger and abounding in lovingkindness
> (Psalm 103:8).

The subject here again is God's superabounding supply of mercy. Notice how it causes Him to act toward us:

> He will not always strive with us;
> Nor will He keep his anger forever.
> He has not dealt with us according to our sins,
> Nor rewarded us according to our iniquities (verses 9-10).

God's mercy restrains Him from giving us what our sins deserve.

This concept is found in other passages of Scripture as well. When Moses pleaded with God to forgive the people rather than destroy them after their exhibition of unbelief at Kadesh-barnea, he made that request on the basis of God's great mercy (Numbers 14:19). When Daniel prayed for forgiveness for his people, it was on the basis of God's mercy (Daniel 9:4,9). Jeremiah probably made it clearer than anyone else when he boldly declared, "It is [because] of the LORD's mercies that we are not consumed" (Lamentations 3:22 KJV).

Some people say, "I don't want any favors from God. I just want what I deserve." People like that really do not understand what they are saying. The human heart is filled with maliciousness, covetousness, selfishness, pride, envy, strife, adulteries, lies, blasphemies, and every form of wickedness. If we got what we deserved we would feel the fury and sting of all God's righteous wrath against sin. It is not justice we need, but mercy—the compassion that shows forbearance when justice demands punishment. If a criminal is found guilty, justice calls for a sentence to be pronounced. The best the convicted felon can hope for is that the judge will suspend the sentence, hold back the penalty he deserves.

God does exactly that. We have been judged guilty. Yet, the Psalmist reveals:

> For as high as the heavens are above the earth,
> So great is His lovingkindness toward those who fear Him.
> As far as the east is from the west,
> So far has He removed our transgressions from us
>   (Psalm 103:11-12).

What magnificent mercy! God looks on us hell-deserving sinners with compassion, sympathizes with us in our plight, then proceeds to remove our transgressions from us as far as our minds can imagine.

Some may protest, "Well, if God's mercy is so great, why doesn't He save everybody?" His mercy is reserved for those who *fear* Him (verse 11), a term that signifies reverential trust. He will not force His mercy on us any more than He will force His grace on us. If we choose to resist Him and spurn His offer of mercy, He will permit us to have justice instead. He asks us to acknowledge our need, then cast ourselves in simple faith upon the divine court for mercy.

There is a sense in which God's mercy is extended to all
His creation (cf. Psalm 119:64; 145:9), as when He gives sun-
shine and rain to both the just and the unjust (Matthew 5:45).
But mercy in this special sense is reserved for believers alone.

> For Thou, Lord, art good, and ready to forgive,
> And abundant in lovingkindness to all who
>   call upon Thee (Psalm 86:5).

The call must be made in faith. There were outstanding
illustrations during the earthly ministry of Christ. On one
occasion after Jesus raised Jairus's daughter from the dead,
two blind men followed Him, crying out, "Have mercy on us,
Son of David" (Matthew 9:27). They were fully aware of their
plight and the distress it had caused them, and they longed
for mercy. "And after He had come into the house, the blind
men came up to Him, and Jesus said to them, 'Do you believe
that I am able to do this?' They said to Him, 'Yes, Lord.' Then
He touched their eyes, saying, 'Be it done to you according
to your faith'" (Matthew 9:28-29). The personal appropria-
tion and enjoyment of the Lord's mercy came when they
believed.

Although that incident has to do with physical healing, the
principle is applicable to salvation as well. God offers deliverance from the just penalty of sin to all those who will acknowledge their need and entrust themselves to His mercy by faith.
It does not matter what background they come from or how
vile their sin may have been. The Apostle Paul called himself
a blasphemer, a persecutor, a violent aggressor, the chief of
sinners. Yet he was shown mercy (1 Timothy 1:13-16). That
same mercy is available to all.

> There's a wideness in God's mercy
> Like the wideness of the sea;
> There's a kindness in His justice
> Which is more than liberty.

For those people who have become the special objects of His mercy, to whom He has extended His merciful salvation, whose debt of sin He has canceled, and upon whom He showers His daily mercies, His mercy takes on yet another dimension.

His Requirement for the Believer

This truth is revealed in Jesus' parable of the unmerciful servant. He owed his master the sum of ten million dollars. We are not told how he incurred a debt of such magnitude, but it is obvious that on a servant's salary of a few cents a day he could never repay it. He was in a miserable predicament. Yet, foolish as it seems, he thought he could somehow pay back the debt, and so he begged for an extension of time: "Have patience with me, and I will repay you everything" (Matthew 18:26). Jesus went on to say, "And the lord of that slave felt compassion and released him and forgave him the debt" (verse 27). That was mercy. First there was the intense feeling of sympathy, followed by an unprecedented act of kindness in which the master held back the punishment he could have exacted and forgave the servant the entire debt, more than he ever could have expected. What a beautiful illustration of mercy!

Yet the poor servant never seemed to grasp the significance of what had happened to him. In fact, it seems as though he never even heard that his debt was wiped out. He went out and found a fellow servant who owed him a mere twenty dollars, took him by the throat and demanded payment. When the fellow servant could not pay, he required the full extent of the law and had him thrown in jail. When the master heard what his servant had done, he was incensed. "Should you not also have had mercy on your fellow slave, even as I had mercy on you?" (Matthew 18:33)

The lesson is clear. We as believers have received an enormous measure of God's mercy. We have been forgiven a debt of sin we could never repay and we have been blessed with daily mercies we can never number. Now God wants us to show the same kind of mercy to others, to have the same tender feelings of sympathy toward them in their misery, the same eagerness to minister to them and help them in their times of distress, the same willingness to hold back retribution and to forgive them when they wrong us. To do anything less reveals that we have little understanding of the immense debt of sin from which we have been released. To be stern and exacting, or to insist on getting even with those who have injured us, exposes a heart that has no concept of its own degradation. When we understand the depths of our own sin and the enormity of God's mercy in forgiving us, we will freely forgive every evil committed against us, great or small.

The prophet Micah reminded God's Old Testament people of this responsibility. He extolled God's mercy when he said, "Who is a God like unto Thee, that pardoneth iniquity, and passeth by the transgression of the remnant of His heritage? He retaineth not His anger for ever, because He delighteth in mercy" (Micah 7:18 KJV). But he also made the application to the lives of the people. "He hath showed thee, O man, what is good; and what doth the LORD require of thee, but to do justly, and to love mercy, and to walk humbly with thy God?" (Micah 6:8 KJV) People who know a merciful God should love mercy. Do we love mercy? Do the needs of other people move us to compassion? Do we have a desire to help relieve human suffering?

The Pharisees of Jesus' day sadly failed the mercy test. Jesus accused them of insisting on every intricate detail of the law while ignoring the more important matter of mercy (cf. Matthew 12:7; 23:23). That could describe some of us as well. We may have long lists of precise rules we try to live by and sometimes force others to observe, yet be unmoved by the misery of other people. Those who have truly experienced God's mercy want to show mercy to others.

I read of a woman at the check-out counter who had groceries which totaled four dollars more than she had in her purse. A stranger behind her relieved her embarrassment by motioning to the clerk to put the amount on his bill. He refused to give her his name so she could pay him back. A few days later the local newspaper reported that a charity had received a check for four dollars with a note which read: "This check is for the man who helped me out of a tight spot. I'm giving it to you as a 'thank you' to him." When we understand what has been done for us, we want to reach out and do the same for others, just as that woman did.

God's merciful heart aches over the misery which man's sin has brought to the world. And when we get to know Him intimately, our hearts will ache as well. Not only will our hearts ache, but our arms will reach out, our homes will open up, our wallets will unfold, and we will find great joy in relieving some of the misery in this world. Our God is called "the Father of mercies" (2 Corinthians 1:3). Meditate on His mercy, and as you grow in His likeness, mercy will become an increasingly significant part of your daily life style. Then the beautiful shepherd psalm will take on new meaning for you: "Surely goodness and mercy shall follow me all the days of my life; and I will dwell in the house of the LORD for ever" (Psalm 23:6 KJV).

Action To Take:

Describe what it means to you personally that God is merciful.

List some specific things you can do to show mercy to others. Now begin to do at least one of them today.

16

SLOW TO ANGER

WHEN WAS THE LAST TIME you felt at the end of your tolerance level with people? "If he says that one more time, I'm going to scream." "If she does that to me again, I'm going to walk right out that door." "If you kids don't quiet down by the time I count to three, I'm going to wale the tar out of you." "If that telephone rings one more time, I'm going to pull it out of the wall." We may not carry through with our threats, but the fact remains, our nerves are frazzled, our patience is exhausted, and we feel we are about to have a nervous breakdown.

Our breaking point probably varies from day to day, and on any given day everybody's breaking point is slightly different. But there is one person whose endurance level is always supremely higher than ours. It is part of God's nature to be slow to anger. We call it His long-suffering.

The Meaning of God's Long-Suffering

If we want to understand God's long-suffering we must go back to His relationship with His Old Testament people Israel. They were about as exasperating as anybody could be, and it was never more evident than when Moses lingered on Mount Sinai, receiving the law from God's hand. Because it took him a little longer than they anticipated, they got edgy and demanded that Aaron fashion them new gods to lead them to their promised land.

185

It was inexcusable! God had performed one miracle after another to deliver them from their bondage and bring them to this place, yet they turned their backs on Him when He did not meet their expectations. That would be enough to try anyone's patience, and it sorely tried God's. "And the LORD said to Moses, 'I have seen this people, and behold, they are an obstinate people. Now then let Me alone, that My anger may burn against them, and that I may destroy them; and I will make of you a great nation' " (Exodus 32:9-10). God said that they were *obstinate*, or more literally, that they had hard necks, necks that would not bow to His will in spite of His goodness to them.

That offer to Moses presented him with a serious test. Which was more important to him, the preservation of the existing nation or the personal honor of becoming the founder of a new nation? He passed the test beautifully and prayed for God to stay His hand of judgment. God answered his prayer. Those people deserved to be punished, but God delayed the application of His righteous indignation against them; that is the essence of long-suffering. The word itself appears for the first time in the Bible just a little later, when Moses returned to the mount to get a firsthand glimpse of God's glory. "And the LORD passed by before him, and proclaimed, The LORD, The LORD God, merciful and gracious, long-suffering, and abundant in goodness and truth" (Exodus 34:6 KJV).

Long-suffering is actually two Hebrew words, the first meaning "long" or "slow," and the second meaning "nostril," "nose," "face," or "anger." Obviously, long-suffering does not refer to a long nose. But it is interesting that the Hebrew uses the same word to mean either nose, face, or anger. Maybe that was because anger is clearly seen on the face and is sometimes expressed by snorting or wheezing through the nose. But anger is the foremost idea in this expression. It means literally "slow to anger" and is so translated in the New American Standard Bible, as well as in several passages of the King James Version (e.g. Nehemiah 9:17; Psalm 103:8; 145:8; Proverbs 14:29; 15:18; 16:32; Joel 2:13; Jonah 4:2; Nahum 1:3). It takes a long-suffering person a long time to get heated up with anger.

The same concept appears in the New Testament as one Greek word, and it conveys exactly the same idea as the Old Testament expression. It means "long tempered," or "slow to express wrath." God's long-suffering has to do with His wrath. He can get angry, as we shall see in the next chapter, but it takes Him an extremely long time to do so. His nature is to delay the expression of His wrath. He is of long endurance. Those obstinate Jews deserved to be destroyed immediately for their rebelliousness and disobedience. They would have driven anybody else to quick retaliation. But God postponed the execution of His judgment because He is a long-suffering God.

Is there a difference between God's mercy and His long-suffering? His mercy involves His restraint toward the blameworthy, and long-suffering means essentially the same thing. They are related terms which often appear together in the Old Testament. But there is a distinction. While both involve restraint toward sinful people, mercy emphasizes the *misery* which our sin causes us, while long-suffering emphasizes the *sin* which causes us our misery. Long-suffering bears patiently with us in our sin, waiting and longing for us to repent.

Our sin is a horrible offense to God's holy nature, and His justice cries out for its punishment. But at the same time, His love is longing to forgive us, His grace is making it possible for Him to forgive us even though we do not deserve it, His mercy is reaching out to us in compassion over the consequences which our sin has caused us, and His long-suffering is delaying the punishment we deserve, giving us the opportunity to repent and trust His grace. What a magnificent God!

There is another related word in the New Testament which must also be distinguished from long-suffering, a word which means literally "to abide under," and which is usually

translated in the King James Version "patience."[1] That word
refers to patience in difficult *circumstances*, while long-suffering
refers to patience with difficult *people*. It is never applied to
God (Romans 15:5 means He *gives* patience, not that He *has*
it.) He does not need patience with circumstances because He
controls them. They cannot resist Him. But He made people
with wills of their own. They can resist Him, and they do.
They wrong Him, offend Him, sin against Him, tempt Him,
and endeavor to provoke Him to wrath. But He is not easily
provoked. He does not quickly explode into a blaze of anger.
He is long-suffering.

God's long-suffering is the attribute which allows Him patiently to endure our offenses and call us to repentance rather
than promptly punish us. It is His self-restraint in the face of
provocation which delays the expression of His wrath. As we
all know, it takes a great deal of power to show restraint when
people are provoking us. Think about the pressure you feel
when your boss criticizes everything you do although you try
desperately to please him, or when your neighbor blasts his
stereo next to your bedroom window long into the night
although you have asked him not to. Sometimes we feel as
though we may not have the power to restrain ourselves. But
God has that power. The prophet Nahum put the two together when he said, "The LORD is slow to anger, and great in
power" (Nahum 1:3).

The Demonstration of God's Long-Suffering

The nation Israel never did stop provoking God. In fact,
God counted ten different occasions, from their exodus from
Egypt through the period of their encampment at Kadesh-
barnea, when they refused to take Him at His Word and do
what He told them (cf. Numbers 14:22). It all came to a head

---

[1] e.g. Romans 5:3; James 1:3-4. The NASB renders it "patience," "perseverance,"
"endurance" or "steadfastness."

when the spies returned from checking out the land and the majority gave a pessimistic report. "Then all the congregation lifted up their voices and cried, and the people wept that night. And all the sons of Israel grumbled against Moses and Aaron; and the whole congregation said to them, 'Would that we had died in the land of Egypt! Or would that we had died in this wilderness! And why is the Lord bringing us into this land, to fall by the sword? Our wives and our little ones will become plunder; would it not be better for us to return to Egypt?' So they said to one another, 'Let us appoint a leader and return to Egypt' " (Numbers 14:1-4).

God's patience was just about exhausted. He again expressed His inclination to destroy them and He repeated His offer to make Moses the founder of a new and greater nation. And again Moses prayed, "But now, I pray, let the power of the Lord be great, just as Thou hast declared, 'The LORD is slow to anger' " (Numbers 14:17-18). Moses appealed to God once more to stay His hand of judgment, and the appeal was made on the basis of God's own self-revelation of His long-suffering character. Again God answered his prayer. It was another display of Moses' total unselfishness and of God's amazing long-suffering.

But there was no end to the abuse God suffered from His people. Paul, in his sermon in the synagogue at Antioch, remarked that God put up with their disgusting behavior for forty years in the wilderness (Acts 13:18). When they finally did reach their promised land, they repeatedly turned away from the Lord and worshiped the gods of the Canaanites. He chastened them for their sin by delivering them into the hands of surrounding nations, but He did not utterly destroy them. Instead, He raised up judges to lead them out of their servitude and misery, and He did it over and over again.

Later in their history, during the period of the kings, several times God delayed His judgment at the hands of the Babylonians. After the Babylonian captivity, when the restored nation rejected His Son and nailed Him to a cross, He waited yet another forty years before allowing the Romans to level Israel's capital city and disperse them to the ends of the earth. His restraint in exercising His wrath against sin went far beyond what we would have expected.

The demonstration of God's long-suffering has not been limited to the nation Israel. There are other dramatic illustrations of it in Scripture; for example, His evaluation of the entire human race in the days of Noah. "Then the LORD saw that the wickedness of man was great on the earth, and that every intent of the thoughts of his heart was only evil continually. Now the earth was corrupt in the sight of God, and the earth was filled with violence. . . . And God looked on the earth, and behold, it was corrupt; for all flesh had corrupted their way upon the earth" (Genesis 6:5,11-12). Yet He waited another one hundred twenty years before He destroyed the population of the earth with a flood, and during that time He had Noah on the earth preaching to them the message of righteousness (cf. 2 Peter 2:5; Genesis 6:3). The Apostle Peter identified that as long-suffering. He referred to that generation as the people who were disobedient, when "the long-suffering of God waited in the days of Noah" (1 Peter 3:20 KJV).

Look at another illustration. God warned Abraham that his descendants would be sojourners in a strange land, but that in the fourth generation they would come out with many possessions and return to their promised land. Then He told him the reason for the delay: "for the iniquity of the Amorite is not yet complete" (Genesis 15:16). Their cup of iniquity was filling up, but it was not yet full. God gave them time to turn from their wickedness, but they refused. In fact, it got worse. Idolatry, child sacrifice, religious prostitution, and every conceivable abomination multiplied with each succeeding generation until their cup was full and God commanded the people of Israel to destroy them. But He had patiently waited, delaying the application of wrath. It is His nature to restrain Himself.

The Apostle Paul said that God "endured with much long-suffering the vessels of wrath fitted to destruction" (Romans 9:22 KJV). There are some people who can be categorized only as vessels of wrath. God has been good to them, yet they have resisted His grace, chosen to defy Him, and immersed their lives in every variety of wickedness. They are worthy of nothing but His wrath, equipped only for eternal ruin. Yet God patiently puts up with them with much long-suffering.

We wonder why He doesn't do something. Why doesn't He oblige the insolent atheist who shouts, "If there's a God, let Him strike me dead right now?" Why didn't He shut the mouth of the brazen Soviet cosmonaut who insisted that God does not exist because He was nowhere to be found a few hundred miles from earth? Why doesn't He strike people with lightning who blaspheme His holy name? It is His nature to be long-suffering. We see it demonstrated all around us every day. Not only does He refrain from punishing them, He gives them rain from Heaven and fruitful seasons, and provides them with food and gladness (Acts 14:17). That is like sending provisions to the enemy who has invaded the land and seeks to destroy it. It makes some wonder whether God really is concerned about sin. But we need not wonder long.

The Challenge of God's Long-Suffering

There is challenge in this doctrine for both the unbeliever and the believer. Think first of the challenge to the unbeliever. The very fact that long-suffering is defined as a delay in the expression of God's wrath implies that eventually His long-suffering will terminate and His wrath will be displayed. This highlights another difference between long-suffering and mercy. Scripture says God's mercy is everlasting (Psalm 100:5). It endures forever (Psalm 106:1). That is never said about His long-suffering. Long-suffering has a terminus point. There comes a time when God's patience with willful, rebellious sinners will run out and He will exhibit His wrath. Solomon wrote,

> A man who hardens his neck after much reproof
> Will suddenly be broken beyond remedy (Proverbs 29:1).

We do not know *when* that will be, but we do know that it *will be*. We can count on it. We cannot trifle with God's long-suffering or try to take advantage of Him.

Because God delays His judgment, sinners may begin to think that He is not aware of their sin, or that He does not care about it, or possibly that He has forgotten it. So they go on sinning without fear of the consequences. After all, if they have gotten away with it this long, who is to say that they will not get away with it forever? Solomon warned us of that attitude: "Because the sentence against an evil deed is not executed quickly, therefore the hearts of the sons of men among them are given fully to do evil" (Ecclesiastes 8:11).

Does God ignore sin? Look again at the Old Testament references to His long-suffering. Right after the golden calf incident and the revelation of God's long-suffering, He immediately adds that He will by no means leave the guilty unpunished (Exodus 34:7). After that gross exhibition of unbelief at Kadesh-barnea, He repeated it again: "He will by no means clear the guilty" (Numbers 14:18). The prophet Nahum assured us that God is slow to anger and of great power, but he immediately added, "And the Lord will by no means leave the guilty unpunished" (Nahum 1:3).

Some human judges may be accused of softness toward sin and leniency toward sinners, but the divine Judge will ultimately punish every unrepentant sinner. He may postpone His judgment for awhile, but He does not forget the sin. Paul reminded the Athenian philosophers of that: "In the past God overlooked such ignorance, but now He commands all people everywhere to repent. For He has set a day when He will judge the world with justice by the man He has appointed. He has given proof of this to all men by raising Him from the dead" (Acts 17:30-31 NIV). A day of judgment is coming when God's wrath will be revealed.

The message of judgment is not any more popular today than it was in Paul's day. It does not calm troubled minds or soothe frazzled nerves. It will not win friends or ingratiate us with people, but it is true. The person who has never turned from his sin or trusted Jesus Christ as his Saviour must not be misled by God's long-suffering. It is not a license to go on sinning. It is the evidence of God's love for sinners and His desire to save them from eternal punishment. He is patiently waiting, holding back His wrath against their sin. It would be wise for them to avail themselves of His gracious delay. God's long-suffering and forbearance are designed to lead them to repentance and eternal salvation (Romans 2:4).

There is in this doctrine a challenge for the believer also. It is, first of all, a challenge *to pray* for those who deserve God's judgment, even as Moses prayed for his people. On two occasions, God restrained His wrath because Moses asked Him to, demonstrating that this is something God is pleased to do in answer to our prayers. Are you longing to see a loved one come to know Christ? Ask God to delay His judgment and to use that demonstration of long-suffering to lead that person to repentance.

Secondly, it is a challenge *to proclaim* the message of God's long-suffering. The world needs to hear that God is patiently waiting, but that the day of His patience will eventually end. Our nation needs to hear that God is graciously restraining His wrath against sin, but that one day the cup of iniquity will be full and He will restrain Himself no longer. As unpopular as the message may be, it must be proclaimed. It is a matter of eternal life and eternal death. If we knew that a dam had cracked and that a great torrent of water would soon sweep through the valley below, destroying everything in its path, we would be quick to warn the inhabitants of that valley. We do know that God's long-suffering may soon give out and that a great torrent of judgment will be poured out on the inhabitants of this earth. Should we be any less quick to warn them?

Finally, it is a challenge *to be long-suffering* in our own personal relationships with others. The Apostle Paul encouraged us to be long-suffering with one another, bearing with one another in love and forgiving one another (cf. Ephesians 4:2; Colossians 1:11; 3:12-13). People often get on our nerves. They irritate us, exasperate us, slight us, provoke us, gossip about us, wrong us, offend us. Our patience wears thin and we want to strike back in anger. God wants us to be long-suffering, to bear those injuries patiently, and to forgive.

Solomon wrote several proverbs extolling the person who has learned this important lesson. They are worth some prayerful meditation.

> He who is slow to anger has great understanding,
> But he who is quick-tempered exalts folly (Proverbs 14:29).

> A hot-tempered man stirs up strife,
> But the slow to anger pacifies contention (Proverbs 15:18).

> He who is slow to anger is better than the mighty,
> And he who rules his spirit, than he who
>   captures a city (Proverbs 16:32).

Being long-suffering with people who exasperate us is not easy, and it is certainly something we cannot do consistently in our own strength. Long-suffering is the fruit of the Spirit (Galatians 5:22). It is produced in us by the Spirit of God as we occupy our minds with Him, grow in our knowledge of Him, and yield ourselves to His control. How can we refuse to do that when we consider His long-suffering with us, His interminable patience with our stubbornness, self-will, and rebelliousness?

The world may not consider long-suffering to be a very important trait, but the believer who has demonstrated it to others will tell you it has brought harmony to his relationships. It helps him to get along with his spouse, to handle his children, to put up with his boss, to deal with his employees, to enjoy his in-laws, and to show his neighbors that the gospel of Jesus Christ makes a difference in his life. As we grow in the likeness of our long-suffering God, we shall show the world that He is real and so bring glory to Him.

Action To Take:

List some specific unbelievers whom you would like to see trust Christ as Saviour. Then begin to pray that God will give them a sense of His long-suffering and use it to bring them to Himself.

Think of some recent occasions when you have been short-tempered with people. Go to them personally, ask their forgiveness, and express to them your desire to become more long-suffering.

17

THE GRAPES OF WRATH

THE LORD JESUS was a great storyteller. One of His stories was about a fig tree growing in a vineyard. As we might expect, the owner of the property kept coming to look for figs from his tree, but he never found any. Finally he said to the keeper of his vineyard, "Behold, for three years I have come looking for fruit on this fig tree without finding any. Cut it down! Why does it even use up the ground?" (Luke 13:7) The keeper of the vineyard requested a little more time, at least another year to dig around the tree and fertilize it. There was nothing to lose. If it bore fruit, everyone would be happy. If not, he could cut it down then.

Jesus told that story to illustrate God's long-suffering with sinners. He delays His judgment and gives them one privilege after another, one revelation of Himself after another, one opportunity to repent after another. Then, as we might expect, He looks for the fruit of a changed life that provides the evidence of eternal salvation. But He does not wait forever. If people go on disregarding His patient and gracious offer of salvation, eventually the ax falls. "Cut it down," He says. "Let the full force of My anger be directed against these unrepentant sinners."

That sounds rather severe. And it is! God can be severe. "Behold then the kindness and severity of God," warned the Apostle Paul (Romans 11:22). We all like to talk about God's kindness, His love, His grace, His mercy, and His long-

197

suffering, but most of us choose not to say very much about His severity. That word means literally "a cutting off." It has to do with retribution—strictly exacting the full penalty of the law, righteously judging sin with perfect justice. It introduces us to another inescapable side of God's character, what Scripture calls His *wrath*.

The first thing that usually comes to mind when we hear the term wrath is violent anger and temper, and somehow that does not sound very becoming for a loving God. We get a little embarrassed for Him when he says to the nation Israel, "And My anger will be kindled, and I will kill you with the sword" (Exodus 22:24); or "So it will be a reproach, a reviling, a warning and an object of horror to the nations who surround you, when I execute judgments against you in anger, wrath, and raging rebukes" (Ezekiel 5:15). Some of us have a secret desire to get rid of those passages and somehow hide the fact that God gets angry. But God does not try to hide it. He is not ashamed of it. He is perfectly willing to make His wrath known (Romans 9:22). In fact, He says more about His wrath than He does about His love.

The Explanation of God's Wrath

Attempts have been made to dilute the Biblical doctrine of wrath, but a study of the Scriptural words that are used for wrath hardly permits us to do that. The most common word is the one that makes up half of the word *long-suffering*, the word that means nose, face, or anger. God's anger is pictured symbolically as smoke pouring from His nostrils. The Psalmist wrote,

> Then the earth shook and quaked;
> And the foundations of the mountains were trembling
> And were shaken, because He was angry.
> Smoke went up out of His nostrils,
> And fire from His mouth devoured;
> Coals were kindled by it (Psalm 18:7-8).

That sounds rather forboding. Other words for wrath in the Old Testament portray the idea of fire, heat, burning, fury, and rage. Again the Psalmist wrote,

> Therefore the LORD heard and was full of wrath,
> And a fire was kindled against Jacob,
> And anger also mounted against Israel (Psalm 78:21).

That does not sound like something we can explain away as a mild slap on the wrist accompanied by a timid rebuke, "I really would rather you didn't do that." God can actually get heated up, and if we want to know Him in truth, we need to understand this side of His nature.

God's wrath is not something limited to the Old Testament. There are two primary New Testament words for *wrath*. Paul applied one of them to God (*orge*) when he warned the Ephesians that the wrath of God comes upon the sons of disobedience (Ephesians 5:6). The word he used referred originally to any passion or impulse, but it came to mean especially anger, the most powerful of all the emotions, an intense feeling of displeasure. A second word for wrath (*thumos*) is used of God only in the book of the Revelation (14:10,19; 15:1,7; 16:1,19; 19:15). It refers to a sudden passionate outburst in contrast to the settled and lingering frame of mind. But the point is, both words are used of God; the passionate eruption as well as the settled feelings. The New Testament does not hesitate to expose this side of God's character.

Is it wrong for God to get angry like that? On the contrary, it is as much a part of His glory and perfection as is His holiness, His justice, or His love. In fact, it is required by all three. Sin is an outrage against God's holiness; His justice requires that He punish it. And His love for His people demands that He destroy sin because it threatens their wellbeing. Wrath is God acting in love to destroy sin, to purge His universe of what is detrimental to its best interests. God cannot love what is good without hating what is evil and moving decisively against it, any more than a parent can love his child without acting quickly and ruthlessly to destroy a wild animal that threatens the life of that child. God's wrath is the perfect response of His perfect being to that which poses a danger to His children.

One of the reasons we have such a problem accepting God's wrath is because we liken it to our own. When we lose our temper and shout at our spouse or our children, we know it is sin. We feel remorse and shame over it after we have cooled down. So how then can a holy God be angry and still maintain His sinlessness? God's wrath is much different from ours.

For one thing, His wrath is not selfish like ours. We usually get angry and bitter at people because they attack our self-esteem, frustrate our attempts to reach some personal goal, threaten us with some personal loss, inconvenience us, treat us unjustly, or fail to meet our needs. God is sovereign, omnipotent, totally self-sufficient; He does what He pleases and has all things in His control. Nobody can frustrate His goals or threaten His well-being, so He has no reason to become selfishly angry and no reason to get bitter or resent-ful. Our anger is usually expressed for our own benefit—to let off steam, to let everybody know how much we have been hurt, to assert our rights, or to get our own way. God is perfect love and so acts for the good of others. His wrath never is selfishly motivated.

Another major difference between God's wrath and ours is that His is always in perfect control. While He acts firmly and decisively, He never acts with unbridled or unrestrained emotion. He does not lose His temper, rant and rave, say foolish things, throw pots and pans, put His fist through walls, or do any of the other senseless things we may do when we get angry. While from man's point of view it may look as though His actions are sudden and unpredictable, He is un-changeable. Every expression of His wrath was known from eternity past and is part of His perfect plan. Though it may seem to be violent from man's perspective, it is actually the settled opposition of His holiness to sin, and the judicial administration of His justice toward sinners. It may be described as hot, fiery, fierce, and furious. But, unlike ours, it is never out of control.

The major reason we try to cover up God's wrath is probably because we have little understanding of the absolute, awesome holiness of His nature and, consequently, have little consciousness of the contemptible, despicable character of our own sin. We see no need for God to get angry. The prevailing opinion of the day seems to be, "So what's a little sin? Why should God get so heated up about that?" A knowledge of His holiness would help us understand the significance and the necessity of His wrath. An old graying dress shirt may look white enough until it is placed beside a brand-new one. Then it may look so grubby and grimy that we decide it must be relegated to the ragbag. Just so, our sin may seem acceptable until we get a glimpse of God's perfect holiness. Then we begin to understand why He finds it necessary to take such drastic action. But against what does He take that action? Against what, specifically, is His wrath revealed?

The Revelation of God's Wrath

The Apostle Paul went straight to the heart of this issue when he said, "For the wrath of God is revealed from heaven against all ungodliness and unrighteousness of men, who suppress the truth in unrighteousness" (Romans 1:18). God does not hide His wrath. He reveals it, that is, He discloses it, brings it to light, makes it known. He expresses it, not in violent, uncontrolled explosions as we have already seen, but nevertheless by definite, observable acts. Whenever it is expressed, it is always against *ungodliness* and *unrighteousness.* Ungodliness involves irreverence, impiety, and blatant disregard for His will. Unrighteousness involves any kind of wickedness, wrongdoing, or injustice. In other words, God's wrath, unlike ours, is always expressed against sin, and particularly the sin of those who suppress His truth by willful wickedness and so do moral damage to others.

When we read through the Old Testament we see some of the ways God revealed His wrath—pestilence, death, exile, the destruction of cities and nations, and the denial of privileges. The Psalmist described the hardhearted Israelites who provoked God in the wilderness and were denied entrance into the Promised Land. He quoted God as saying,

> Therefore I swore in My anger,
> Truly they shall not enter into My rest (Psalm 95:11).

It was God's anger or wrath revealed against their stubborn, willful disbelief that kept them from enjoying what they might have had. To allow them to enter the land with their rebellious attitudes would probably have brought them more unhappiness than wandering in the wilderness brought them, so even in wrath His mercy was evident. Just so, those who refuse to accept God's offer of Heaven by faith in the death of His Son will suffer eternal wrath. The holiness of Heaven would be agony for them in their unregenerate state.

Another way we see God's wrath revealed is by observing the earthly life of God incarnate, the Lord Jesus Christ. There were occasions when He was clearly angry. The first one was at the outset of His public ministry. He had come to Jerusalem for the Passover and found the temple of God invaded by profiteers who were taking advantage of the people and exploiting the things of God for personal gain. So He made a scourge of cords and drove them out of the temple, along with their sheep and oxen, pouring out the coins of the moneychangers and overturning their tables (John 2:15-16). It was an unmistakable expression of anger, as His disciples themselves testified. They reflected on a passage in the psalms about the zeal of God's house consuming Him (John 2:17) (cf.

Psalm 69:9). That word *zeal* is a word of passion and indignation. God gets angry when people use spiritual things for
personal profit, whether it be the businessman who uses his
church affiliation to fatten his bank account or the preacher
who uses his position to enhance his image. Eventually God
does something about it.

Jesus got angry on another occasion as well, this time in
the synagogue at Capernaum. A man was there with a para-
lyzed hand, and the Pharisees were watching to see if Jesus
would heal on the sabbath day so they could find some
excuse to condemn Him. "And after looking around at them
with anger, grieved at their hardness of heart, He said to the
man, 'Stretch out your hand.' And he stretched it out, and his
hand was restored" (Mark 3:5). Jesus was angry because of
their spiritual insensitivity and utter lack of concern about the
man's need. This kind of pharisaism probably angers God as
much as anything else—maintaining the outward traditions
of religion, clinging tenaciously to religious rules and regula-
tions, but lacking a life-changing faith that shows itself in
compassion toward people in need. Eventually He does something about it. This unbelieving nation was removed from its
privileged position and scattered to the ends of the earth.
"Cut it down," God said, revealing His wrath.

The revelation of God's wrath has been observed throughout human history in a myriad of ways, but Scripture indicates that we have not yet seen the worst. God is still restraining
His wrath to a large degree, giving men an opportunity to
trust Him. But the day is coming when He will restrain it no
longer.

The Culmination of God's Wrath

Several passages in Scripture speak of "the wrath to come."
John the Baptist used that phrase when he saw the Pharisees
and Sadducees coming to his baptism. "You brood of vipers,
who warned you to flee from the wrath to come?" (Matthew

3:7) Evidently a day is coming when God's wrath is going to be revealed in an unparalleled way.

Paul also spoke of a future day of wrath: "But because of your stubbornness and unrepentant heart you are storing up wrath for yourself in the day of wrath and revelation of the righteous judgment of God" (Romans 2:5). People with hard and impenitent hearts are accumulating wrath against themselves for that day. It sounds as though there is a storehouse where all the wrath that sin deserves is piling up. God's long-suffering is presently restraining it, but someday the storehouse will be full, the doors will burst open, and all that accumulated wrath will pour out. It is as though a great dam is holding back the angry waters of retribution. But a day of wrath is coming when the dam will break and the waters will be released.

When will that day be? It seems significant that when the seals of judgment are opened, in the book of the Revelation, the inhabitants of the earth cry out to the rocks and mountains, "Fall on us and hide us from the presence of Him who sits on the throne, and from the wrath of the Lamb; for the great day of their wrath has come; and who is able to stand?" (Revelation 6:16-17) That time, known in the Old Testament as the time of Jacob's trouble (Jeremiah 30:7 KJV), called by Jesus a time of great tribulation (Matthew 24:21), is here described as the great day of God's wrath. The meek and mild Lamb of God, who willingly submitted Himself to the abuse and humiliation of men at His first coming, is going to become the instrument of God's wrath. The wrath of the Lamb will be so fierce that men will endeavor to flee from His presence and seek death rather than face Him.

The chapters that follow in the Revelation describe unprecedented wrath. The great majority of the earth's population is killed in calamities such as the world has never seen. And references to the wrath of God keep turning up in this account (e.g. 11:18; 14:10,19; 15:1,7; 16:1,19). Then the Son of God Himself appears as John described in prophetic vision:

"And from His mouth comes a sharp sword, so that with it He may smite the nations; and He will rule them with a rod of iron; and He treads the wine press of the fierce wrath of God, the Almighty" (Revelation 19:15). The cup of iniquity is full, the grapes of wrath are ripe, and now God crushes them in awesome judgment. Those who have rejected His grace feel the terror of His wrath.

But the end is not yet. The scene changes to a great white throne where the unbelieving dead of all the ages have been raised to stand before God for judgment. "And if anyone's name was not found written in the book of life, he was thrown into the lake of fire" (Revelation 20:15). The lake of fire, where there shall be torment day and night for ever and ever (Revelation 20:10), is the ultimate expression of God's wrath. Some have wondered how God can be glorified through people suffering in the lake of fire for eternity. We cannot deny that it will display the glory of His holiness, His righteousness, and His justice.

Punishment in the lake of fire seems to be much more severe than most human crimes deserve, however. We cringe at the thought of it. Yet the violation of God's infinitely holy nature demands an infinite penalty. Beyond that, Scripture assures us that eternal wrath is something men choose for themselves. They have expressed their preference for living apart from God by rejecting the light He has given them. As we have seen, God allows them to have what they prefer. But there is no reason why anyone should have to suffer God's wrath. Deliverance is available.

The Salvation from God's Wrath

In perfect, infinite, unselfish love, God has laid the curse of His offended holiness on His own Son who willingly bore it for us (cf. 2 Corinthians 5:21; Galatians 3:13). He provided the sacrifice by which His holiness could be satisfied and His wrath avoided. The Apostle Paul explained it: "But God demonstrates His own love toward us, in that while we were yet sinners, Christ died for us. Much more then, having now been justified by His blood, we shall be saved from the wrath of God through Him" (Romans 5:8-9). Because the infinitely holy Son of God died in our place and paid for our sins, we may be forgiven, declared righteous, and made acceptable to God. We can be delivered from the awful wrath that has been stored up because of our sin. That is the essence of the gospel.

When the Thessalonians heard Paul preach that message, they received it and were delivered from the wrath to come (1 Thessalonians 1:6,10). God is willing to do the same for us. Those who acknowledge their sin and put their trust in Christ's death for forgiveness are no longer destined for wrath, "but for obtaining salvation through our Lord Jesus Christ" (1 Thessalonians 5:9). There is no wrath for the child of God—only for those who reject His Son. "He who believes in the Son has eternal life; but he who does not obey the Son shall not see life, but the wrath of God abides on him" (John 3:36).

Some are certain they have nothing to worry about since they have escaped God's wrath thus far. They are sure that God, if there is a God, does not care about their sin, and they can live as they please without fear of wrath. But that is a dangerous delusion. Donald Grey Barnhouse told the story of some godly farmers who, when they drove up to their little country church one summer Sunday morning, observed the owner of the forty acres across the road busily plowing his field. He was careful to plow the portion immediately adjacent to the church during services, flaunting his disregard for God. After the harvest he wrote a letter to the editor of the local weekly newspaper boasting that he had the highest yield per acre of any farm in the county even though he had done most of his work on Sundays. He asked the editor how the Christians could explain that. The editor answered with one brief but incisive comment: "God does not settle His accounts in the month of October."

Do not mistake God's long-suffering for lenience with your sin. He patiently waits for you to repent of your sins and turn to Him in faith. If you refuse, you will one day experience His wrath. The choice is yours.

Action To Take:

If you are a believer, thank God right now for laying on His Son all the wrath which your sin deserves.

Determine that by God's grace you will take advantage of every opportunity you can to share His message of salvation, so that others as well may be delivered from the wrath to come.

18

HE WILL ABUNDANTLY PARDON

COUNSELORS ARE CONVINCED that the overwhelming majority of troubled people who walk into their offices for help are suffering from some degree of guilt which has contributed significantly to their problem, be it a spiritual, emotional, or interpersonal problem. Guilt has a way of dominating our lives and disrupting our relationships. It preys on our minds, fills us with anxiety and fear, makes us defensive, irritable, and judgmental, drives us to punish ourselves in various ways, and may even make us physically sick. It is one of life's most destructive emotions.

Not all guilt is true guilt. It is sometimes difficult to distinguish feelings of inferiority, failure, shame, or poor self-image from real guilt. They all register on our minds in much the same way and cause us to say much the same things, such as, "I never do anything right; I make a mess of everything I put my hand to; I can't get along with anybody; I'll never amount to anything; I'm just no good."

Feelings like that usually find their roots in our upbringing, particularly our efforts to please a parent who was difficult to satisfy, one who seldom gave encouragement or commendation, but rather condemned, blamed, and accused excessively, and conditioned our acceptance and approval on our performance. That kind of environment produces false guilt, a feeling of blame over things that do not violate any principle in God's Word and for which we may not even know the cause.

People with false guilt usually view God as a mean old man who will be nice to them if they measure up to His standards, but nasty to them if they don't. They see His standards as impossibly high and the potential for pleasing Him practically hopeless, so they have resigned themselves to living in His disfavor. They do not like it, but they see no other way. Bible-centered counsel may help them learn to accept themselves and to relate positively to God.

But there is also real guilt. We may feel guilty because we *are* guilty. We have broken God's laws and we know it. The Bible says that the whole world is guilty before Him (Romans 3:10-20). We have all fallen short of His standard (Romans 3:23), and because we are guilty we deserve to be punished (Romans 6:23). An infinitely holy God must express His wrath against sin. God's critics will be quick to attack Him at this point. "See, God is a rigid, demanding, intolerant, perfectionist judge who refuses to accept us if we fail to live up to His expectations." The critics are right to a degree. God cannot condone sin or allow it to enter His presence. He must judge it. But what they fail to see is that He is also loving, gracious, merciful, and kind, and that those traits motivate Him to forgive us.

The God which men have created in their own image is harsh, vindictive, and punitive. But the true God who has revealed Himself in His Word is forgiving and accepting. When He passed by Moses on the mount and made His glory known, He proclaimed it for all to understand: He is the God "who forgives iniquity, transgression, and sin" (Exodus 34:7). David reiterated it plainly in a beautiful prayer of worship: "For Thou, Lord, art good, and ready to forgive" (Psalm 86:5). God is forgiving by nature. Forgiveness is the essence of His being. That is about the best news we guilty human beings could ever hear. God is not set on punishing us. He wants to forgive us and accept us warmly and freely.

Forgiveness is a most misunderstood concept. Some people have the notion that forgiving means simply overlooking a wrong. They say, "Everybody does things they don't mean in moments of stress. So I'll just pretend that I didn't see it, and act as if it didn't happen." Nothing could be further from true forgiveness, which is neither passive nor indifferent, but decisive and dynamic. We learn what it involves by watching our forgiving God in action. There are at least five essential elements to His forgiveness.

The Removal of the Sin

Nowhere do we see a more graphic picture of God's forgiveness than on Israel's day of atonement, the day God dealt with the nation's sins for another year. After the high priest offered a sacrifice for his own sins, he secured two goats, one to be sacrificed as a sin offering and the other to be used as a scapegoat. Then he slaughtered the sin-offering goat, brought its blood inside the veil of the tabernacle and sprinkled it on and in front of the mercy seat to "make atonement for the holy place, because of the impurities of the sons of Israel, and because of their transgressions" (Leviticus 16:16). The word translated "make atonement" is also translated "forgive" in the Old Testament (e.g. in Psalm 78:38). It means, basically, "to cover." The blood of that goat was not actually the basis for the Israelites' forgiveness, but it dramatically pictured the important fact that God would cover their sins.

Under the mercy seat, in the ark of the covenant, were the symbols of Israel's sin—the manna about which they murmured and complained, the tables of the law which they broke, and Aaron's rod that budded when they rebelled against their divinely appointed leaders. But all those sins were covered by the blood of the goat. In like manner, when God forgives our sins, He covers them with the blood of His Son; He hides them from view. Micah said, it is as though He casts them into the depths of the sea (Micah 7:19). What a relief to know that the sins which have haunted us, burdened us, and grieved us are permanently removed from view, perfectly covered. David expressed that relief when he exclaimed,

> How blessed is he whose transgression is forgiven,
> Whose sin is covered! (Psalm 32:1)

But that is not all God did on the day of atonement. When the high priest finished making an atonement in the holy place, he laid both of his hands on the head of the live goat and confessed over it the sins of the nation, then sent it away into the wilderness (Leviticus 16:20-22). As he placed his hands on the goat's head, it was as though he were lifting the sins of the people and placing those sins on a substitute. Then as he let the goat go into the wilderness, it was as though those sins were being removed far away. He lifted them up, then he let them go.

Two Sides of Forgiveness

It is interesting that of the two major words translated "forgiveness" in the Old Testament, one means literally "to lift up" and the other "to let go." The most common New Testament word for forgiveness likewise means "to let go" or "to send away." When God forgives us, He lifts our sins from us and sends them far away. David said,

> As far as the east is from the west,
> So far has He removed our transgressions
> from us (Psalm 103:12).

He chose an analogy that describes a place infinitely beyond which anybody could ever find our sins. While we know where north stops and south begins, nobody can determine precisely where east stops and west begins. Why should we bear a burden of guilt any longer when God has taken the trouble to remove our sins that far from us and cover them so thoroughly? The first great blessing of knowing a God who forgives is the complete removal of our sin from us.

The Remission of the Debt

When somebody wrongs us, we usually consider him to be indebted to us. He owes it to us to right the wrong, or he owes us an apology. If we commit a crime and are apprehended, tried, and convicted, we must pay our debt to society. We understand that principle clearly; it permeates our culture— sin incurs a debt. When we sin against the God who made us and gave us life, we are indebted to Him. If He wants to forgive us, He must cancel that debt.

This facet of forgiveness is beautifully illustrated in Jesus' parable of the unmerciful servant, the man who owed his king ten thousand talents, the equivalent of approximately ten million dollars in our money (Matthew 18:21-35). It is inconceivable that a servant could accumulate a debt of that magnitude, but Jesus chose such an extraordinary figure to emphasize how much we owe God because of our sin. Fur- thermore, there was no way a servant could possibly repay such a debt on a meager salary of a few pennies a day, and that too is part of the point Jesus made. We can never repay the debt we owe God. An eternity of torment in hell will not even begin to satisfy the extent of His offended holiness.

Like the servant in the story, some of us think we can repay God what we owe Him. We say as he said, "Have patience with me, and I will repay you everything" (Matthew 18:26). We think that given enough time we can do enough good works and keep enough of His commandments to compen- sate God for all the debt of our sin. That attitude displays our gross failure to grasp the awesomeness of His holiness and the awfulness of our sin. God knows it can never be done. So in the story, the master took pity on his servant and canceled his debt for him. That is exactly what God does for us. He cancels the debt of our sin, and that is an essential element of forgiveness.

But how can God do that? His infinite holiness has been violated and His justice demands that the debt be paid. He cannot simply ignore it. Who will pay it? In infinite love and grace, He decided to pay it Himself. In the story, it cost the king ten million dollars that was rightfully his in order to forgive his servant. We often overlook the inescapable fact that forgiveness always costs somebody something. If an offense has been committed, somebody has to pay. When justice is served, the one who has committed the offense pays. When forgiveness is granted, the one who has been offended pays. Guilt cannot be transferred to a third party. The Psalmist said,

> No man can by any means redeem his brother,
> Or give to God a ransom for him (Psalm 49:7).

Sometimes we think we have forgiven a person who has wronged us, but yet we are subconsciously looking for some way to reclaim from him what we have lost, whether it be our reputation, our money, our pride, or whatever else he might have taken from us. We are looking for a way to make him pay; and that is not forgiveness. When we forgive him, we pay in full for his wrong. Since God is forgiving by nature, He pays in full for our sins. That is what Jesus Christ was doing on that cross. He was not a third party trying to get God and man together. He was the offended One, God in flesh, who came to earth to pay for man's forgiveness. As the Apostle Paul put it, "God was in Christ reconciling the world to Himself, not counting their trespasses against them" (2 Corinthians 5:19). When He bowed His head and voluntarily dismissed His Spirit, He cried, "It is finished." That statement is one word in the Greek text, a word that was used in business transactions meaning "paid in full." The obligation which our sins incurred was paid in full at Calvary's cross. God took our place and paid our debt as our substitute.

Did you ever have a debt canceled? What a happy experience it is! When I was a seminary student, my wife and I scraped and scrounged to get the money together for my tuition one semester. I approached the business office to pay my bill, but when the girl behind the counter found my record she happily announced, "We don't need your money. Your bill has already been paid." I have never found out who paid that money, but I am still grateful to that unknown person. We were able to continue eating for awhile, much to our delight. As wonderful as that experience was, it is still infinitely greater to know that the eternal debt of our sin has been canceled. When God forgives, He not only takes away our sin, He also cancels our debt. But there is still more to His forgiveness.

The Repeal of the Penalty

The debt of a broken law is called a penalty, so if the debt is canceled, it is obvious that the penalty must also be re-voked. While the two are related, it is essential that we under-stand both aspects of forgiveness. As we have seen, on the day of atonement one of the goats was killed as a sacrifice for the sins of the people. It pictured the punishment of a substi-tute. The goat's blood could not in itself pay for Israel's sins (cf. Hebrews 10:4), but blood did have to be shed neverthe-less. The penalty for sin is death, and only death could satisfy that requirement (cf. Hebrews 9:22). The death of that goat portrayed to the people of Israel that God Himself would suffer the penalty of their sin.

That is exactly what Jesus Christ was doing on the cross. Isaiah predicted that He would be pierced for our transgres-sions and crushed for our iniquities, that the penalty of our sins would fall on Him (Isaiah 53:5-6). Peter described how it happened: "And He Himself bore our sins in His body on the cross" (1 Peter 2:24). He died for our sins, "the just for the unjust" (1 Peter 3:18). The basis for our eternal forgiveness is the blood of Jesus Christ, and nothing could be clearer in Scripture (cf. Ephesians 1:7). Jesus Himself declared, "For this is My blood of the covenant, which is poured out for many for forgiveness of sins" (Matthew 26:28).

Believers never again need to fear punishment from God. The penalty for our sins has been assessed and fully satisfied by God's Son. "There is therefore now no condemnation for those who are in Christ Jesus" (Romans 8:1). No punishment! No penalty! No eternal judgment! The penalty has been paid. The case is settled and will never come up for review. There is no possibility of appeal to any higher court. We as God's children are free from sin's penalty, free from all fear of punishment. He may lovingly discipline us to help us grow in Him and so experience greater satisfaction and joy in living, but we never need to fear His retribution.

Some professing Christians find that difficult to believe. They are still afraid that God is going to punish them. They live much like the child who has been promised a spanking after school. It ruins his whole day. He is tense and irritable, he does poorly in his school work, he feels a strain with his friends, he dreads coming home. When he finally does come home, there is no communication with his parents, no freedom to grow in his relationship with them, just apprehension and latent hostility—until the ordeal is over. He may decide to run away because he cannot face them, but that only compounds his problem. Some professing Christians are trying to hide from God because they are afraid that He has not really rescinded sin's penalty, that eventually He is going to punish them. Believe it, Christian! There is no condemnation for those who are in Christ Jesus. The penalty has been repealed.

The Release from Guilt

Fear of punishment can be damaging to our emotional and spiritual well-being, but our greatest danger probably comes from guilt. Guilt can be constructive, one of the tools God uses to help us see our need for forgiveness and acknowledge our sin. But after we have seen it and have received His forgiveness by faith, the guilt is gone forever. We never need to struggle with its venomous effect again.

> "Come now, and let us reason together,"
> Says the LORD,
> "Though your sins are as scarlet,
> They will be as white as snow;
> Though they are red like crimson,
> They will be like wool" (Isaiah 1:18).

Guilt is viewed as a red stain. That would be most appropriate if the crime were murder, as Shakespeare's character Macbeth could well attest. But it may also be a fitting description of any sin against God's holiness. It is a blot, a blemish, a taint, a flaw, a stigma, a red stain that dirties our lives and contaminates our relationships. God's forgiveness washes that ugly stain as white as snow. Before the days of air pollution, there was nothing purer or cleaner than fresh fallen snow. That is how clean we are when God forgives us. The blood of Jesus Christ washes us and cleanses us (1 John 1:7). It leaves us pure and blameless. What a relief! "Blessed is the man whose sin the LORD does not count against him" (Psalm 32:2 NIV). His nagging guilt is gone.

We read that and we really may believe it. But somehow when our minds are occupied with our sins, we tend to forget it and we still feel guilty. Satan works very hard at making us feel guilty, accusing us, and condemning us, trying to convince us that God could never forgive the awful things we have done. He knows that when we wallow in guilt, we become discouraged and defeated and are of little use to God. We may begin to say things like, "I'm no good. I never will get victory over this sin, so I might as well go ahead and enjoy it." And our spiritual power plummets to new lows.

Satan also knows that when we fail to accept God's forgiveness, we will not be able to forgive ourselves. And when we do not forgive ourselves, we will not be able to forgive others. We will be harsh, demanding, overbearing, intolerant, and punitive in our relationships. Remember Christ's parable of the unmerciful servant. Because the servant never grasped the reality of his forgiveness, he grabbed one of his fellow slaves by the throat and tried to choke him, demanding payment for the mere twenty dollars he was owed (Matthew 18:28-30). There have been some fierce battles precipitated by professing believers who have never learned to enjoy their freedom from guilt. Satan's advantage is to hold us in that bondage to guilt. Do not let him do it. God has forgiven you. Accept His forgiveness, and then forgive yourself. It will help you forgive others who have wronged you and treat them with kindness, patience, and tolerance. People who know a forgiving God will forgive others. If you have been experiencing conflicts, your new attitude will help to bring peace to your relationships.

The Restoration To Fellowship

It is difficult to look people in the eye when we know that we have wronged them. We wonder if they know what we have done, whether or not they are holding it against us, or what they might try to do to get back at us. But if we are sure they have forgiven us, the barriers are gone and we are free to enjoy an open and cordial relationship with them once again.

In like manner, sin builds a barrier that hinders our fellowship with God. Isaiah said to the people of his day, "your iniquities have made a separation between you and your God" (Isaiah 59:2). He likens those sins to a thick cloud that blocks the rays of the sun. But just as a cloud can be dispelled by the sun or the wind, so God dispels our cloud of sin when he forgives us.

> I have wiped out your transgressions like a thick cloud,
> And your sins like a heavy mist.
> Return to Me, for I have redeemed you (Isaiah 44:22).

With the cloud of sin removed, the debt canceled, the penalty satisfied, and the guilt gone, we are free to come boldly into His presence and enthusiastically enjoy His fellowship.

And it will ever be so. God assures us that when He forgives our sins, He remembers them no more (cf. Isaiah 43:25; Jeremiah 31:34; Hebrews 8:12; 10:17). He will never allow them to come between us again. Why then should we? The child of God stands forgiven for all time. Paul says we have been forgiven of all our trespasses, and that includes sins that are past, present, and future (Colossians 2:13; cf. also Psalm 103:3). When we believe that, we can come joyfully and confidently into His presence.

Remember that while our forgiving God has provided for our eternal forgiveness, He still reserves the right to establish the condition by which we may experience that forgiveness. Peter mentioned the condition as he preached in the house of Cornelius, the Roman centurion. He was speaking about the Lord Jesus when he said, "everyone who believes in Him receives forgiveness of sins" (Acts 10:43). Belief in Christ— that is the condition. Forgiveness is offered to all, but it is only experienced by those who will turn from their sin and place their personal trust in Jesus Christ as the One who can deliver them from its guilt and penalty.

> Let the wicked forsake his way,
> And the unrighteous man his thoughts;
> And let him return to the LORD,
> And He will have compassion on him;
> And to our God,
> For He will abundantly pardon (Isaiah 55:7).

Abundant pardon is pardon that is multiplied over and over, pardon that has no limit. It is ours for the believing. If you have never done so before, avail yourself by faith of God's offer.

Action To Take:

If you have trusted Christ as your Saviour, thank God right now for your total forgiveness. Whenever Satan tries to make you feel guilty over some past sin, remind yourself that you have been fully forgiven.

Now think about someone who has wronged you and forgive him for what he has done; that is, decide that you will pay for his offenses in full. And remember to treat him as fully forgiven.

19

GOD IS SO GOOD

JESUS was on the road, making His final journey to Jerusalem to celebrate the Passover. This time He Himself would
be the Passover Lamb, slain for the sins of the world. As
He walked along with His disciples, a young man ran up to
Him, knelt down in front of Him and asked, "Good Teacher,
what shall I do to inherit eternal life?" (Mark 10:17)

"Good Teacher"—that was an unusual form of address. In
all of Jewish religious literature, no rabbi was ever called
good. Only God and His law were considered to be good.
Was this a case of empty flattery, or had this young man
become convinced of something that the rest of the religious
establishment had refused to admit—that Jesus Christ was
actually God in flesh?

"Why do you call Me good?" Jesus asked. "No one is good
except God alone" (Mark 10:18). His comment was not a
denial of His deity, as some have suggested, but rather an
opportunity for the rich young ruler to confess his faith in
Christ's divine person. That confession never came, indicating the man's lack of spiritual understanding. But Christ's
statement tells us something about God that we need to
consider if we ever hope to know Him intimately. God is
good, and beyond that, He is the only one who can rightfully
be called good.

The Nature of God's Goodness

The word for *good* which Jesus used refers to what is excellent in its character or constitution and beneficial or useful in its effect. The Old Testament equivalent means pleasant, agreeable, excellent, valuable, benevolent, and kind. Two separate ideas begin to surface as we examine these words that describe God's goodness. One has to do with the perfections of His person and the other with the kindness of His acts.

Both ideas occur together in one verse in the psalms: "Thou art good and doest good" (Psalm 119:68). First of all, God Himself is good; that is, He is everything that God should be—the ideal person, the sum total of all perfection. There are no defects or contradictions in Him, and nothing can be added to His nature to make Him any better. He is excellence to an infinite degree, possessing every desirable quality, and therefore of inestimable value. God is good.

Because God is Himself the highest and greatest good, He is also the source and fountain of all other good. He does good things. He extends His goodness to others. It is His nature to be kind, generous, and benevolent, to demonstrate good will toward men, and to take great pleasure in making them happy. Because God is good, He wants us to have what we need for our happiness and He sees that it is available to us. Every good thing we now enjoy or ever hope to enjoy flows from Him, and no good thing has ever existed or ever will exist that does not come from His good hand.

That is why Jesus could say to the rich young ruler, "No one is good except God alone." No other being is infinitely and innately and immutably good. All goodness that exists outside of Him finds its source in Him. Even a man as godly as the Apostle Paul had to admit that in his natural being there was no good thing (Romans 7:18), and we have to admit it too. If there is any good to be found in us, it had to come from God, for we are incapable of producing it ourselves.

In addition, everything God does is good—specially tailored for our benefit. Asaph began Psalm 73 by stating quite literally, "Only God is good to Israel." In other words, God is nothing but good. He can do nothing but what is absolutely best.

A little fellow was heard praying at bedtime, "Help me to be a good boy—but you be a good God too." But there is no need to remind God to be good. He cannot possibly be otherwise.

If everything God does is good and all His acts are the outflowing of His goodness, it would seem that this attribute embraces all His other attributes. There is some Biblical evidence for that. God promised Moses that he would make all His goodness pass before him (Exodus 33:19). When God did pass before him the next morning on Mount Sinai, He revealed His compassion, His graciousness, His long-suffering, His mercy, His truth, and His forgiveness (Exodus 34:5-7). Evidently all those attributes were summed up in His goodness.

We readily can see the relationship between goodness and some of God's other attributes. For example, when His goodness gives of itself unconditionally and sacrificially, it is love. When it shows favor to the guilty and undeserving, it is grace. When it reaches out to relieve the miserable and distressed, it is mercy. When it shows patience toward those who deserve punishment, it is long-suffering. When it reveals to us the way things are, it is truth. When it bears the offense of our sin and absolves us of our guilt, it is forgiveness. When the Bible says that God is good, it is referring to all these qualities and more.

> Praise the LORD, for the LORD is good;
> Sing praises to His name, for it is lovely (Psalm 135:3).

The Expression of God's Goodness

Although God's goodness is unfolded in all that He is and all that He does, the Bible reveals some specific expressions of it. For one, it is demonstrated in His creation. Seven times in Genesis God said that what He made was good (Genesis 1:4,10,12,18,21,25,31). The final statement sums it up: "And God saw all that He had made, and behold, it was very good" (Genesis 1:31). No one can observe the grandeur of God's handiwork and deny that it is good. Even though man has managed to mar it considerably, it was good the way God made it and it still reflects that goodness: blue skies studded with fluffy white clouds by day and spangled with sparkling bright stars at night; glistening snow-covered mountain peaks; fields and trees with infinitely varied shades of green and gold; brilliant, multi-colored flowers with lovely fragrances. There is no end to the goodness we enjoy in God's creation: "the earth is full of the goodness of the LORD" (Psalm 33:5 KJV). The beauty of God's earth reminds us of His goodness.

Then there is man, the zenith of God's creative genius. God made him with eyes to behold the beauty of nature, ears to hear its lovely sounds, nostrils to enjoy its pleasant aromas, taste buds to relish its infinite variety of eatable delights, a sense of touch to help communicate love to someone precious to him, and a mind to comprehend the meaning of it all, to name just a few evidences of God's goodness. He affords us no end of good things: the warmth of sunlight, the joy of loving family and friends, the satisfaction of productive labor, the exhilaration of physical exercise and recreation, the refreshment of a good night's sleep, provision for our daily needs, and so many others that enrich our lives. These blessings turn our minds to Him in adoration and gratitude.

These "good things" are blessings God bestows on all mankind. They are not reserved for believers alone. King David wrote:

The LORD is good to all,
And His mercies are over all His works (Psalm 145:9).

The eyes of all look to Thee,
And Thou dost give them their food in due time.
Thou dost open Thy hand,
And dost satisfy the desire of every living thing (15·16).

Jesus said He makes the sun rise on the evil as well as on the good, and sends the rain on the unrighteous as well as on the righteous (Matthew 5:45). He deals bountifully and kindly even with ungrateful and wicked men (Luke 6:35). Paul said in a message to a group of unbelievers at Lystra, "He did good and gave you rains from heaven and fruitful seasons, satisfying your hearts with good and gladness" (Acts 14:17).

Unbelievers have a tendency to take God's goodness for granted and exploit it for their own ends. But the person who knows Him personally, who understands and appreciates His goodness, will not only enjoy His blessings fully, but use them thankfully and unselfishly, giving glory to Him. The Apostle Paul wrote to Timothy, "For everything created by God is good, and nothing is to be rejected, if it is received with gratitude" (1 Timothy 4:4).

Along with the general benefits which God has bestowed on all people, the believer has additional good things to enjoy. For example, he has in his possession the Word of God which is described as good (Hebrews 6:5). He can know and do the will of God which is called good (Romans 12:2). He has the assurance that his good God will work every detail of his life together for good (Romans 8:28), the minor annoyances as well as the major crises. The expressions of God's good-ness to His children are endless.

How great is Thy goodness,
Which Thou hast stored up for those who fear Thee,
Which Thou hast wrought for those who take refuge in Thee,
Before the sons of men! (Psalm 31:19)

The Psalmist goes further: "No good thing does He withhold from those who walk uprightly" (Psalm 84:11).

Our family has seen innumerable evidences of God's goodness through the years. One small but unforgetable incident occurred when our youngest son was about five years old. We were spending the week at a Bible conference and Tim had gained a new friend named Peter. One evening we overheard him say, "Peter, let's pray that we will find a treasure on the beach tomorrow."

My wife and I thought that maybe we ought to plant something in the sand for him to find, in order to help God out a little and bolster our young son's budding faith, but we completely forgot about it. As we relaxed on the beach the next afternoon we heard Tim suddenly exclaim, "I found it! I found a treasure!" He had dug a nickel out of the sand, and as an added bonus it had been minted in the year of his birth. It was just a little thing—but another evidence that a good God loves to do good things for His own.

The Objections To God's Goodness

Of course, not everybody agrees that God is good, and it should be no surprise that His goodness is being called into question today. It was probably the first attribute of God to be attacked in human history. When Satan met Eve in the garden, he implied that God was less than good for denying her the luscious fruit of that one forbidden tree (cf. Genesis 3:1-5). Men have been challenging God's goodness ever since. How can a good God allow evil to exist in His world? How can He permit disease, pain, suffering, poverty, hunger, prejudice, greed, exploitation, crime, violence, war, bloodshed, catastrophe, and destruction? They argue, either He is not very good or He does not have the power to stop it.

It is difficult for us to understand how these human tragedies can possibly be good, and quite frankly, we may never fully understand it. God tells us that His ways are higher than our ways and His thoughts are higher than our thoughts (Isaiah 55:8-9), therefore we cannot expect to understand everything. We do know, however, that God is not the author of sin (Habakkuk 1:13; James 1:13; 1 John 1:5). We also know that God in His sovereign good pleasure created man with volition—the ability to choose good or evil. The first man chose evil of his own will, and his sin affected all of God's creation. All of the heartache and suffering in this world today are the direct result of that choice, the consequence of living in a world affected by sin.

In addition, our suffering is intensified by repeated sinful choices; not only our own, but those of individuals and nations around us. We may suffer when a drug addict decides to secure the money he needs for his next fix or when the leaders of some nation decide to enlarge their sphere of influence. The only way to remove all suffering from the world would be to deny everyone all of their freedom, to make them all automatons. None of us would opt for that.

God knew before He created him that man would choose evil, but He also knew that creating him was the best way to demonstrate the greatness of His person and the perfections of His nature—in other words, to show who He really is and to bring glory to Himself. He even has the power to overrule man's sin to accomplish that good purpose. In fact, He promises to overrule all things for good: "And we know that God causes all things to work together for good to those who love God, to those who are called according to His purpose" (Romans 8:28). That is so difficult to accept in times of great trial, even for true Christians. "If God is so good, why did He let my mate get cancer, or why did He allow my child to be taken away from me, or why did He let my marriage fall apart, or why did He let me lose my job, or why did He let me lose my life savings? I'm not guilty of any great sin."

The cause of our dilemma is our failure to understand what is truly good for us. We may have the notion that our ultimate good would be to have things go smoothly for us all the time, to do anything we please, knowing that everything we do will turn out for our happiness, comfort, convenience, health, affluence, and success. But God in His omniscience knows that the choices we make in our human wisdom and with our sinful natures will not always make us truly happy in the end.

God's good goal for us is to make us like His Son. We should never separate verse 28 from the great promise of Romans 8:29: "For whom He foreknew, He also predestined to become conformed to the image of His Son, that He might be the first-born among many brethren." Our highest good is conformity to the model of humanity that Jesus presented to us. That will bring us maximum happiness. We can be growing toward that goal daily; any choice we make that fails to contribute to that goal is going to increase our unhappiness. In other words, we do not always know what is best for us.

Parents especially understand that. Children think they know what will make them happy, but since parents have lived a few more years and know a little more about life, they know better what produces true happiness. So they insist on what they know will be for their children's good, because they love them. Sometimes parents even have to make life unpleasant for them so they will learn to do what is best. To do less than that would be inconsiderate and neglectful.

When I was sixteen years old I wanted to buy a motorcycle. I pleaded with my dad for permission, but he refused to grant it. As I look back, I know his decision was best. With the lack of responsibility I had at that age, I probably would have killed myself on a motorcycle. I couldn't understand it at the time, but now I know that what he did was good and has worked out for my benefit.

Let me illustrate it from the world of medicine. Medical studies have determined that the disease known as Hansen's disease or leprosy does not damage the limbs and make the fingers and toes drop off as people historically have believed. It attacks the nervous system and destroys the victim's ability to feel pain. As a result, lepers damage their own limbs by such careless practices as grasping things too tightly, cutting themselves seriously and not treating the wound, or putting their hands in a fire to pluck something out. On some occasions their limbs have actually been chewed off by rats while they slept, and they never felt a thing.

Medical technicians have experimented with devices that inflict an electric shock whenever a vulnerable part of the patients' bodies is being abused. But the patients would switch off the current whenever they anticipated doing anything that might produce an unpleasant sensation, so the device did them no good. The only way a patient could be protected from destroying his own body and thus adding to his misery was to put the signal out of his reach. The pain of that electric shock, as unpleasant as it might have been for the moment, proved to be good and contributed to his ultimate happiness.[1]

Most of us would like God to turn off the current, to turn down the heat, to get us out from under our burdens. But that would not necessarily be good. It might be inconsiderate and neglectful. If we had an on/off switch, we could take care of it ourselves, but that would not be very smart. True happiness can be found only when we get to know God and grow in the likeness of His Son. Nothing reminds us of that more dramatically or encourages us to grow in Him more effectively than pain and suffering. Without it we might drift away, live our lives apart from Him, and never know true happiness. Suffering does not cast doubt on God's goodness; it demonstrates it. The Psalmist saw it clearly:

> It is good for me that I was afflicted,
> That I may learn Thy statutes (Psalm 119:71).

Not only do we learn the truthfulness of His Word, we also learn firsthand the joy of His presence and the reality of His

---

[1]Related by Philip Yancy in *Where Is God When It Hurts?* Zondervan, 1977.

grace. It is often through suffering that we begin to appreciate God's goodness as never before.

Our Response To God's Goodness

When we become aware of God's goodness, it should elicit a certain kind of response from us. We see the proper response in a group of weary exiles who had made their way back to their promised land after seventy years of Babylonian captivity. Their goal was to rebuild the temple of God. Progress was slow, but in the second year of their restoration the foundation was finally completed. Those who had lived long enough to see Solomon's temple knew that this one would not begin to compare with it in size or beauty. But that made little difference to them. They were back in their land, and their temple was under way. "And they sang, praising and giving thanks to the LORD, saying, 'For He is good, for His lovingkindness is upon Israel forever.' And all the people shouted with a great shout when they praised the LORD because the foundation of the house of the LORD was laid" (Ezra 3:11). God's goodness prompted songs of praise and thanksgiving. And that is exactly what it should do for us.

> Praise the LORD!
> Oh give thanks to the LORD, for He is good;
> For His lovingkindness is everlasting (Psalm 106:1).

(Cf. also Psalm 100; 107:1; 118:1,29; 135:3; 136:1; 1 Chronicles 16:34; 2 Chronicles 5:13.)

The word *praise* comes from a root that means "to be boastful." When we praise God, we are boasting in the good things He has done, not necessarily because He has done them for us (as though we deserved anything), but simply because they demonstrate who He is. People who know a good God have no cause to grumble and complain. Praise becomes a way of life for them.

Our response to God's goodness is not only praise, but also thanksgiving. If we take a few minutes each day to do nothing but thank God for some of the good things He has done, we may never get depressed again. So take a thanksgiving break! Thanksgiving is like a tonic that brightens the entire complexion of our lives. Learn to practice it. It may require discipline at first, but soon it will become a joyful and satisfying way of life. There is no better way to get it flowing than to rehearse the evidence of God's goodness.

God is so good! If you have not yet discovered it, heed the exhortation of the Psalmist:

> O taste and see that the LORD is good;
> How blessed is the man who takes refuge
>   in Him! (Psalm 34:8)

Action To Take:

Sit down with someone close to you and rehearse some of the good things God has done for you through the years. Then respond to Him with thanksgiving and praise. If you are presently facing some trial, think of some of the good things God could be teaching you through it.

20

A JEALOUS GOD

JEALOUSY IS AN UGLY WORD. "It is the green-eyed monster," said Shakespeare in *Othello*. It has overtones of selfishness, suspicion, and distrust, and implies a hideous resentment or hostility toward other people because they enjoy some advantage. It is possessive, demanding, and overbearing; and that is repulsive. It stifles freedom and individuality, it degrades and demeans, it breeds tension and discord, it destroys friendships and marriages. We view jealousy as a horrible trait and we hate it.

We do not read very far in the Bible before we hear God saying, "You shall not make for yourself an idol, or any likeness of what is in heaven above or on the earth beneath or in the water under the earth. You shall not worship them or serve them; for I, the LORD your God, am a jealous God" (Exodus 20:4-5). A jealous God! How can a God who is holy, just, loving, gracious, merciful, and long-suffering possibly be jealous? We need to explore a side of jealousy that may have escaped us.

The Meaning of God's Jealousy

The root idea in the Old Testament word *jealous* is to become intensely red. It seems to refer to the changing color of the face or the rising heat of the emotions which are associated with intense zeal or fervor over something dear to

us. In fact, both the Old and New Testament words for
jealousy are also translated "zeal." Being jealous and being
zealous are essentially the same thing in the Bible. God is
zealous—eager about protecting what is precious to Him.

One thing He views as especially important to Him in the
Old Testament is the nation Israel. She belongs to Him as His
special possession, His unique treasure.

> For the LORD has chosen Jacob for Himself,
> Israel for His own possession (Psalm 135:4).

In fact, He views her as His wife. Through the Prophet
Hosea He said to the nation, "And I will betroth you to Me
forever" (Hosea 2:19).

No man with any moral fiber wants to share his wife with
another man, and neither does God. He expects exclusive
devotion from her. When she goes after other lovers, that is,
when she worships other gods and thus commits spiritual
adultery, He is said to be jealous. When the term jealousy is
applied to God in Scripture it is usually because His people
are worshiping idols. In the second of His ten commandments He warned them not to do that, but they failed to listen
to Him.

> For they provoked Him with their high places,
> And aroused His jealousy with their graven
> images (Psalm 78:58).

That same idea is present in the New Testament. After a
discussion of idolatry in the church of Corinth, Paul asks, "Or
do we provoke the Lord to jealousy?" (1 Corinthians 10:22)

The marital relationship may be the best way to help us
understand the difference between sinful jealousy and righteous jealousy. I can be jealous over my relationship with my
wife in a wrong way or in a right way. For example, if I feel
resentment or anger merely because I see her talking to

another man, that would be self-centered possessiveness and unreasonable domination—in other words, sinful jealousy. It would stem from my own selfishness or insecurity rather than from my commitment to her and to what is right.

But, on the other hand, if I see some man actually trying to alienate my wife's affections and seduce her, then I have reason to be righteously jealous. God gave her to me to be my wife. Her body is mine just as my body is hers. I have the exclusive right to enjoy her fully, and for someone else to assume that right would be a violation of God's holy standards. I am zealous for the exclusiveness and purity of our marriage, and that is a righteous jealousy. Jehovah feels the same way about His relationship with His "wife." There is no selfishness in His jealousy. It is the appropriate expression of His holiness.

There is a difference between jealousy and envy in Scripture. They are two entirely different words in the Greek New Testament. Jealousy involves the desire to have what somebody else has. That may be wholesome, particularly when we desire to develop in our own lives the positive spiritual qualities we see in others, or when we seek to enjoy the spiritual riches which are ours in Christ just as we see others enjoying them. In like manner, God wants what is His: the exclusive devotion of His people. It is only right and good that He should. But for us, jealousy may degenerate into something bad, as when we feel frustrated and bitter because we cannot obtain what we want, or when we find fault with those who have what we want or who keep us from getting it. God is not capable of experiencing that sinful jealousy. The point is, jealousy can be either good or bad.

On the other hand, envy is nearly always bad. It is a feeling of displeasure over the blessings others are enjoying and it makes us want to deprive them of that enjoyment. Jealousy wants what others have, while envy wants to keep them from having it. It is a vicious and malicious trait which Solomon calls "rottenness to the bones" (Proverbs 14:30 KJV).

There are some notorious examples of sinful jealousy and envy in Scripture. For example, because of Joseph's favored position with his father and because of the regal coat which Jacob gave him, "his brothers were jealous of him" (Genesis 37:11). Their sinful attitudes resulted in sinful acts; first they plotted his death, then cast him into a pit, and finally sold him into slavery. Selfishness and sinfulness were written all over their lives.

Another example of sinful jealousy is found in the book of Acts when the apostles preached with power and performed miracles of healing. Multitudes were added to the Lord and the Jewish religious rulers were furious over this threat to their position and authority. Scripture records, "they were filled with jealousy" (Acts 5:17). First, they threw the apostles into prison and later had them flogged. Their selfish motives were unmistakable.

When we are jealous in a sinful way, we often try to hurt others, just as Joseph's brothers and the Jewish religious leaders did. We pick at them, find fault with them, and gossip about them. Critical attitudes toward other people are often spawned by selfish jealousy. But there is not a trace of selfishness in God's jealousy. It is perfectly pure, as its expressions reveal.

The Manifestation of God's Jealousy

He Is Jealous for His Holy Name. It wasn't long after God first spoke of His jealousy that He had occasion to demonstrate it. Moses had come down from the mount with the two tablets of the law in his hands only to find the people of Israel carousing in idolatrous worship before the golden image of a calf. He dashed the tablets to the earth, burned the calf and ground it to powder, then commanded the Levites to discipline the people. It was a vivid expression of God's jealousy operating through His servant Moses.

When the crisis was past, God invited Moses back to the

mount for a fresh encounter with Himself. That was when He revealed His glory to Moses as no one had ever seen it before. Moses saw Him as a compassionate, gracious, long-suffering God who abounds in mercy and truth (Exodus 34:6). The culmination of that revelation came a few moments later when God said, "Watch yourself that you make no covenant with the inhabitants of the land into which you are going, lest it become a snare in your midst. But rather, you are to tear down their altars and smash their sacred pillars and cut down their Asherim—for you shall not worship any other god, for the LORD, whose name is Jealous, is a jealous God" (Exodus 34:12-14).

God's name is the epitome of who and what He is, and He says His name is Jealous. Jealousy is not merely a passing mood with God. It is the essence of His person. He cannot be other than jealous. Since He is the highest and greatest being there is, infinitely holy and glorious, He must be passionately committed to preserving His honor and supremacy. He must zealously desire exclusive devotion and worship. To do less would make Him less than God. He said about Himself:

> I am the LORD, that is My name;
> I will not give My glory to another,
> Nor My praise to graven images (Isaiah 42:8).

God is sovereign and supreme over all. Were He to share His glory with other so-called gods, He would be elevating them to a position that would not be consistent with their true nature, and it likewise would be making Him untrue to His own nature—less than the preeminent God He is. He must be faithful to Himself and maintain His high and holy position, and He wants His creatures to attribute to Him that degree of honor. Basically, that is what He means when He says, "I shall be jealous for My holy name" (Ezekiel 39:25). His jealousy does not grow out of insecurity, anxiety, frustration, covetousness, pride, or spite, as ours usually does. It is the natural and necessary by-product of His absolute sovereignty and infinite holiness.

If God, by virtue of His essential being, must be jealous for His uniqueness and His supremacy above all, then those who know Him and want to please Him should be just as jealous for Him. If we are serious about our relationship with Him, we shall exalt Him above everyone and everything else in our lives; we shall be absolutely dedicated to living for His honor; we shall be zealously committed to doing His will. The primary goal of our lives will be to show the world that our God is the one true and living God—that He alone makes life meaningful and worthwhile.

That is the way the prophet Elijah lived his life. He risked his physical safety to prove that Jehovah is God when he stood alone against the prophets of Baal and called down fire from Heaven on his water-soaked sacrifice. The fire of the Lord did fall, and it consumed the sacrifice, the wood, the stones, the dust, and licked up the water in the trench around the altar. "And when all the people saw it, they fell on their faces; and they said, 'The LORD, He is God; the LORD, He is God' " (1 Kings 18:39). It was a spectacular victory for the Lord over the pagan idols of the Canaanites. And it all happened because that one lone prophet could say, "I have been very jealous for the LORD God of hosts" (1 Kings 19:14 KJV).

We live in a pagan society where money is god and material possessions are the chief object of man's worship. We need people who will be very jealous for the Lord God of hosts, people who will stand alone if need be against this insidious and contagious brand of idolatry and show the world that the Lord is God, people who will adopt a simpler life style and use their resources for His glory rather than for their own comforts and pleasures.

In our pagan society, Satan holds the adoration of some and superstition grips the hearts of others, alternative brands of idolatry which suggest that supernatural forces other than

God have ultimate control of our lives. We need a nucleus of people who will be jealous for the Lord God of hosts, who will stand against every expression of idolatry, who will look solely to the Lord and His Word for guidance and strength rather than to horoscopes or lucky charms, and who will allow Him to control their lives so thoroughly that His sovereign power is evident to all who observe them.

The Apostle Paul qualified for that company. "According to my earnest expectation and hope, that I shall not be put to shame in anything, but that with all boldness, Christ shall even now, as always, be exalted in my body, whether by life or by death. For to me, to live is Christ, and to die is gain" (Philippians 1:20-21). His great desire was to bring glory to Jesus Christ, to show the world by the way he lived and by the way he died the magnificence and preeminence of the Saviour. That is being jealous for God.

We see it again in Paul's last visit with the Ephesian elders: "But I do not consider my life of any account as dear to myself, in order that I may finish my course, and the ministry which I received from the Lord Jesus, to testify solemnly of the gospel of the grace of God" (Acts 20:24). The focus of his life was communicating the truth of God's grace. He let nothing interfere with that overriding purpose. Whatever else he had to do was always secondary to and supportive of accomplishing that goal, and he maintained it even to death. That is what it means to be jealous for God.

Forty great soldiers from Cappadocia in Rome's vaunted twelfth legion shared Paul's jealousy for God some two hundred fifty years after his death. Licinius was reigning over the eastern portion of the empire but was sensing an increasing military threat from the west. He became more and more repressive in his policies, particularly toward Christians. To solidify his strength, he called on his armies to demonstrate their support by offering a sacrifice to the pagan gods.

Most of the legion stationed at Sebaste, a city south of the Black Sea, dutifully complied, but the forty Cappadocians, all

Christians, respectfully declined. For more than a week they were placed under guard, where they sang and prayed together continually. Their captain pleaded with them: "Of all the soldiers who serve the emperor, none are more loved by us and more needed right now. Do not turn our love into hatred. It lies in you whether to be loved or hated." "If it rests with us," they replied, "we have made our choice. We shall devote our love to our God."

It was sundown when they were stripped and escorted shivering to the middle of a frozen lake with guards stationed along the shore. A heated Roman bathhouse stood ready at the shore for any of them who were prepared to renounce their faith in Christ and offer a pagan sacrifice. Their jailer stood by with arms folded, watching, as a bitter winter wind whipped across the ice. But through the whistling wind the soldiers could be heard singing:

> Forty good soldiers for Christ!
> We shall not depart from You as long as You give us life.
> We shall call upon Your Name whom all creation praises:
>   fire and hail, snow and wind and storm.
> On You we have hoped and we were not ashamed!

As midnight approached, their song grew more feeble. Then a strange thing happened. One of the forty staggered toward shore, fell to his knees and began crawling toward the bathhouse. "Thirty-nine good soldiers for Christ!" came the weakening, trembling song from the distance. The jailer watched the man enter the bathhouse and emerge quickly, apparently overcome by the heat, then collapse on the ground and expire. The other guards could not believe what they saw next. The jailer wrenched off his armor and coat, dashed to the edge of the lake, lifted his right hand and cried, "Forty good soldiers for Christ!" then disappeared over the ice into the darkness.

All forty were dead by the next day, but it was the jailer

who caught the captain's notice as their bodies were being carted away. "What is he doing there?" he demanded. One of the guards replied, "We cannot understand it, Captain. Ever since those Christians came under his care, we noticed something different about him." The martyrs of Sebaste were jealous for the name of their God, and it had a profound impact on that jailer who looked on. Our jealousy for God will have a similar effect on the people around us.[1]

We should be reminded, however, that it is possible to be jealous for God in the wrong way. Paul accused the Jews of his day of having a misdirected jealousy: "For I bear them witness that they have a zeal [jealousy] for God, but not in accordance with knowledge" (Romans 10:2). The Jews thought they were exalting the Lord above all gods, but in their system of salvation by performing religious rituals and deeds they actually exalted themselves above God. It was a jealousy for God all right, but not consistent with the knowledge God has revealed about Himself in His Word.

The discovery that God is jealous for His holy name is not a challenge to become religious. It is a challenge to put our trust in God's gracious provision for our salvation—the death of His sinless Son—and a challenge to develop a way of life that reveals Him to a lost world.

He Is Jealous for Our Best Interests. Not only is God jealous for Himself, but He is also jealous for us. He has a passionate, consuming zeal for our best interests, and He wants us to share that zeal by being jealous for one another.

When the mighty Assyrians threatened to destroy the city of Jerusalem, King Hezekiah brought their insolent threats before the Lord in prayer. God's answer, delivered by the prophet Isaiah, reassured Hezekiah that God would put a hook in the nose of Assyria's king and lead him right back to where he came from (Isaiah 37:29). Jerusalem would be saved. "For out of Jerusalem shall go forth a remnant, and

[1]Related in *Decision*, December 1963, page 8.

out of Mount Zion survivors. The zeal of the LORD of hosts shall perform this" (verse 32). Because God was jealous for His people and wanted them to have what was best for them, He would protect them through that siege and deliver them from destruction.

Later God allowed the nation Israel to be disciplined by the Babylonians. He loved them dearly and His discipline was the expression of that love. But then He was ready to restore them and bless them, so he said, "I am exceedingly jealous for Jerusalem and Zion" (Zechariah 1:14). Then He described what He was about to do: He will return to Jerusalem with mercy and rebuild His house there. He will cause the towns of Israel to overflow with prosperity and provide comfort for Zion once more (Zechariah 1:16-17). God is jealous for those whom He loves and takes positive steps to help them, just as we are jealous for those whom we love when they are threatened, wronged, or abused. He wants only the best for us, and at this very moment He is planning things that will bring benefit and blessing to our lives.

God wants us to have the same attitude toward each other as fellow believers: to be jealous for one another's best interests. Paul said Epaphras felt that way toward his Christian friends at Colosse: "For I bear him record, that he hath a great zeal for you, and them that are in Laodicea, and them in Hierapolis" (Colossians 4:13 KJV). His jealousy for them led him to pray for them daily, as the context indicates. If we shared God's jealousy for other believers, we would be busily engaged in intercessory prayer, faithfully bringing their needs to God's attention. Our prayer lives would not be wholly occupied with our own problems, but we would beseech God on behalf of the specific needs of others in the body of Christ.

The Apostle Paul also shared God's jealousy for other Christians. When his converts at Corinth began to fall for the subtle perversion of the gospel being propagated by Satan's servants who had infiltrated the church, Paul said, "For I am jealous for you with a godly jealousy; for I betrothed you to one husband, that to Christ I might present you as a pure virgin" (2 Corinthians 11:2). As their spiritual father, he had promised them to Christ, their spiritual bridegroom, and it was his desire to present them to their husband as a pure bride, untainted with the distorted doctrine of those false apostles. For that reason, he faithfully taught them the truth at great personal sacrifice and encouraged them to submit to it.

If we shared God's jealousy for others, we too would be filling our minds with God's truth and graciously sharing it with those whom God sends our way. We would want what is best for them, and we know that patterning their lives according to His Word will always result in their greatest possible good. If we cared enough we would share the very best—the eternal truths of God's Word.

So our God is a jealous God! The truth of His jealousy challenges us to give God His due and to put Him before all else. But it likewise guarantees that He is looking out for our best interests. Getting to know Him as a jealous God will increase our level of devotion to Him, deepen our trust in Him, and strengthen our dedication to pray for others and faithfully share His truth with them.

Action To Take:

Examine your life style prayerfully. Have other things assumed a more prominent place in your life than your relationship with the Lord Himself? If so, take some decisive and concrete steps to put Him in the position He deserves to be.

Are you jealous for the spiritual welfare of other believers? If you have never done so, begin making a list of others' needs and bring them before the Lord daily in prayer.

21

TREASURES OF WISDOM

SUPPOSE THAT YOU OWNED one of those famous magic lamps, and your own private genie promised to grant you anything in this world you desired. What would you ask for? Wealth would probably be one of the most popular requests. Some think more money would solve almost all their problems. Good health might also rate high, particularly among those who have lost it. Happiness would be the leading desire for others. One worldwide poll of young people revealed happiness as the number one goal in life.

There was a man who had such a choice offered him, not by a fictitious genie, but by the true and living God. God appeared to King Solomon one night and said, "Ask for whatever you want me to give you." Solomon answered, "Give me wisdom and knowledge, that I may lead this people, for who is able to govern this great people of Yours?" (2 Chronicles 1:7,10 NIV) God was pleased that Solomon asked for wisdom rather than riches, honor, long life, or victory over his enemies, so He granted his request. Scripture testifies that all Israel "saw that *the wisdom of God* was in him" (1 Kings 3:28).

God has wisdom, infinite and perfect wisdom. Job was willing to admit that, even while he was enduring grievous affliction that made no sense at all to him. "With Him are wisdom and might," he declared (Job 12:13). The Prophet Daniel said much the same thing after God supernaturally revealed to him Nebuchadnezzar's dream and its meaning: "wisdom and power belong to Him" (Daniel 2:20). The fact is well established in Scripture—our God is distinguished by wisdom.

The Meaning of God's Wisdom

What is wisdom? The words used in Scripture have the idea of skill and expertise. For example, Bezalel had the wisdom to make artistic designs in gold, silver, bronze, stone, and wood for the tabernacle (cf. Exodus 31:1-5). When he did his work, he had a goal in mind, a plan to reach that goal, the proper materials to use, and the skill to bring it all about. When applied to God, wisdom seems to refer to His establishing the best goals and choosing the best and most effective means to accomplish them.

Wisdom is mental excellence in its greatest sense, more comprehensive and far-reaching than mere knowledge. Knowledge is an awareness and understanding of the facts. Wisdom is the ability to adapt those facts into accomplishing a desired end. God knows all the facts, but also has the ability to work everything He knows into a perfect plan that accomplishes His perfect purpose.

Wisdom implies a final end or goal. So if we ever hope to understand God's wisdom, we must first understand the primary goal toward which He is moving. God is infinitely holy and righteous, He is sovereign, the highest and greatest, infinite goodness. In other words, He Himself is best. If God exists for what is best and He Himself is best, then He must of necessity exist for Himself. He lives to demonstrate His own glory.

That may sound selfish, but it really is not. It is essential because of who God is, and it is to our advantage for Him to be who He is. If He existed for anyone outside of Himself, then the one for whom He existed would be greater than He, and therefore god, and we could not be certain who he is or whether he is interested in our welfare. But that cannot be. God is God and there is none greater. His chief end must therefore be to bring glory to Himself. He has the skill to weave everything there ever was or ever will be into the ultimate accomplishment of His glory. That is His wisdom.

God never faces a situation He cannot handle or a problem He cannot solve. We certainly do. I ofen get myself into predicaments where I simply do not know which way to turn or what action is best to take. When I face a major decision I try to gather all the facts, because a person's decisions are only as good as his information. But even with all the facts, I still may not know the best course to take, because I lack the wisdom God has. But God is the master of every situation. He knows all the facts, and He knows how to use every one of them to attain the perfect results. Nobody else can do that. God's wisdom is unique. That is why Paul called Him "the only wise God" (Romans 16:27). God alone has perfect wisdom in and of Himself. All other wisdom is merely a reflection of His.

The Expressions of God's Wisdom

Everything that God does reveals His wisdom, but several specific things are mentioned in Scripture. For instance, *creating the world* was an expression of His wisdom.

> O LORD, how many are Thy works!
> In wisdom Thou hast made them all;
> The earth is full of Thy possessions
> (Psalm 104:24 cf. Proverbs 3:19).

God put the universe together in such a manner that it displays not only His goodness, but also His wisdom. And that brings glory to Him.

> The heavens are telling of the glory of God;
> And their expanse is declaring the work of His hands
>   (Psalm 19:1).

A second expression of God's wisdom was *sending His Son.* Jesus Christ is the personification of God's wisdom. In the eighth chapter of the book of Proverbs, wisdom cries out for men to hear. It seems to be a person, and the further we read the more convinced we become. He existed from everlasting, before the earth was. He was the Father's delight and rejoiced in the Father's presence (Proverbs 8:22-23,30). Wisdom can be none other than the eternal Son of God. The Apostle Paul calls Him "the wisdom of God" (1 Corinthians 1:24). In Him "are hidden all the treasures of wisdom and knowledge" (Colossians 2:3).

If you want to get to know the God of wisdom, study the life of Jesus Christ. As a boy, He "kept increasing in wisdom and stature, and in favor with God and men" (Luke 2:52). When He began His public ministry, He taught with such penetrating perception and amazing authority that people asked, "Where did this man get this wisdom, and these miraculous powers?" (Matthew 13:54) He confronted the hypocritical scribes and Pharisees with such crisp thinking that they could not answer Him (e.g. Matthew 22:46). They had the finest theological minds of the day, but their mouths were stopped before the wisdom of Jesus Christ. God gave the world the most complete and comprehensive demonstration of His wisdom possible when He sent His Son to earth. And it brought great glory to Him. Near the end of Christ's life He could say to His Father, "I have brought you glory on earth" (John 17:4 NIV).

However, that was not the final expression of God's wisdom. He likewise discloses it by *redeeming the lost.* "For since in the wisdom of God the world through its wisdom did not come to know God, God was well-pleased through the foolishness of the message preached to save those who believe"

(1 Corinthians 1:21). The people of the world think they can get to know God by using their own human wisdom. God knows they cannot, so in perfect wisdom He has provided a way. His wisdom seems like foolishness to them, but through it, He manages to deliver people from their bondage to sin and bring them into a satisfying relationship with Himself. How does He do it? Paul goes on to tell us: "For indeed Jews ask for signs, and Greeks search for wisdom; but we preach Christ crucified, to Jews a stumbling block, and to Gentiles foolishness, but to those who are the called, both Jews and Greeks, Christ the power of God and the wisdom of God" (1 Corinthians 1:22-24).

Christ crucified! That is the means God has provided for mankind to know Him. To the average unbeliever it seems ridiculous to think that God's Son should have to die on a cross to pay the penalty for man's sin. But that is the heart of God's wisdom, the message that brings eternal salvation. The death of God's sinless Son was necessary to satisfy His offended holiness, deliver mankind from bondage to sin, and open the door to His presence.

Those who believe that message are brought into a living union with God through Jesus Christ and become members of His Church. Nothing displays God's wisdom and demonstrates His glory more dramatically than that body of redeemed sinners who have been eternally forgiven and accepted by His grace. "His intent was that now, through the church, the manifold wisdom of God should be made known to the rulers and authorities in the heavenly realms" (Ephesians 3:10 NIV). Because it displays His wisdom it also glorifies Him. "Unto Him be glory in the church by Christ Jesus throughout all ages, world without end. Amen" (Ephesians 3:21 KJV).

God has another way of expressing His wisdom—by *ordering the lives of believers.*

Man's steps are ordained by the Lord,
How then can man understand his way? (Proverbs 20:24)

God in wisdom has already mapped out the course of our lives to bring the greatest glory to Himself. His wise plan even includes the means by which He will use our volitional choices, some of which may be contrary to His desires, in order to achieve His perfect end, as difficult as that may be for us to understand.

His plan also includes the means by which He will use the trying circumstances in our lives to achieve His perfect goal. We can trust Him in the dark places of life, because He in His wisdom knows the way through the darkness. Maybe you have visited one of the world's famous caverns. If you have, you were probably led through it by a guide. You trusted him and committed yourself to him because you were confident that he knew the way. To refuse to follow him would not only have endangered your own life, it would have insulted his wisdom. To do anything less than commit ourselves completely to our Lord in simple trust during the troubling times in our lives is to insult His wisdom. To resist Him, question Him, doubt Him, or criticize what He allows in our lives is to deny that He is the only wise God, and claim that we are wiser than He.

We may not always enjoy what God does, but our enjoyment is not His primary goal. Our happiness will come, but it will come as we grow in the likeness of His Son. That is His great goal for our lives, because as we grow to be more like Jesus, not only will we experience greater happiness ourselves, but God's principal goal of bringing glory to Himself will also be fulfilled. Allowing trials to enter our experience is part of His wise plan to accomplish His perfect end. To understand His wisdom in ordering our lives will help us to lay hold of His peace in the disturbing circumstances of life.

The Enjoyment of God's Wisdom

The most exciting aspect of God's wisdom is that He offers to share it with us. Many of us would be willing to admit that we could use a large supply of it in order to handle the circumstances we confront daily. Having God's wisdom does not necessarily mean we will know *why* God allows certain things to happen to us or *how* He will work them together for good. It simply means that we will know the right thing to do in each situation, the thing that will bring the greatest glory to Him.

Scripture makes it clear that we need divine wisdom. Solomon devoted nearly nine chapters in the book of Proverbs to the need for wisdom. Just as He sought it from God, so He encourages us to do likewise: "Wisdom is supreme; therefore get wisdom. Though it cost all you have, get understanding" (Proverbs 4:7 NIV). The New Testament echoes that need: "Therefore be careful how you walk, not as unwise men, but as wise, making the most of your time, because the days are evil. So then do not be foolish, but understand what the will of the Lord is" (Ephesians 5:15-17). Again, real wisdom is basically knowing the right thing to do in every situation—knowing and doing the will of God.

Scripture suggests that we especially need God's wisdom in our encounters with unbelievers (Colossians 4:5), when wrestling with trials (James 1:2-5), and in the use of our tongues (James 3:8-13). But there are countless other occasions as well when we desperately need wisdom. We know it comes from God, "For the LORD gives wisdom" (Proverbs 2:6). But how do we get it? There are several basic prerequisites.

The first is to *admit our need*. Solomon said, "with the humble is wisdom" (Proverbs 11:2). The humble are those who do not think more highly of themselves than they should. They are willing to admit that they do not have all the answers, that their opinions may not always be right, and that they need to know the mind of God. In other words, they have a teachable spirit. They are willing to learn and are open to change. We will enjoy God's wisdom only if we admit that we need it.

The second prerequisite is to *fear the Lord.* The Psalmist

said, "The fear of the LORD is the beginning of wisdom" (Psalm 111:10). To fear God is not to cower before Him in terror, but to bow before Him in awe, respect, and total trust in His purposes for our lives. Just as we will put our confidence in a guide's wisdom and follow him through a dark cave only when we respect him, so we will be open to receiving and following God's wisdom only when we respect Him and believe that He will not lead us astray. To fear Him, then, is to submit ourselves to Him. We need not only teachable spirits, but broken wills.

The third prerequisite is to *study God's Word*. By loving God's Word and meditating on it daily, the Psalmist discovered that he was wiser than his enemies, that he had more insight than his teachers, and more understanding than the aged (Psalm 119:97-100). Through the Word, he found wise guidance in life:

> Thy word is a lamp to my feet,
> And a light to my path (Psalm 119:105).

God's wisdom is revealed in His Word and that is where we must find it.

The final prerequisite is to *pray*. "But if any of you lacks wisdom, let him ask of God, who gives to all men generously and without reproach, and it will be given to him" (James 1:5). Sometimes praying for wisdom is the last thing we think to do when we face a knotty problem, a difficult decision, a pressing emergency, or an alarming crisis. The Lord is standing ready to give us His wisdom and we often think about everything we can do to work out the problem except talking to Him about it. Regardless of how big or how little the matter may be, He invites us to ask Him for wisdom.

Ask Him for wisdom in the business deal with which you have been struggling. Ask Him for wisdom in handling the problems you encounter in raising your children. Ask Him for wisdom concerning the information on which you should concentrate for that upcoming exam at school. Ask Him for wisdom in working out the tension and hard feelings you have been experiencing with another believer. Ask Him for wisdom in coping with your pain or sorrow. Ask Him for wisdom in balancing your checkbook. Ask Him for wisdom concerning what to prepare for dinner. Ask Him for wisdom concerning the right things to say to your wife when she is feeling blue. He cares about all those things, and more.

The Recognition of God's Wisdom

How do we know whether the wisdom we are exercising is from God or from men, whether it is divine wisdom or human wisdom? One way will be to compare it to the truth of God's Word. His wisdom will always be consistent with all of His Word. But there is one special passage in the Word that tells us particularly how to identify God's wisdom: "But the wisdom from above is first pure, then peaceable, gentle, reasonable, full of mercy and good fruits, unwavering, without hypocrisy" (James 3:17). Here is the acid test.

First, God's wisdom is *pure*, unmixed with error, untainted by immorality, unclouded by selfish motives, cleansed of all personal ambition. If we are looking out for our own interests, we are probably operating by man's wisdom rather than God's. Secondly, God's wisdom is *peaceable*, not quarrelsome, contentious, or cutting, but promoting the harmony and peace that draws people together. If our words or actions are arousing antagonism in others, we are probably operating by man's wisdom rather than God's. Thirdly, God's wisdom is *gentle*, that is, fair, moderate, forgiving, forbearing, and considerate in the demands it puts on others. If we are putting pressure on others to conform to our way of thinking, we are probably operating by man's wisdom rather than God's. Fourthly, God's wisdom is *reasonable*, easy to be entreated, not stubborn or inflexible, but pliable and willing to listen to reason. If we have already made up our minds and refuse to be influenced by any more facts, we are probably operating by man's wisdom rather than God's.

Fifthly, God's wisdom is *full of mercy and good fruits.* It shows genuine concern and extends practical help toward others in need, even when they have wronged us. Sixthly, God's wisdom is *unwavering,* not hesitant or vacillating, but standing firm on Biblical principles, undivided in allegiance to God and consistent from day to day. And finally, God's wisdom is *without hypocrisy.* When we are operating by God's wisdom we do not wear masks, play roles, or deceive people by putting on a good front. We do not try to conceal our true thoughts, feelings, or motives in order to make ourselves look good or to accomplish our own ends. We are open, honest, and straightforward.

Here is God's standard for measuring His wisdom. When we begin to get our wisdom from Him, our homes will be happier, our lives more effective, and our God greatly glorified. And there is really no time to lose. As the Psalmist put it, "So teach us to number our days, that we may apply our hearts to wisdom" (Psalm 90:12 KJV).

Action To Take:

What difficulties are you presently facing? Ask God for wisdom in handling them. Measure your words and actions by the sevenfold standard of divine wisdom revealed in James 3:17. If you have doubt about whether you are operating by man's wisdom or God's wisdom in any one of the seven, ask other members of your family what they think, then prayerfully consider their advice.

22

LET GOD BE TRUE!

WHEN OUR LORD JESUS stood trial, the civil judge in the case was a puzzling and pathetic figure named Pontius Pilate, the Roman procurator of Judea. He had little understanding of the Jewish people and had gained a reputation for total insensitivity to their customs and manner of life. Yet he feared the damage they could do to him by their continual complaining to Rome, so when he heard the case against Christ, he was torn between displeasing the Jews and condemning an innocent man.

He thought that a personal conversation with the accused might help him make a more intelligent decision, so he retreated from the crowd and entered into the palace to talk with Jesus privately. "Are You the King of the Jews?" he asked. After Jesus explained that His kingdom was not of this world, Pilate persisted with his questioning: "So You are a king?" Jesus replied, "You say correctly that I am a king. For this I have been born, and for this I have come into the world, to bear witness to the truth. Everyone who is of the truth hears My voice." At that, Pilate threw up his hands and exclaimed in total exasperation, "What is truth?" Then he went back outside to the Jews, never waiting for Jesus to answer his question (cf. John 18:33-38).

"What is truth?" It was a good question and it deserved an answer. Christ could have given Pilate one if he had waited just a moment longer. But he did not really want an answer.

He was not honestly seeking the meaning of truth. Like many people today, he was expressing skepticism about the whole subject of truth. He was doubtful that there was any such thing, or that anyone could know it if there were.

Statements like, "This is true," or "This is right," are meaningless to some intellectuals, those who deny the possibility of absolute truth. They insist that truth is relative, that what is true for one may not be true for another, or what may have been true in the past is not necessarily true today. They claim that it's all in the way you see it, and it really does not matter how you see it because, in the final analysis, nobody has any ultimate answers. Some would even say that life is a laugh, death is a bad joke, and everything is quite absurd.

But above this din of confusion and despair, another voice is heard, the voice of this same Jesus ministering to His disciples on the night before His trial in Pilate's court: "I am the way, and the truth, and the life" (John 14:6). It was the same claim made by Jehovah when He revealed Himself to Moses on Mount Sinai centuries before. He called Himself "The Lord, the Lord God, compassionate and gracious, slow to anger, and abounding in lovingkindness and truth" (Exodus 34:6). There is such a thing as truth, and it resides in a person, a person whom King David called the "God of truth" (Psalm 31:5). What does it mean that God is truth?

He Is the Truth

"But the Lord is the true God," declared the prophet Jeremiah (Jeremiah 10:10). The New Testament echoes that same message. For example, Jesus referred to His Father as "the only true God" (John 17:3). Paul commended the Thessalonians because they "turned to God from idols to serve a living and true God" (1 Thessalonians 1:9); (cf. also John 3:33; 1 John 5:20-21). The meaning is clear—the God they trusted is the only real God. All other so-called gods are really not gods at all, but woefully inadequate imitations of the one genuine God. When we read that He is the true God, it is usually because He is being contrasted to false gods, particularly to idols.

Listen to Jeremiah again as he describes the gods men fashion with their own hands:

> Like a scarecrow in a cucumber field are they,
> And they cannot speak;
> They must be carried,
> Because they cannot walk!
> Do not fear them,
> For they can do no harm,
> Nor can they do any good (Jeremiah 10:5).

Why worship gods who cannot communicate with us, minister to us, or even transport themselves from one place to another? "They are worthless, a work of mockery" (Jeremiah 10:15). The word *worthless* refers to a vapor, something unsubstantial or unreal. Worshiping an idol makes no more sense than swearing your allegiance to a zucchini squash.

But what a contrast is the Lord, the true God, the living God, the everlasting King. He made the earth by His power and established the world by His wisdom. He stretched out the heavens by His understanding. He causes the clouds to ascend from the end of the earth, makes lightning for the rain, and brings the wind from His storehouses (Jeremiah 10:10-13). He is the only God who has done what God must do to be God. His actions substantiate who He says He is. We can understand that from the physical world. For instance, we may claim to have pure gold in our possession, but pure gold must be gold not only in appearance but also in true reality. It must have all the properties and characteristics of pure gold. So the true God must be God not only in name, but in truth and actuality.

The same idea is suggested when He is called the God of truth, as in Psalm 31:5. The Old Testament word for truth comes from a root indicating firmness, stability, or a reliable basis for support. It refers to something that rests on trust-worthy facts. The New Testament word has the idea of being open and unconcealed, and therefore being real and genuine rather than false or imaginary. The God of truth is the God whose disclosures about Himself are consistent with the facts and with the nature of things as they are. He has integrity. He is who He says He is.

Isaiah also called Him "the God of truth" (Isaiah 65:16), but he used a different word which is translated "amen" every time it occurs in the Old Testament. Isaiah called Him literally "the God of the Amen." The word *amen* means "verily" or "truly," and refers simply to something that is so. When God says "amen," He is asserting that something is and shall be so. When we use the term, we are saying essentially, "Let it be so." But when it is applied to God as a title, it means He is the God who truly is, the only true God, the God of truth, the God who is truth.

Interestingly enough, Jesus is also called the Amen (as in Revelation 3:14). He is the embodiment of all God is. That is why He could say to His disciples, "I am the truth," and why He could tell Pilate that He came to bear witness to the truth. That is why John could say, "grace and truth were realized through Jesus Christ" (John 1:17). He is the visible manifesta-tion of the eternal God. He is no imposter or deceiver. Jesus Christ is the God of truth. The Apostle John stated it power-fully: "And we know that the Son of God has come, and has given us understanding, in order that we might know Him who is true, and we are in Him who is true, in His Son Jesus Christ. This is the true God and eternal life" (1 John 5:20). Jesus Christ is the true God.

He Knows the Truth

God not only *is* the truth but He *knows* the truth. The Psalmist went so far as to say that His truth reaches to the skies (Psalm 108:4), another way of stating that it is complete, perfect, and unlimited.

We can illustrate that from the human realm also. Some people are mechanically inclined and enjoy building things. I have a friend who likes to restore antique cars. He tears them apart and puts them back together again. He knows them inside and out, right down to the last nut and bolt. People are normally familiar with the things they build. Scripture teaches that God created all things (e.g. Ephesians 3:9). Since He obviously knows all there is to know about everything He made, we are driven to the inescapable conclusion that He has complete and accurate information about everything there is. The Psalmist said, "The truth of the LORD is everlasting" (Psalm 117:2). He has all the true facts; they will always be true, and He will never forget any of them.

I certainly cannot make that claim. I am not very mechanically inclined, and when I put something together there is no guarantee that I will remember how it works the next time I use it. Some time ago I purchased a bicycle rack for my automobile so my wife and I could get away and enjoy a little togetherness. I followed the instructions carefully, installed the rack on my car, and we had a great time together. It was nearly a year before I tried to use it again, and I could not figure out how to attach it to my car. I had to find the instructions and read them again. Facts do not always stay with me very long. Just because I prepare and preach a sermon does not necessarily mean that I will remember everything I said the next time I need that information. But all truth resides in God permanently.

All truth is God's truth and we are totally dependent on Him for our knowledge of truth. Since He is the author of truth and since He created our capacity to grasp truth, we can come to a knowledge of things as they are only through Him. Anything we think we know to be true must coincide with the truth He possesses; that is, it must be in accord with reality as He knows it.

He Reveals the Truth

God has no intention of hiding His truth from the people He made. His desire is for everyone to come to a knowledge of the truth (1 Timothy 2:4), so He takes the initiative and reveals Himself to us. The fact that He is truth guarantees that He will reveal Himself as He really is, that His revelation will be perfectly reliable, that what He says will correspond exactly to the way things are. A God of truth will never deceive us or reveal to us error or falsehood. He must speak the truth. At least four times in Scripture we are assured that God does not lie (Numbers 23:19; 1 Samuel 15:29; Titus 1:2; Hebrews 6:18).

People lie. We all know that. We have all been lied to and we have all distorted the truth for our own advantage at one time or other. Whatever men may be like, we have no reason to question God. The Apostle Paul said, "Let God be found true, though every man be found a liar" (Romans 3:4). When He speaks, it is true, accurate, and correct to an infinite degree.

But how does God reveal His truth to us? One major method is through His Word. "All Scripture is God-breathed" (2 Timothy 3:16 NIV). It actually "proceeds out of the mouth of God" (Matthew 4:4). It was revealed when "men spoke from God as they were carried along by the Holy Spirit" (2 Peter 1:21 NIV). So we would expect Scripture to be true. And that is exactly what it claims for itself:

> The words of the LORD are pure words;
> As silver tried in a furnace on the earth,
>   refined seven times (Psalm 12:6).

> The fear of the LORD is clean, enduring forever;
> The judgments of the LORD are true;
>   they are righteous altogether (Psalm 19:9).

Thou art near, O LORD,
And all Thy commandments are truth
   (Psalm 119:151).

The sum of Thy word is truth,
And every one of Thy righteous ordinances
   is everlasting (Psalm 119:160).

Jesus added His divine testimony: "Sanctify them in the truth; Thy word is truth" (John 17:17).

If God's Word is truth, then it is necessarily without error. Truth and error are antithetical and mutually exclusive. If it is true, then it cannot be in error, and if it is in error, then it cannot be true. Yet there are some who claim to be Christians who insist that it is unnecessary to believe in an inerrant Word from God. They say that the Bible is inspired by God, but they consider it to be no problem if it contains historical, scientific, numerical, or chronological mistakes. The subject of inerrancy has become one of the major theological issues among evangelicals in our generation, and it is not an issue on which we can afford to remain neutral. To weaken the Biblical doctrine of inerrancy is to set us adrift on a sea of human speculation and rob the Christian message of its uniqueness and power.

If parts of the Bible are true and parts are false, what criteria can we use for determining which parts we can accept as correct? Who will make that decision? The parts that are false cannot be from God since He is the God of truth, so they must be of human origin. Yet Scripture claims to be from God in its entirety. If we are the ones who determine what is true and what is false, then we are elevating ourselves above Scripture, and ultimately above God Himself.

If the Bible is not true in its historical facts, then we cannot be sure it is true when it speaks about eternal salvation or daily responsibility. We are left with no sure word from God. We cannot be certain that anything about the Biblical message is true, and we are free to follow the spirit of our age. Some professing Christians who have denied the inerrancy of Scripture have already adopted the world's standards in matters such as homosexuality, abortion on demand, and divorce and remarriage for any cause.

The Bible was written by human authors who left their mark on the finished product by their own individual personalities, literary styles, and particular emphases. But what they wrote in its original form was exactly what God wanted it to be. It is His truth and it cannot be diluted with falsehood.

Admittedly, there are problem passages in the Bible, but none of them is without some reasonable answer. We must acknowledge that some passages are open to varying interpretations, but careful study with hearts that are open to God's Spirit and wills that are yielded to Him can lead to an accurate understanding of their meaning. There may be some passages on which we all will never agree here on earth, due possibly to our deeply ingrained presuppositions or prejudices. But God still knows what He means, and someday we shall all understand it as He does.

The Bible obviously includes some of the erroneous ideas of Satan and self-willed men, but it is still an accurate account of what they said or thought. It does not tell us everything there is to know, but what it does tell us is truth. If man is ever to know God and have the assurance of eternal life, then God must speak to him, and a God of truth will speak the truth, without error, fraud, or deceit. First believe Him, then spend time studying His Word and come to a knowledge of the truth.

He Requires the Truth

Unfortunately, believing in an inerrant Bible alone is not going to impress a lost world very much. The people of the world can find somebody who believes almost anything, and one religious opinion is just as good as another, as far as they are concerned. People want to see something that works in everyday living. When God's truth is demonstrated by a life of honesty, integrity, and absolute truthfulness, then people will notice. And that is what God desires of us.

David learned that lesson after a major crisis in his life. He had committed the sin of adultery, then tried to cover it by dishonesty and deceit. The whole sickening affair had brought reproach on the name of God. But David had repented and was reflecting on his relationship with the Lord when he made this incisive observation: "Behold, Thou dost desire truth in the innermost being" (Psalm 51:6). When we fulfill God's desire and allow His truth to become a part of our inner person, then we will be able to speak truthfully and act truthfully toward others. They will see the reality of God's presence in our lives and turn to Him.

> Then I will teach transgressors Thy ways,
> And sinners will be converted to Thee (Psalm 51:13).

The Apostle Paul put it like this: "Therefore, laying aside falsehood, SPEAK TRUTH, EACH ONE of you, WITH HIS NEIGHBOR, for we are members of one another" (Ephesians 4:25). That kind of living will have an impact on the world. When a Christian businessman tells the truth about his product and can be trusted to do what he promised to do, people will notice the difference. When a Christian employee is honest about reporting the number of hours he works and how he uses those hours, unbelieving employers will notice the difference. When a Christian student is honest at examination time even when he has opportunities to cheat, others will feel the impact of his witness. When a Christian family is truthful with the neighbors about the damage their dog did to the neighbor's flower garden, or when the twelve-year-old boy in the family is honest about the window he broke when nobody was home to see him, then those neighbors will begin to listen to a testimony about a God of truth whose message of truth can bring the assurance of everlasting life.

Living in the knowledge of God's absolute truth has other far-reaching implications for our lives as well, such as bowing to His authority over us. If everything God says in His Word is absolutely true, then we are responsible to act on the basis of it, to do what He tells us to do. Something that is true requires that we heed it. For example, if a sign says, "Dangerous Curve Ahead, Maximum Safe Speed 15 M.P.H." and it is true, then we had better reduce our speed to 15 miles per hour. Truth demands compliance. Many of us resist that. We live in an age of rebellion against authority. Some of us reserve the right to live as we please and seek our own happiness anywhere we think we can find it. But a true God whose Word is truth demands our total submission and faithful obedience. That may sound oppressive and burdensome but, on the contrary, it is the only way our lives can operate smoothly and effectively.

Most products work better when we use them according to the manufacturer's instructions. We are free to ignore the manual if we choose, but that does not always turn out to be true freedom. It may restrict the product's usefulness and the satisfaction it brings. One of my sons purchased a thirty-five millimeter camera and took it with him on a once-in-a-lifetime trip. But on one roll of film he failed to heed the instructions, did not engage the gear in the film properly, and did not check to see if the spool was turning as he advanced the film. By the time he reached forty exposures he realized there was something wrong, but by then it was too late. He had taken forty never-to-be-repeated shots on the same frame. He was free to ignore the instructions, but the end result was frustrating.

Just so, our lives operate most satisfactorily when we live by the principles which our Maker has revealed in His manufacturer's manual, the Bible. To ignore His truth leads not to freedom, but to bondage, frustration, and failure. Jesus said, "and you shall know the truth, and the truth shall make you free" (John 8:32). By letting His truth find expression in our lives, we can be free to live and grow and become all we were meant to be.

Action To Take:

How much time do you give to reading and studying the Bible in an average week? If you have not already done so, build into your daily schedule some time to spend in God's Word.

Examine your life prayerfully for possible areas of dishonesty, then determine before God to correct them.

23

GREAT IS THY FAITHFULNESS

WHEN GOD PREDICTS that He will cause a son to be born to a husband and wife who are nearly one hundred years old, more than just His power is in question. His credibility is likewise at stake. Is He reliable? Is he trustworthy? Can we expect Him to do what He says He will do? When that promise was made to Abraham, he literally fell on his face and laughed (Genesis 17:17). Abraham had not yet fully come to believe that God's Word could be trusted. And neither had Sarah, his wife. When she heard the same promise, she too laughed (Genesis 18:12). Her faith had not grown beyond the example she observed in her husband.

The narrative in Genesis does not record specifically when it happened, but at some point in their walk with God, both Abraham and Sarah became convinced that God would do what He promised to do. The Apostle Paul told us about Abraham: "And without becoming weak in faith he contemplated his own body, now as good as dead since he was about a hundred years old, and the deadness of Sarah's womb; yet, with respect to the promise of God, he did not waver in unbelief, but grew strong in faith, giving glory to God, and being fully assured that what He had promised, He was able also to perform" (Romans 4:19-21).

The writer to the Hebrews tells us the story from Sarah's perspective: "By faith even Sarah herself received ability to conceive, even beyond the proper time of life, since she considered Him faithful who had promised" (Hebrews 11:11). She not only believed that God *could* give her a son, but also that He *would* because He is a faithful God. His Word is reliable and His promises are trustworthy.

The faith of Abraham and Sarah was not misplaced. "Then the LORD took note of Sarah as He had said, and the LORD did for Sarah as He had promised. So Sarah conceived and bore a son to Abraham in his old age, at the appointed time of which God had spoken to him" (Genesis 21:1-2). It happened just exactly *as* God said it would and *when* He said it would. God is truly faithful.

The Explanation of God's Faithfulness

The Old Testament word for faithfulness is related to the word for truth. They both come from the same root which means "firmness" or "stability." Faithfulness actually grows out of truth. What is true must also be trustworthy. Even a pagan soothsayer named Balaam had to admit that the God who tells the truth will also keep His Word. He said to the king of Moab,

> God is not a man, that He should lie,
> Nor a son of man, that He should repent;
> Has He said, and will He not do it?
> Or has He spoken, and will He not make
>   it good? (Numbers 23:19)

Since God cannot lie, we can count on Him to do exactly what He promised—to be perfectly reliable, always steady and stable, never fickle or vacillating. That is His faithfulness. His Word is infallible and unfailing. Since it is without error, it will surely come to pass.

It is interesting to note how often faithfulness and truth are used together in Scripture. For example, Isaiah said, "Thy counsels of old are faithfulness and truth" (Isaiah 25:1 KJV).

The Apostle John also said that God's words are "faithful and true" (Revelation 21:5; 22:6). He said that Jesus Christ, the living Word in flesh, is "the faithful and true Witness" (Revelation 3:14), and that at His return to the earth He will actually bear the title, "Faithful and True" (Revelation 19:11).

All of God's attributes operate in conjunction, never in isolation. If everything about Him is true, then He has no alternative but to be faithful. We sometimes go back on our word because we are unable to do what we intended to do, such as when we have been hindered by a storm from taking our children on a picnic we promised them. But God is *omnipotent*. He can do anything He pleases, even control the weather. He has no reason to be unfaithful. We may also be unfaithful because we are influenced by others. For instance, a wife may have promised her husband that she would prepare his favorite dish for dinner. But some socially prominent women, whose acceptance and friendship she desires, have invited her for coffee. The time has gotten away from her and it is too late to keep her word. But God is totally *self-sufficient*. He does not need anyone else's approval to meet His needs. He is His own reason for everything He does.

We may fail to keep our word because we lose interest, like the husband who promised his wife he would build her some new kitchen cabinets, but simply got tired of carpentry and sold his tools. God never loses interest. He is *immutable*. He never changes His mind. We may not follow through because it no longer suits our selfish purposes. One couple said they would assume responsibility for a Sunday school department, but failed to follow through because they acquired a new motor home and decided they did not want to be tied down on weekends. But God is *love*; He acts for the good of others rather than for His own selfish interests.

Scripture extols God's faithfulness. The Psalmist said it surrounds Him (Psalm 89:8); that is, it is part of His being and affects everything He does. Moses assured the people of Israel that because God is faithful He could be expected to keep His covenant and carry out His promises (Deuteronomy 7:9). He has done exactly that. For example, He gave them the land He promised them, He gave them victory over their enemies, and He gave them rest from their conflicts just as He said He would. "Not one of the good promises which the LORD had made to the house of Israel failed; all came to pass" (Joshua 21:45). That is the essence of God's faithfulness.

God's faithfulness to His covenant promises is assured even if His people forsake His law, refuse to walk in His judgments, violate His statutes, and break His commandments (Psalm 89:30-37). Although He will discipline them, He will not violate His covenant, alter the utterance of His lips or, as He says, "deal falsely in My faithfulness" (Psalm 89:33). He can be counted on to do what He promises.

God's faithfulness is unlimited (Psalm 36:5). The Psalmist went so far as to say,

> Forever, O LORD,
> Thy word is settled in heaven.
> Thy faithfulness continues throughout all
>   generations (Psalm 119:89-90).

Because God has spoken in truth and His word is sure, every generation can count on what He has said. No wonder Jeremiah exclaimed with joy, "Great is thy faithfulness" (Lamentations 3:23).

The Extent of God's Faithfulness

Since God's faithfulness is part of His essence, it affects everything He says and everything He does. Several specific applications of His faithfulness are made in the New Testament.

First of all, He is faithful in *assuring our salvation*. The spiritual lives of the Corinthian Christians left much to be desired, but Paul commends them for "awaiting eagerly the revelation of our Lord Jesus Christ, who shall also confirm you to the end, blameless in the day of our Lord Jesus Christ. *God is faithful*, through whom you were called into fellowship with His Son, Jesus Christ our Lord" (1 Corinthians 1:7-9). Paul is confident that the Lord will make them steadfast and pre-serve them from falling away, right up to the moment they enter His presence. That confidence does not rest in the strength or ability of the Corinthians, but in the faithfulness of God. If He promised eternal life to those who receive His Son, then He will deliver what He promised. He will never allow them to perish.

A similar assurance is expressed about the Thessalonians: "Now may the God of peace Himself sanctify you entirely; and may your spirit and soul and body be preserved com-plete, without blame at the coming of our Lord Jesus Christ. *Faithful is He* who calls you, and He also will bring it to pass" (1 Thessalonians 5:23-24). Paul longs to see every one of them standing before the throne of God, wholly set apart unto the Lord, perfectly pure and blameless. He is confident that they will, not because they have the innate power to make them-selves holy, but because the One who called them is faithful. God promised to glorify every person He called and justified— every one without exception (Romans 8:29-30). God does what He says He is going to do.

What a satisfying assurance! Once we have acknowledged our sin and trusted Christ as our Saviour, there is no need ever again to worry and fret over our eternal destiny. Our faithful God confirms us in Him forever, and with that issue eternally settled, we can give our attention to growing in our knowledge of Him.

I have talked to people who have struggled for years about the assurance of their salvation. They have been perpetually preoccupied with whether or not they really are saved, and this has hindered them from growing in God's grace. They will not graduate from that plateau until they take God at His Word and realize their salvation is settled forever. It is like a marriage in which the wife is asking herself, "Does my husband really love me? Is he really committed to this marriage?" As long as those doubts persist, she will never be free to grow in her relationship with her husband. Similar doubts keep us from growing in our relationship with the Lord. "Believe in the Lord Jesus, and you shall be saved" (Acts 16:31). A faithful God will do what He promises. He will save you when you trust His Son. You can count on it, because He is faithful.

Secondly, He is faithful in *providing for our victory*. God wants us to enjoy victory over sin and triumph through trials, but He has not left us on our own to achieve it. He offers us help. "No temptation has overtaken you but such as is common to man; and *God is faithful*, who will not allow you to be tempted beyond what you are able, but with the temptation will provide the way of escape also, that you may be able to endure it" (1 Corinthians 10:13). The word *temptation* may refer either to a trial from God who seeks to purify and strengthen us, or a solicitation to sin from Satan who seeks to destroy us. In either case, God promises to protect us from more than we can bear and to provide with every tempation or testing a way of escape. His faithfulness guarantees it.

The term *way of escape* was used of a narrow mountain pass through which a trapped army might escape an impossible situation. God always has an escape available when temptation strikes. When we yield to temptation, it is because we have ignored His provision and refused to take His way out. In the case of trials, the way of escape may simply be the strength to endure, but it will be there. We can count on it. A God who never fails to keep His Word has promised it.

A similar promise was made to the Thessalonians: "But the Lord is faithful, and He will strengthen and protect you from the evil one" (2 Thessalonians 3:3). God promised to guard them against Satan's attacks by strengthening them, buttressing their faith, and providing the support they required. When I have succumbed to temptation, it has not been because God failed to keep His Word, but because I chose at that moment to ignore what He had made available. The mountain pass to freedom was in sight, but I closed my eyes to it and walked headlong into Satan's trap. God's strength was accessible, but I chose to handle the situation myself.

God has been faithful to His promise. He has given us His Spirit to live in us and help us, and He is the Spirit of power. He has equipped us with His Word which sets Satan on his heels. He is continually available for communication through prayer. He has created us with a human will by which we may choose to flee from the enticement to sin (cf. 1 Corinthians 6:18; 10:14; 1 Timothy 6:11; 2 Timothy 2:22). When we step out by faith to obey Him, He meets us there with His strength. These are resources which He has faithfully provided, and when we use them we enjoy His victory.

In the third place, He is faithful in *forgiving our sins.* Unfortunately, most of us only use God's resources for victory intermittently, and as a result we sin. But God's faithfulness reaches us even then. "If we confess our sins, *He is faithful* and righteous to forgive us our sins and to cleanse us from all unrighteousness" (1 John 1:9). In that verse our sins are viewed both as a debt that needs to be forgiven and as a stain that needs to be cleansed. We can enjoy blessing in both of these circumstances, when we acknowledge our sins to God, when we agree with Him that they are vile and repulsive, an offense to His holy nature.

God forgives us on the basis of two aspects of His character. One is His righteousness or justice. He has already punished His Son in our place, so justice has been served and He now has no reason to withhold forgiveness. The second is His faithfulness. When He looked ahead to Israel's new covenant nearly six hundred years before Christ, He said, "I will forgive their iniquity, and their sin I will remember no more" (Jeremiah 31:34). We share in the benefits of that new covenant (cf. 2 Corinthians 3:6). Though our sins seem so horrible that God could never be expected to forgive them, He says

He will, and He is always faithful to His Word. Confess your sins to Him, then take Him at His Word. Believe that He has forgiven you and cleansed you from all unrighteousness.

Finally, God is faithful in *sustaining us through suffering.* One of the times we are most tempted to doubt God's faithfulness is when suffering strikes our lives. It often makes no sense to us and we see no reason for it. We may search our lives, and although we find some sins which we have previously over-looked, we still cannot believe we deserve what God has allowed to happen to us. We begin to think that He has forgotten us or really does not care about us.

The people of Jerusalem in Isaiah's day were beginning to think that way. Israel was a tiny nation surrounded by giant powers which were continually menacing her. Listen to her complaint:

> But Zion said, "The LORD has forsaken me,
> And the Lord has forgotten me" (Isaiah 49:14).

But the Lord was right there with words of encouragement.

> Can a woman forget her nursing child,
> And have no compassion on the son of her womb?
> Even these may forget, but I will not forget you.
> Behold, I have inscribed you on the palms of My hands;
> Your walls are continually before Me (verses 15-16).

He had allowed them to suffer, but He could never forget them in their suffering because He is faithful. And He does not forget us. He really does care.

How can we appropriate this great doctrine of God's faithfulness and enjoy calmness and contentment when hard times come? The only way is to do what Peter suggested: "There-fore, let those also who suffer according to the will of God entrust their souls to a faithful Creator in doing what is right" (1 Peter 4:19). As the Creator, God has the power to carry out

His perfect plan for our lives and to accomplish His perfect purposes through our suffering. And as the *faithful* Creator, He can be counted on to do it. Therefore we can consciously entrust ourselves to His care with complete confidence, and hand the safekeeping of our lives over to Him, believing that He will do what is best. When we do that, we will have peace in the midst of adversity.

I recently met a successful salesman who was struck totally blind at the age of forty-four. Not only was his sales ability hindered but his enjoyment of sports and his capacity to appreciate the great outdoors seemed to be terminated. His anger with God was intense. On one occasion he laid on the floor and cried, begging God to take his life and threatening to commit suicide. It seemed as though God said to him, "Don, trust Me. I have a great plan for your life." But still the resentment lingered.

A short time later he insisted on going for a walk. When no one in the house was free to take him, he angrily fumbled around and found his cane, located the front door, and against his wife's protests made his way down the front steps and across the yard, determined to prove something to himself and his family. He crossed the road, and in a state of disorientation accidently stumbled into a creek. As he sat there waist-deep in the water, it seemed as though God was saying, "Are you cooled down now, Don? Trust me. I have a great plan for your life." That was the moment he entrusted himself to his faithful Creator. A few years later he was serving the Lord effectively as a representative for a mission to the blind, finding more joy and satisfaction in his Christian life than he had ever known before. God is faithful in sustaining us through suffering.

The Encouragement of God's Faithfulness

God will not only be faithful in assuring our salvation, providing for our victory, forgiving our sins, and sustaining us through suffering, but He will also be faithful in keeping every promise He has ever made. That is the greatest encouragement we could possibly have. The Bible contains thousands of precious promises from God, and at least one of them will have application to every conceivable situation we can possibly encounter—financial reversal, terminal illness, the loss of a loved one, family tensions, or anything else. A faithful God can be trusted to keep every promise. The writer to the Hebrews encouraged his readers with these words: "Let us hold fast the confession of our hope without wavering, for He who promised is faithful" (Hebrews 10:23).

After assuring the Corinthians of God's faithfulness, Paul makes this astounding statement: "For as many as may be the promises of God, in Him they are yes; wherefore also by Him is our Amen to the glory of God through us" (2 Corinthians 1:20). The words "in Him" refer to Christ. Jesus Christ is the absolute certainty that all God's promises will be fulfilled. A God who loves us enough to give us His Son will certainly keep all His other promises as well. Christ's coming was as though God had written beside every promise in the Bible, "Yes, so be it, I will keep My Word." When we believe His promises, our lives bring glory to Him—as Paul said, "to the glory of God through us."

People in the world today are fed up with empty religious claims. They want to see something that does what it says it will do. Few things give evidence to the reality of life in Christ more powerfully than a believer who exhibits genuine peace in trying circumstances. That is the by-product of knowing a faithful God and believing His promises. When we are assured that He cares because He is loving and good; when we are convinced that He is in control because He is omnipotent; when we believe that He is with us and knows all about the problem because He is omnipresent and omniscient; when we believe that He is working everything together for good because He is sovereign and wise; then we will have peace when things around us are falling apart. And that will make a powerful impact on the world.

It is important to understand that some of God's promises are conditional. If we fail to keep the conditions, and as a result God does not fulfill the promise, His faithfulness obviously can not be impugned. We must study the context to see if there are any conditions stated or implied.

Many other promises in the Word are absolute and unconditional. God is going to keep them whether we believe He will or not. He will fulfill His Word whether we are faithful to Him or not. The Apostle Paul said, "If we are faithless, He remains faithful; for He cannot deny Himself" (2 Timothy 2:13). To be faithless may also mean to be unbelieving. When God's promises are unconditional, neither our faithlessness nor our unbelief will affect His faithfulness. They will rob us of our peace, our joy, and our testimony, but He will just keep right on doing what He promised to do, keep right on being faithful to His Word. What a wonderfully faithful God! Believe Him. Experience the peace, the joy, and the power which faith in His Word will bring. Then you too will exclaim enthusiastically, "Great is Thy faithfulness!"

Action To Take:

Think back to a time in your life when you doubted God's faithfulness. Now list the ways He has since proven Himself faithful, the things He has done which He promised in His Word He would do.

24

THE KING OF GLORY

WHEN YOUNG PEOPLE want us to know that something is of major importance, they sometimes say, "Man, that's heavy." The subject of glory is in that category. It is heavy! As a matter of fact, the most common word for glory in the Old Testament comes from a root that means literally "to be heavy." In Old Testament times, a person's weight was his glory.

Now please let me explain that statement. It does not mean that overweight people were any more glorious than under-weight people, or that we all ought to start eating more in order to increase our glory. It simply means that a person who was considered to have glory in that day was usually one who had some kind of weight, such as the weight of riches, the weight of power, or the weight of position. A man's glory referred to what he was and what he had—his honor, his reputation, or his possessions.

The Biblical References To God's Glory

When we read through the Old Testament, it does not take long to discover that God has glory. It was first mentioned when the people of Israel grumbled because they had no food. Moses promised them a miraculous provision of manna from Heaven which would be an evidence of the glory of the Lord (Exodus 16:7). God's faithful provision for His people was part of His weight of glory.

As the Old Testament progresses, it becomes evident that God not only *has* glory, but also that He *is* glorious. David calls Him "the God of glory" (Psalm 29:3), and later declares, "For great is the glory of the LORD" (Psalm 138:5). The phrase "the glory of the LORD" appears with such frequency, we begin to suspect that it refers to more than just one attribute of God. It is the Lord Himself in all His intrinsic and eternal perfections, the sum and substance of all His attributes, the totality of all His inherent majesty. God's glory is who He is, what He possesses, and what He is like. God's glory is God Himself in His essential being.

When God promised to show Moses His glory, He revealed His mercy, His grace, His long-suffering, His goodness, His truth, His forgiveness, and His righteous wrath against sin (Exodus 33:22; 34:6-7). When David asked, "Who is the King of glory?" the answer came back, "The LORD strong and mighty" (Psalm 24:8). His glory in that case referred primarily to His power. When the Psalmist said, "Tell of His glory among the nations" (Psalm 96:3), and "Ascribe to the LORD the glory of His name" (verse 8), things such as His honor, His majesty, His strength, His beauty, His sovereignty, His justice, His righteousness, and His faithfulness were mentioned (verses 6,10,13). God's glory is all that He is.

Furthermore, He can never lose any of His glory and still be God. That is not true of human beings. We can lose anything we might be known for—our position, our reputation, our money, or anything else—and still be as human as we ever were. But God would not be God if He lost His glory. That is one reason why He cannot share any of it with any other god.

> I am the LORD, that is My name;
> I will not give My glory to another,
> Nor My praise to graven images (Isaiah 42:8).

God must exercise His wrath against people who exchange

His glory for images (Romans 1:18-23). He cannot allow any-one to diminish His worth or detract from His majesty.

There have been occasions in human history when God has allowed His glory to take limited visible form, and it has always been revealed in terms of brightness and radiant light. The Psalmist said, "For the LORD God is a sun and a shield" (Psalm 84:11). Evidences of His brilliance are found all through the Bible. For instance, when He gave the law to Moses on Mount Sinai, His glory covered the mount like a consuming fire (Exodus 24:16-17). When Moses came down from that encounter with God "the skin of his face shone" (Exodus 34:29), another indication that God had revealed Himself to Moses in resplendent light.

When the people of Israel finished constructing the taber-nacle, an amazing thing happened. "Then the cloud covered the tent of meeting, and the glory of the LORD filled the tabernacle. And Moses was not able to enter the tent of meeting because the cloud had settled on it, and the glory of the LORD filled the tabernacle" (Exodus 40:34-35). That cloud of glory seems to have been brilliant light, so bright that Moses could not look at it or stand before it. It was called by the Jews the Shekinah, a non-Biblical term derived from a Hebrew verb meaning "to dwell," emphasizing God's pres-ence among His people in that shining cloud of glory. The same Shekinah glory filled Solomon's temple years later when it was completed (1 Kings 8:10-11). When Ezekiel saw a vision of the glory of the Lord, he too described it in terms of brightness: "As the appearance of the rainbow in the clouds on a rainy day, so was the appearance of the surrounding radiance. Such was the appearance of the likeness of the glory of the LORD" (Ezekiel 1:28).

A similar idea is present in the New Testament word for glory, a verb that means "to think." It referred to a man's self-evaluation (what he *thought* of himself), or his reputation (what others *thought* of him). When it is applied to God, it carries over the Old Testament idea of His majesty and splendor, the totality of His essence—what He is and how He expresses Himself. It does not take long before His glory is visibly manifested in brilliant light. When a group of shepherds heard the announcement of Messiah's birth from an angel of God," the glory of the Lord shone around them" (Luke 2:9). God's glory shines!

The Apostle John wrote that "God is light" (1 John 1:5). He predicted that the New Jerusalem will not need the sun or moon, "for the glory of God has illumined it" (Revelation 21:23). The Apostle Paul taught that God "dwells in inapproachable light; whom no man has seen or can see" (1 Timothy 6:16). All through the Bible God is depicted as light. Just as no man can look directly at the brightness of the sun with his naked eye without destroying his eyesight, so no mortal man can gaze at the undiminished brightness of God's glory without being consumed (Exodus 33:20). Yet, there have been sufficient veiled glimpses of His radiant glory through history to give men some idea of the majesty and splendor of His being. Even today, we see the evidences of His glory.

The Present Revelation of God's Glory

God must exist to glorify Himself. There is no one higher or greater for Him to glorify, so we can expect Him to keep on demonstrating the perfections of His person and revealing the radiance of His glory. He does this in several ways, the first being *in creation.* Just as we saw God's goodness and His wisdom revealed in creation, so also do we see His glory.

> The heavens are telling of the glory of God;
> And their expanse is declaring the work
> of His hands (Psalm 19:1).

It is impossible to contemplate the starry heavens and fail to see the glory of God. They reveal that He exists, for such a glorious creation demands a Creator. They reveal His power, for such a powerful effect demands a more powerful cause. They reveal His wisdom, for their amazing design demands an all-wise divine Designer. And they reveal His infinity, for their extent defies discovery by man's best scientific efforts.

But the heavens are only the beginning. The earth likewise reveals His glory: one of the seraphim cried to Isaiah in his vision of God, "The whole earth is full of His glory" (Isaiah 6:3). It is impossible to contemplate the beauty of a flower, the perfection of a snowflake, the loveliness of a tree, the strength of the mountains, the vastness of the oceans, or the amazing instincts of the animal kingdom and fail to see the glory of God.

But the highest of God's glorious creation is man. He reflects the very image of God (Genesis 1:26-27). David wrote concerning him:

> Yet Thou hast made him a little lower than God,
> And dost crown him with glory and majesty! (Psalm 8:5)

It is impossible to contemplate the intricacies of the human body, the capabilities of the human mind, or the complexities of the human personality and fail to see the glory of God. No man can contemplate God's dealings with the human race through history and fail to see His glory, particularly His love, His grace, His mercy, His long-suffering, as well as His wrath against sin.

Nothing, however, can possibly reflect the glory of God like the God-man Himself—*Jesus Christ*. Christ claimed to have possessed equal glory with the Father before the worlds were formed (John 17:5). When He came to earth, those who saw His glory recognized it for what it was: "glory as of the only begotten from the Father, full of grace and truth" (John 1:14). His divine glory was veiled by human flesh throughout His earthly life, but on one momentous occasion that veil was pulled aside: "And He was transfigured before them; and His face shone like the sun, and His garments became as white as light" (Matthew 17:2). Peter, James, and John beheld the magnificent glory of the eternal God that day. When Peter wrote, years later, about his thrilling experience, he said, "we were eyewitnesses of His majesty. For when He received honor and glory from God the Father, such an utterance as this was made to Him by the Majestic Glory, 'This is My beloved Son with whom I am well-pleased' " (2 Peter 1:16-17).

All other manifestations of God's glory grow dim in the light of this revelation in Jesus Christ. The writer to the Hebrews called Him "the radiance of His glory and the exact representation of His nature" (Hebrews 1:3). Just as surely as the radiant light that flooded the Old Testament tabernacle was the visible manifestation of God's glory, so was Jesus Christ. He is the Shekinah glory of God because He is God in flesh, the express image of God's person, the very impress of God's being. In the same way an image on a coin exactly matches the mold from which it was cast, so Jesus Christ bears the exact stamp of God's nature. He is, as the Apostle Paul called Him, "the Lord of glory" (1 Corinthians 2:8). Since He is continually being revealed to us in His Word, we have the exciting prospect of personally beholding the very glory of God as we get to know Jesus Christ. "For God, who said, 'Light shall shine out of darkness,' is the One who has shone in our hearts to give the light of the knowledge of the glory of God in the face of Christ" (2 Corinthians 4:6).

The Proper Response To God's Glory

I had a professor in seminary who used to say, "Revelation demands response." The primary reason God reveals His truth to us is to transform our lives. If we profess to know the truth, but refuse to let it affect the way we live, we are guilty of hypocrisy. God has revealed to us His glory. What then should our response be? What are we going to do about it?

If God's ultimate goal for all things is His own glory, and

if He goes to great lengths to manifest His glory, then we as His children should also establish as our highest goal in life the demonstration of God's glory. We should live to glorify Him. The Apostle Paul said that very explicitly: "Whether, then, you eat or drink or whatever you do, do all to the glory of God" (1 Corinthians 10:31; cf. also Romans 15:6; 1 Peter 4:11).

To glorify God simply means to bring His innate glory to light, to expose it, manifest it, reveal it, demonstrate it, make it known. It is to put God on display and show Him off for who He is. Suppose you decide to take up painting and you work very hard to develop your talent as an artist. You finally reach a stage of proficiency that permits you to produce a masterpiece. What are you going to do with it? Hide it in the attic? Hardly! That painting gives testimony to your talents. It is your glory. You hang it in a prominent place so others can see it. You show it off. In the same way, when we glorify God, we bring His glory to light for others to see. We make His attributes prominently known.

There are several ways by which we do that. The first is by *heartfelt worship.* When Moses saw the glory of the Lord, there was no question in his mind about what he should do: "And Moses made haste to bow low toward the earth and worship" (Exodus 34:8). To worship God is simply to acknowledge His glory. The Psalmist said,

> Ascribe to the LORD the glory due to His name;
> Worship the LORD in holy array (Psalm 29:2).

God wants us to acknowledge who He is, to confess that we understand who He is, and to bow in submission to Him as He is. That is true worship.

Some people think worship is merely following a prescribed form of service in the proper building, saying the right thing, and singing the right song in the right order. Worship may take place in that setting, but it does not necessarily happen that way. Worship is basically the joyful response of our hearts to the revelation of who God is and what He has done. It can take place any time, anywhere, and should take place regularly—not just when we are in a church building. But it cannot take place unless we are growing in our knowledge of the Lord. When we know Him and rehearse His attributes and acts in appreciation, gratitude, praise, and adoration, He is glorified.

One lone Samaritan leper showed us how. Jesus had healed ten lepers and sent them to the priests for the cleansing ceremony. "Now one of them, when he saw that he had been healed, turned back, glorifying God with a loud voice, and he fell on his face at His feet, giving thanks to Him. And he was a Samaritan." Jesus asked, "Was no one found who turned back to give glory to God, except this foreigner?" (Luke 17:15-16,18) By rehearsing God's love, His mercy, His goodness, and His power, and by thanking Him for His act of healing, that leper gave glory to God. People learned something about God that day through the leper's thanksgiving, and in that way God was glorified. The Lord said, "Whoso offereth praise glorifieth Me" (Psalm 50:23 KJV).

The second means by which we can glorify God is *holy living*. Jesus said, "By this is My Father glorified, that you bear much fruit, and so prove to be My disciples" (John 15:8). The fruit Jesus spoke of may have included converts brought to Him through our witness (John 4:36), or contributions made for the needs of others (Romans 15:28), but it certainly includes a Christlike character (Galatians 5:22), as well as conduct that honors Him (Colossians 1:10)—in other words, holy living. Jesus was also talking about the way we live when He said, "Let your light shine before men in such a way that they may see your good works, and glorify your Father who is in heaven" (Matthew 5:16). The quality of our lives should be such that the very character of the Lord is displayed to the people around us.

The Apostle Paul was talking about moral purity when he

exhorted us to glorify God in our bodies (1 Corinthians 6:20). We can actually display the holiness of God by keeping ourselves from sexual immorality. We can demonstrate other aspects of God's character as well by the way we live. When we submit to His will, we display His sovereignty. When we accept others unconditionally, we display His love. When we show kindness to those who have wronged us, we display His grace. When we reach out to those in need, we display His mercy. When we are honest, we display His truth. When we pray, we display His power. When we trust Him, we display His faithfulness. In all these, He is glorified.

When we fail to glorify God because of sin in our lives, we must confess and forsake that sin in order for Him to be glorified. A greedy Israelite named Achan took clothing, silver, and gold for himself during the conquest of Jericho, contrary to God's command. Joshua confronted him: "My son, I implore you, give glory to the LORD, the God of Israel, and give praise to Him; and tell me now what you have done. Do not hide it from me" (Joshua 7:19). When we acknowledge our sin and turn from it, our holy God is glorified.

The most significant means by which we can glorify God is simply *getting to know Him* as He is. The source of many of our problems as Christians is our unwillingness to accept God as He is. We want to remake Him as we would like Him to be so that we can live as we want to live, and the result is heartache and tragedy. Paul wrote to the Corinthians, "But we all, with unveiled face beholding as in a mirror the glory of the Lord, are being transformed into the same image from glory to glory, just as from the Lord, the Spirit" (2 Corinthians 3:18). As we focus our attention on God's glory and get to know Him as He truly reveals Himself, we become progressively more like Him. His character rubs off on us and we begin to display Him more perfectly. That brings glory to God.

We will never give much time or attention to knowing God, however, as long as we are glorying in ourselves or in any earthly thing. "Thus says the LORD, 'Let not a wise man boast of his wisdom, and let not the mighty man boast of his might, let not a rich man boast of his riches; but let him who boasts boast of this, that he understands and knows Me, that I am the LORD who exercises lovingkindness, justice, and righteousness on earth; for I delight in these things,' declares the LORD" (Jeremiah 9:23-24). Life's greatest joy is knowing God in a personal, precious, loving, intimate, yet submissive relationship. It is not that "good buddy" relationship which some talk about flippantly and irreverently. It is not that "get God on my side" attitude which is motivated by a desire for success in worldly pursuits. It is a Creator-creature relationship that recognizes His lordship, His right to be God in our experience. When we abdicate the throne of our lives and let Him be our sovereign Ruler, our King of glory, then and then alone will He be glorified.

Most of us will struggle with this until our dying day. As our knowledge of God grows, we will discover additional areas of our lives which have not yet been brought under His sovereign control. Every new challenge will meet with new resistance from our sinful natures and will require new surrender to His lordship over our lives.

But someday the struggle will be over and we ourselves shall be glorified (cf. Romans 8:29-30). That does not mean we shall take the place reserved only for God, but that our stubborn natures will be changed and we shall be made like our glorious Saviour (cf. 1 Corinthians 15:52; Philippians 3:21; 1 John 3:2). We shall become vessels that are perfectly fitted to express His glory throughout eternity. Then God's purpose for saving us will have been fully realized; our entire existence will be perfectly and uninterruptedly directed to the praise of His glory forever (cf. Ephesians 1:6,12,14).

"Now to Him who is able to keep you from stumbling, and to make you stand in the presence of His glory blameless with great joy, to the only God our Saviour, through Jesus Christ our Lord, be glory, majesty, dominion and authority, before all time and now and forever. Amen" (Jude 24-25).

Action To Take:

List some of the things you are doing which you believe bring glory to God. Thank Him for the desire, the ability, and the privilege of so glorifying Him.

List some of the things in your life which do not glorify God. Ask Him to help you change them.

HELPFUL BOOKS ON THE
ATTRIBUTES OF GOD

Bavinck, Herman. *The Doctrine of God.* Grand Rapids, Michigan: Baker Book House, 1951.

Berkhof, Louis. *Systematic Theology.* Grand Rapids, Michigan: Wm. B. Eerdmans Publishing Company, 1949.

Boettner, Loraine. *Studies in Theology.* Phillipsburg, New Jersey: Presbyterian Reformed Publishing, 1953.

Buswell, James Oliver, Jr. *A Systematic Theology of the Christian Religion.* 2 vols. Grand Rapids, Michigan: Zondervan Publishing House, 1962.

Chafer, Lewis Sperry. *Systematic Theology.* 8 vols. Dallas, Texas: Dallas Theological Seminary Press, 1948.

Charnock, Stephen. *The Existence and Attributes of God.* Grand Rapids, Michigan: Baker Book House, 1958.

Clarke, William Newton. *The Christian Doctrine of God.* New York: Charles Scribner's Sons, 1909.

Culver, Robert Duncan. *The Living God.* Wheaton, Illinois: Victor Books, 1978.

De Haan, Dan. *The God You Can Know.* Chicago, Illinois: Moody Press, 1982.

Hodge, Charles. *Systematic Theology.* 3 vols. Grand Rapids, Michigan: Wm. B. Eerdmans Publishing Company, 1952.

Hook, Phillip. *Who Art in Heaven.* Grand Rapids, Michigan: Zondervan Publishing House, 1979.

Kerr, William F., ed. *God, What Is He Like?* Wheaton, Illinois: Tyndale House Publishers, 1977.

Packer, J. I. *Knowing God.* Downers Grove, Illinois: InterVarsity Press, 1973.

Pentecost, J. Dwight. *The Glory of God.* Portland, Oregon: Multnomah Press, 1978.

Phillips, J. B. *Your God Is Too Small*. New York: The Macmillan Company, 1954.

Pink, Arthur W. *The Attributes of God*. Grand Rapids, Michigan: Baker Book House, 1975.

Rees, Paul Stromberg. *Stand Up in Praise to God*. Grand Rapids, Michigan: Wm. B. Eerdmans Publishing Company, 1960.

Shedd, William G. T. *Shedd's Dogmatic Theology*. 3 vols. Nashville, Tennessee: Thomas Nelson, Inc.

Strauss, Lehman. *The First Person*. Neptune, New Jersey: Loizeaux Brothers, 1967.

Strong, Augustus Hopkins. *Systematic Theology*. 3 vols. Old Tappan, New Jersey: Fleming H. Revell.

Thiessen, Henry Clarence. *Lectures in Systematic Theology*. Grand Rapids, Michigan: Wm. B. Eerdmans Publishing Company, 1949.

Toon, Peter. *God Here and Now*. Wheaton, Illinois: Tyndale House Publishers, 1979.

Tozer, A. W. *The Knowledge of the Holy*. New York: Harper and Row Publishers, 1961.

INDEX OF SCRIPTURE REFERENCES